NATIONAL GEOGRAPHIC KIDS™

ALMANAC 2012

NATIONAL GEOGRAPHIC

A red panda munches on bamboo in the Wolong Nature Reserve in Sichuan Province, China.

NATIONAL GEOGRAPHIC
KIDS™
ALMANAC 2012

NATIONAL GEOGRAPHIC
WASHINGTON, D.C.

National Geographic Children's Books
gratefully acknowledges the following people for their help with the
National Geographic Kids Almanac 2012.

Curtis Malarkey, Julie Segal, and Cheryl Zook
of the National Geographic Explorers program;
Truly Herbert, National Geographic Communications;
and Chuck Errig of Random House

Going Green

Eric J. Bohn, Math Teacher, Santa Rosa High School

Stephen David Harris, Professional Engineer,
Industry Consulting

Brad Scriber, Senior Researcher,
NATIONAL GEOGRAPHIC magazine

Cid Simões and Paola Segura,
National Geographic Emerging Explorers

Dr. Wes Tunnell, Harte Research Institute for
Gulf of Mexico Studies, Texas A&M
University-Corpus Christi

Amazing Animals

Dr. Thomas R. Holtz, Jr., Senior Lecturer, Vertebrate
Paleontology, Dept. of Geology, University of Maryland

Dr. Luke Hunter, Executive Director, Panthera

"Dino" Don Lessem, President, Exhibits Rex

Kathy B. Maher, Research Editor,
NATIONAL GEOGRAPHIC magazine

Kathleen Martin, Canadian Sea Turtle Network

Barbara Nielsen, Polar Bears International

Andy Prince, Austin Zoo

Julia Thorson, translator, Paris, France

Chris Sloan, NATIONAL GEOGRAPHIC magazine

Dr. Sylvia Earle,
National Geographic Explorer-in-Residence

Dennis vanEngelsdorp, Senior Extension Associate,
Pennsylvania Department of Agriculture

Culture Connection

Dr. Wade Davis,
National Geographic Explorer-in-Residence

Deirdre Mullervy, Managing Editor,
Gallaudet University Press

Super Science

Tim Appenzeller, Chief Magazine Editor, NATURE

Dr. José de Ondarza, Associate Professor,
Department of Biological Sciences, State University
of New York, College at Plattsburgh

Lesley B. Rogers, Managing Editor,
NATIONAL GEOGRAPHIC magazine

Abigail A. Tipton, Director of Research,
NATIONAL GEOGRAPHIC magazine

Erin Vintinner, Biodiversity Specialist,
Center for Biodiversity and Conservation at the
American Museum of Natural History

Barbara L. Wyckoff, Research Editor,
NATIONAL GEOGRAPHIC magazine

Dr. Enric Sala, National Geographic Visiting Fellow

Wonders of Nature

Anatta, NOAA Public Affairs Officer

Douglas H. Chadwick, wildlife biologist and contributor to
NATIONAL GEOGRAPHIC magazine

Drew Hardesty, Forecaster, Utah Avalanche Center

Dr. Robert Ballard,
National Geographic Explorer-in-Residence

Awesome Adventure

Jen Bloomer, Media Relations Manager,
The National Aquarium in Baltimore

Dereck and Beverly Joubert,
National Geographic Explorers-in-Residence

History Happens

Dr. Gregory Geddes, Lecturer, Department of History,
State University of New York, College at Plattsburgh

Dr. Robert D. Johnston,
Associate Professor and Director of the
Teaching of History Program,
University of Illinois at Chicago

Dr. Fredrik Hiebert, National Geographic Visiting Fellow

Sylvie Beaudreau, Associate Professor, Department of
History, State University of New York

Karyn Pugliese, Acting Director, Communications,
Assembly of First Nations

Parliamentary Information and Research Service,
Library of Parliament, Ottawa, Canada

Micheline Joanisse, Media Relations Officer,
Natural Resources Canada

Geography Rocks

Dr. Mary Kent, Demographer,
Population Reference Bureau

Dr. Walt Meier, National Snow and Ice Data Center

Dr. Richard W. Reynolds,
NOAA's National Climatic Data Center

United States Census Bureau, Public Help Desk

Dr. Spencer Wells,
National Geographic Explorer-in-Residence

Carl Haub, Senior Demographer, Conrad Taeuber Chair of
Public Information, Population Reference Bureau

Glynnis Breen, National Geographic Special Projects

4

Contents

Your World 2012

8

Going Green

18

Amazing Animals

38

Culture Connection

Super Science

The Little Big Book of Fun

Wonders of Nature

COOL CLICK

Throughout this book, our virtual pet,
Zipper the dog, alerts you to cool clicks—
Web links that will help you find out more!

Lions are causing an uproar! In the 1940s, there were about 400,000 lions on Earth. Today, there may be as few as 20,000. Every cub brings new hope for these beautiful cats. Scan the QR code or go to the link on this page to help save big cats!

Your World
2012

Got a smart phone?
SCAN THIS to find out
how to save big cats!
(See instructions inside the front cover.)

No smart phone? Go online.
kids.nationalgeographic.com/almanac-2012

Supersmart Dolphins

Dolphins COMMUNICATE using SQUEAKS, WHISTLES, and BODY LANGUAGE.

Recent research suggests that dolphins take high marks in the smarts department, coming in close to humans in brainpower. Using MRI scans of dolphin brains, scientists were able to determine that their brains are four to five times larger than those of other animals of similar size. (Humans also have an impressive brain-to-body ratio.) And not only are their brains big, they're also highly developed, allowing dolphins to demonstrate sophisticated skills like problem-solving and communication. They even display distinct personalities.

Another example of the dolphins' intelligence? Their ability to recognize themselves in a mirror. When researchers marked two bottlenose dolphins on different parts of their bodies with temporary ink, each of the dolphins parked themselves in front of mirrors installed in their pool and studied the markings. This behavior, called mirror self-recognition, is unusual among animals—just going to show how bright those dolphins truly are.

Olympic Fever

IN THE SUMMER OF 2012,

London will become the only city to host the Olympics three times. The games also took place in London in 1908 and 1948. When the 30th Olympic Games kick off on July 27, 2012, eight million ticket holders will watch athletes from around the world compete in 26 different sports. Which sports are new this year? Women's boxing and mixed doubles tennis. What's out? Baseball and softball. But the Olympics are still sure to be a home run!

Where's Wenlock?

The mascot for the 2012 Olympics really has his eye on the prize. Wenlock's giant single eye doubles as a camera, which takes pictures wherever he goes. You can check out Wenlock's photos, along with snapshots from Mandeville (the mascot for the Paralympic Games, which begin on August 29), on Twitter and Facebook, or check out the mascots' very own website! (www.mylondon2012.com/mascots/)

I KNEW I FORGOT TO SCREW SOMETHING ON TODAY!

China's Cheng Fei performs an artistic gymnastics routine at the 2004 Summer Olympics in Athens, Greece.

I ROCK THE HIGH JUMP AND THE HIGH NOTES. OOOOAAH!!

Russia's Andrey Silnov wins the gold medal in the men's high jump final at the 2008 Summer Olympics in Beijing, China.

Animal Discoveries

From MONKEYS to MICRO-FROGS, here are some species recently found in the wild.

Fathead Sculpin Fish

Just call him "Mr. Blobby"! The discovery of this floppy fish was part of the 10-year Census of Marine Life that uncovered 6,000 new species of sea dwellers. Now preserved in 70 percent ethyl alcohol at an Australian museum, Mr. Blobby has become a worldwide phenomenon and even has his own Facebook page!

THIS ISN'T REALLY A NOSE, IT'S A FLAP OF FLABBY SKIN.

Caquetá Titi Monkey

Scientists spotted these cat-size primates deep within the Amazon rain forest in Colombia. One of about 20 species of titi monkeys, the Caquetá has a bushy red beard, purrs like a kitty, and mates for life.

Bornean Micro-frog

It's slimy, it's speckled, and it's the size of a pea. Spotted on plants in Malaysian rain forests on the island of Borneo, the *Microhyla nepenthicola* is considered to be one of the smallest frogs in the world. It's tiny enough to sit comfortably on the tip of a pencil, so it's no wonder these frogs went unidentified for centuries!

Yeti Crab

This fuzzy creature lives in the balmy South Pacific, but its snowy look earned it the nickname Yeti—another name for the Abominable Snowman. This crazy crustacean, discovered deep in the ocean in the warm waters south of Easter Island, has a white shell and fur-like filaments covering its arms and legs. The small, blind crab is so unusual that a whole new family of animals, called Kiwaidae, had to be created to classify it.

COLOSSAL Crater!

After a recent tropical storm ripped through Guatemala City, Guatemala, a gigantic hole mysteriously appeared in a city street—it was big enough to swallow a three-story building! Scientists believe that excess water from the storm combined with a burst pipe or storm drain underground to make the pebbly ground give way. Amazingly, no one was hurt! But that's one storm that really made an impression.

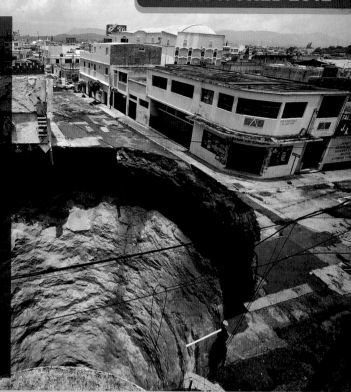

HOT MOVIES in 2012*

ICE AGE: CONTINENTAL DRIFT

- *Madagascar 3*
- *The Hobbit: Part One*
- *Ice Age: Continental Drift*
- *Brave*
- *Men in Black III*
- *Ghostbusters III*

*release dates and titles subject to change

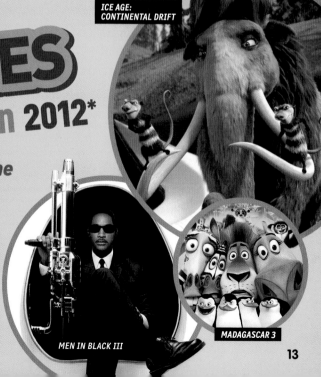

MEN IN BLACK III

MADAGASCAR 3

13

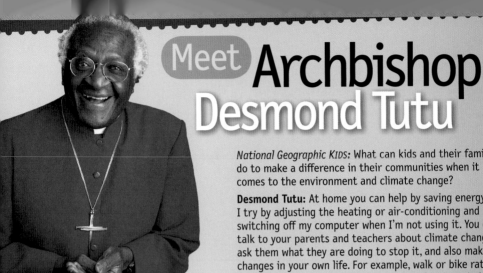

Meet Archbishop Desmond Tutu

National Geographic KIDS: What can kids and their families do to make a difference in their communities when it comes to the environment and climate change?

Desmond Tutu: At home you can help by saving energy. I try by adjusting the heating or air-conditioning and by switching off my computer when I'm not using it. You can talk to your parents and teachers about climate change, ask them what they are doing to stop it, and also make changes in your own life. For example, walk or bike rather than use a car, eat less meat, and remember to switch off the lights.

NGK: What advice can you offer to those who want to promote peace and justice in their schools and community?

Desmond Tutu: I don't want to tell you what to do—young people are so much more creative and energetic than us oldies! I would just encourage you to not be afraid to stand up for what you know is right. Share your passion and creativity with others. And don't forget to laugh. I love to laugh!

NGK: Who is your hero?

Desmond Tutu: My mother. She was not well educated but was caring and compassionate. I have always wanted to emulate her.

NGK: If you were to encourage kids to do just one thing to make a difference in their world, what would it be?

Desmond Tutu: Love life; respect yourself and the environment in which you live.

The Archbishop of South Africa, Desmond Tutu is an advocate for peace, justice, and protection of the environment. A winner of the Nobel Peace Prize and the Presidential Medal of Freedom, Tutu is perhaps best known for his efforts to promote human rights and equality worldwide. In February 2011, Tutu retired from public life. *NG KIDS* was lucky enough to catch up with him to find out what legacy he'd like to leave children around the globe.

Crab Crossing Guards

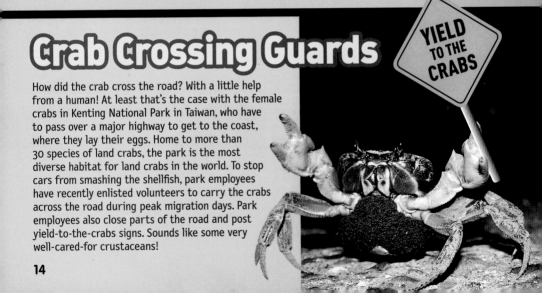

YIELD TO THE CRABS

How did the crab cross the road? With a little help from a human! At least that's the case with the female crabs in Kenting National Park in Taiwan, who have to pass over a major highway to get to the coast, where they lay their eggs. Home to more than 30 species of land crabs, the park is the most diverse habitat for land crabs in the world. To stop cars from smashing the shellfish, park employees have recently enlisted volunteers to carry the crabs across the road during peak migration days. Park employees also close parts of the road and post yield-to-the-crabs signs. Sounds like some very well-cared-for crustaceans!

THE *TITANIC:*
100 YEARS LATER

On April 14, 1912, the R.M.S. *Titanic*—a luxury cruise ship thought to be "unsinkable"—collided with an iceberg in the northern Atlantic Ocean on its maiden voyage and sank to the bottom of the sea. Its wreckage was discovered in 1985 by Robert Ballard, now a National Geographic Explorer-in-Residence, and French explorer Jean-Louis Michel.

Today Expedition Titanic is documenting the ship's site some 2.4 miles (3.8 km) underwater using advanced technology such as robots that can capture images of the wreck. New high-definition video is helping scientists determine how quickly the ship is deteriorating. It has also revealed a few surprises—such as the captain's bathtub, now visible due to the collapse of his stateroom wall.

Despite these new discoveries, some people want the *Titanic* to remain an undisturbed final resting place for the passengers who lost their lives. Others hope that future expeditions can reveal even more of the *Titanic's* secrets—or even help preserve the ship—before it's lost to decay.

THE BOW OF THE R.M.S. *TITANIC* IN 1912

THE BOW OF THE R.M.S. *TITANIC* ON THE OCEAN FLOOR IN 2010

TAKE FLIGHT

Running late? Strap on a Martin Jetpack. Soar over trees and rooftops with this new invention, which reaches about 60 miles an hour (95 kph) and travels up to 30 miles (48 km) on a tank of gas. Driving it is like playing a video game—a joystick-like handle on the left moves you forward, back, left, and right, while the stick on the right lets you go up and down. A thrill like this doesn't come cheap—Martin Jetpacks could sell for $100,000 once they are publicly available!

2012: What's Ahead

JANUARY

1st
Brrrr! About 2,000 brave swimmers plunge into the icy English Bay for the annual POLAR BEAR SWIM in Vancouver, Canada.

FEBRUARY

6th
England's Queen Elizabeth II marks 60 years on the throne today.

MARCH

12th
HAPPY BIRTHDAY! The Girl Scouts of America is 100 years old.

APRIL

12th
Bon anniversaire! Disneyland Paris turns 20.

MAY

early May
Have a blast at **BUN BANG FAI—** Thailand's **Rocket Festival!**

JUNE

5th
Celebrate World Environment Day! Plant a tree, pick up trash, be good to the Earth.

JULY

July 27th-August 12th
Head to London, England, to see the **Games of the XXX OLYMPIAD.**

AUGUST

29th
Opening ceremonies launch **2012 SUMMER PARALYMPICS IN LONDON.**

SEPTEMBER

3rd
RUB A DUB DUB, RACE IN A TUB during the annual **BATHTUB RACE** in Nome, Alaska.

OCTOBER

5th
Say Cheese! It's WORLD SMILE DAY.

NOVEMBER

6th
ELECTION DAY! Votes are cast across the United States for the presidential election.

DECEMBER

14th
Spot a warrior at Tokyo, Japan's **SAMURAI FESTIVAL.**

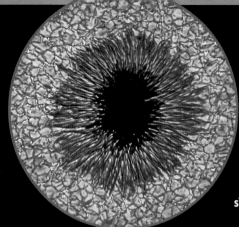

SEEING SPOTS

Believe it or not, this golden image is actually a close-up shot of a sunspot—or a dark area on the sun's surface. Captured by a high-powered solar telescope in Big Bear Lake, California, U.S.A., the shot is considered to be the most detailed picture ever taken of the sun in visible light. Measuring about 8,000 miles (12,800 km) in diameter, this sunspot is slightly bigger than Earth!

FLOATING HOME

Pools and playgrounds are so yesterday. At the Citadel, the fun is right outside your window. A Dutch concept, the Citadel is a floating apartment complex. It's not only a neat place to live, it's part of a growing trend toward environmentally friendly housing. During wet weather, the lake surrounding the Citadel absorbs excess rainfall, which prevents flooding. The apartments rise and fall with the changing water level. The Citadel consumes 25 percent less energy than regular apartment buildings, thanks to solar panels, heat from nearby greenhouses, and the lake itself, which helps warm and cool the floors. A bridge lets you walk or bike to land—but why bother with roads when you can swim over to a friend's house or sail to baseball practice?

HERE'S THE LATEST SCOOP ON DOG DROPPINGS

THEY CAN DOUBLE AS AN ENERGY SOURCE! A man displayed the wonders of dog waste by converting it into energy used to light a park lamp in Massachusetts, U.S.A. Dog owners simply pitch the waste into a tank and stir its contents with an attached handle. This mixing action allows microbes—or tiny bacteria—to convert the waste into methane gas, which is then used to light the lamp. The process is just another example of humans creating biofuel in an effort to go green. Three barks for cleaner, well-lit parks!

17

Going Green

A northern spotted owl swoops through a redwood forest in California, U.S.A.

COOL GREEN inventions

ECO-CAR

Like the wings of an insect, the doors of your car lift upward. As you step onto the sidewalk in front of the movie theater, a crowd gathers around, staring at your awesomely cool set of wheels. The Aptera looks like something from the year 2030, and its futuristic design is all about the environment. Its light weight —about 1,000 pounds (450 kg) less than an average small car—and three-wheeled, flat design minimize wind resistance. Instead of wasting energy pushing against the wind, the Aptera glides through it. It runs on a battery that goes about 100 miles (160 km) before it needs recharging. Panels on the roof convert solar energy into electricity to power the radio, air conditioner, and headlights. Even the plastics in the seats, dashboard, and carpet are eco-friendly: They're made from recycled soda and water bottles. This car is green inside and out.

LOOK INSIDE!

FLYING ON BATTERIES

The Oxyflyer is the first plane to take to the sky on traditional batteries alone. Using 160 special higher-powered AA batteries, the Oxyflyer stayed in the air for 59 seconds and covered 1,284 feet (390 m), beating the Wright brothers' record of 852 feet (260 m) in 1903. Because batteries tend to add a lot of weight, the Oxyflyer is designed to be lightweight with a sprawling 100-foot (30.5 m) wingspan that gives it more lift. Now that the Oxyflyer has proven it's possible to fly this way, the efficient aircraft has inspired other environmentally friendly planes. So someday you'll be able to fly *green* skies!

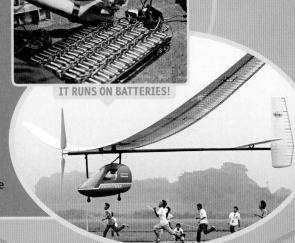

IT RUNS ON BATTERIES!

GREEN
HOUSE

In this deluxe tree house, the walls can't talk, but they are alive. Conceived by a team of researchers at MIT, the Fab Tree Hab is a house constructed with living materials. The outer part is made up of large trees. The trunks of the trees provide structural support, while their branches form an archway. The shell of the house is inside the trees. It's made by weaving plants into a dome-shaped structure. The interior walls are covered in straw and plaster, and the floors are clay tile or stone. The Fab Tree Hab is just a concept for now, and the abode would take about five to ten years to grow. So you've got plenty of time to pack for the move.

RIVER-CLEANING
BOAT

It may float, but this is not your ordinary boat. The translucent, curvy *Physalia* (just a concept now) is a floating museum and research lab. Its mission: to make the planet greener. How? As it glides down a dirty river, the river water is pumped to *Physalia*'s rooftop garden. Plants filter and purify water, which then flows back into the river. The boat powers itself; solar panels on top capture energy from the sun while hydro-turbines underneath convert moving water into electricity. As the boat's scientists study the river's ecosystem, visitors hop aboard to view exhibits and relax.

ABOARD
PHYSALIA

21

GREEN HOUSE

THE LATEST ECO-TECHNOLOGY FOR YOUR HOME

You just moved into the coolest house on the block. From top to bottom, inside and out, your green house cuts natural resource use and decreases CO_2 emissions by using smart design and construction that emphasize renewable resources. Your house is all about recycling, which significantly decreases waste that would otherwise go to landfills. Check out some of the sustainable and biodegradable items in your unique eco-friendly home.

1 A ROOFTOP GARDEN provides insulation for the house, makes oxygen, and absorbs CO_2.

2 SOLAR PANELS facing south use sunlight to generate electricity for the whole house.

3 DOUBLE-PANED WINDOWS reduce the need for heating and air-conditioning systems, keeping your house comfortable year-round.

4 The TALL DESIGN OF THE HOUSE uses less land.

5 BRICKS for the exterior walls are made from recycled materials.

6 You have CHAIRS made from recycled seat belts and LAMPS made of RECYCLED CHOPSTICKS.

7 STRATEGICALLY PLACED TREES provide indoor climate control by shading out summer heat and letting in light and warmth when the leaves fall in autumn.

8 The DECK is made from recycled plastic.

9 A PASSIVE SOLAR SYSTEM uses concrete, brick, stone, and tile to absorb and maintain heat from the sun.

10 WOOD for the stairways and furniture comes from trees grown specifically for harvest, not from old-growth forests.

11 SOFT, NATURAL-FIBER BEDDING is made from bamboo, a renewable resource.

12 CEILING FANS circulate air and help keep rooms cooler in warm weather.

13 In the bathrooms, you use BIODEGRADABLE SOAPS AND SHAMPOOS that won't add chemicals to streams, rivers, and oceans. DUAL-FLUSH TOILETS choose the amount of water you need for flushing. BIODEGRADABLE TOILET PAPER is made from recycled paper. Your shower curtain is made of HEMP, a renewable resource.

14 Energy-saving light switches called OCCUPANT SENSORS automatically turn lights on when you enter the room and off when you leave. COMPACT FLUORESCENT BULBS in all the light fixtures use less energy and last ten times longer than standard bulbs.

15 To water your garden, you use the rainwater that collects in OUTDOOR HOLDING TANKS.

16 The FRONT-LOADING WASHING MACHINE uses less water than a top-loading one.

17 The kitchen COUNTERTOP is made of reclaimed granite salvaged from discarded granite products. The APPLIANCES are certified energy savers. AERATORS conserve water by reducing faucet flow.

18 Your whole family's stylish clothing is made from RENEWABLE, NATURAL FIBERS, such as organically grown cotton.

19 The dog and cat eat ORGANIC PET FOOD. The pets use HEMP collars, beds, and toys. The KITTY LITTER comes from recycled paper.

20 SOLAR GARDEN LIGHTS store energy for nighttime use.

21 Your family's new HYBRID CAR emits very little CO_2.

22 RECYCLING BINS make it easy for you to sort glass, plastic, aluminum, and paper.

OCEAN ALERT!

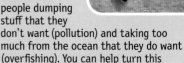

It may seem as if the world's oceans are so vast that nothing could hurt them. Unfortunately, that's not true. The oceans suffer from people dumping stuff that they don't want (pollution) and taking too much from the ocean that they do want (overfishing). You can help turn this problem around.

You probably already know how to help fight pollution: Participate in stream, river, and beach cleanups; don't litter; and don't dump things into storm drains. But you may not realize that too many fish are taken from the sea. Some overfished species are disappearing, such as sharks and the bluefin tuna (above.)

Many fish are slow-growing and live decades or even centuries. Chilean sea bass live up to 40 years. Orange roughies can live to be more than 100 years old. And, rockfish can live to be 200! When there aren't enough of these slow-growing fish, the species is threatened because the fish often are taken from the sea before they are old enough to reproduce. These species could disappear.

PROTECT THE FISH! You can be part of the solution if you choose carefully what fish to eat. Some are okay to eat; others you should avoid because they're overfished or caught in ways that harm the ocean. Encourage your parents to consult this guide when they buy fish at the market or order it at a restaurant. Ask a grocer or chef where and how the fish was caught. Saving marine life is hard, but if everyone helps, it will make a difference.

BEST CHOICES

abalone (farmed)
barramundi (U.S.)
catfish (U.S.)
caviar / sturgeon
  (farmed)
char, Arctic (farmed)
clams (farmed)
clams, softshell
crab, Dungeness
crab, stone
crawfish (U.S.)
halibut, Pacific
lobster, spiny
  (Australia, Baja, U.S.)
mackerel, Atlantic
mahimahi (U.S. troll)
mullet (U.S.)
mussels (farmed)
oysters (farmed)
pollock, Alaska

sablefish / black cod
  (Alaska, Canada)
salmon (Alaska wild)
salmon, canned
  pink / sockeye
sardines (U.S.)
scallops, bay (farmed)
shrimp, pink (Oregon)
shrimp (U.S. farmed)
spot prawn (Canada)
squid, longfin (U.S.)
striped bass
  (farmed)
tilapia (U.S.)
trout, rainbow
  (farmed)
tuna, albacore
  (Canada, U.S.)
tuna, yellowfin
  (U.S. troll)

WORST CHOICES

caviar / sturgeon
  (imported wild)
Chilean sea bass
cod, Atlantic
crab, king (imported)
crawfish (China)
flounder / sole
  (Atlantic)
grouper
haddock (trawl)
halibut, Atlantic

mahimahi
  (imported longline)
monkfish
orange roughy
rockfish
  (Pacific trawl)
salmon (farmed
  or Atlantic)
shark
shrimp / prawns
  (imported)

skate
snapper (red or
  imported)
swordfish
  (imported)
tilapia (Asia)
tuna, bigeye
  (longline)
tuna, bluefin
tuna, yellowfin
  (imported longline)

DEFINITIONS

FARMED: fish raised commercially in enclosures
LONGLINE: fishing with a long line — up to 50 miles (80.5 km) long — that has short lines attached with baited hooks
TROLL: to fish with lines towed by a boat
TRAWL: to fish with a cone-shaped net dragged behind a boat

THE DANGERS OF
Deepwater Drilling

An oily wave approaches Gulf Shores, Alabama, U.S.A., on June 25, 2010.

IN TOO DEEP?

Energy companies are drilling deeper into the earth and farther offshore for oil. It's estimated that by 2020, 10 percent of the world's oil will come from wells nearly a quarter mile (400 m) deep. And the deeper the rigs go, the bigger the risk. Why? For starters, drilling so far out is not easy, as operating a rig is more challenging in extreme water conditions. And if something goes wrong, accidents can be dangerous for both the ecosystem of the surrounding area and the people on the rigs.

Oil in the Gulf

On April 20, 2010, a massive explosion on the *Deepwater Horizon* oil rig, stationed off the coast of Louisiana, U.S.A., sent oil leaking into the Gulf of Mexico. With a total of 207 million gallons gushing into the Gulf, the spill became the worst accidental marine oil spill in world history. The spill had an impact on the ecosystem, including causing thousands of birds to grow sick or die in the oily water. It also took a heavy toll on tourism in an area already hit hard in 2005 by Hurricane Katrina, considered to be one of the costliest and deadliest natural disasters in United States history.

Relief wells were drilled into the damaged well and filled with mud and cement to stop oil flow. After three months, the leak was permanently plugged using a cement cap. But the efforts to clean up the Gulf will be ongoing. Experts say it may take years to restore its water and shores.

GETTING RID OF THE OIL

Oil, oil everywhere—how to clean it up? It took thousands of people to tackle the tough task of removing the leaked oil from the Gulf. In the water, what didn't evaporate, dissolve, or disperse was burned and skimmed off the surface. The Gulf's petroleum-eating bacteria helped cleanup efforts as well. On the beaches, cleanup crews scooped up tons of oil, oily debris, and tar balls along the shore. And as for the animals, rehabilitators tried to rescue oil-covered creatures using vats of warm water and mild detergents. But with so much oil spilled, scientists still aren't sure how much they missed. Only time will tell how long the effects of this spill will linger.

1

GET MOVING.
BIKE OR WALK AS MUCH AS POSSIBLE TO KEEP CAR POLLUTION FROM BEING ABSORBED INTO WATERWAYS.

2

PARTICIPATE
in a cleanup at a river, lake, or beach.

3

Turn off the water when you're brushing your teeth.

4

TAKE SHORT SHOWERS
instead of baths. Set a timer to see how clean you can get in five minutes.

20 WAYS YOU CAN BE A WAT

5

NEVER RELEASE HELIUM BALLOONS INTO THE AIR.
If they fall into the water, animals can mistake them for food.

6

DO LESS WORK! Wash only full loads in the washing machine or dishwasher.

7

MAKE YOUR OWN SOAP
out of leftover soap slivers to keep pieces of soap from going down the drain—and possibly into waterways. Squish the slivers into cool shapes when they're wet.

9

Paint "no dumping" art on storm drains by joining a stenciling program with your city. This encourages people to keep paint, trash, and soapy water from car washes out of storm drains, which often flow into lakes, rivers, and oceans.

NO DUMPING
THIS DRAINS TO OCEAN

10

DRINK FROM A REUSABLE WATER BOTTLE.
All those single-serving bottles take water to produce.

8

WHEN YOUR FAMILY STAYS AT A HOTEL, **REUSE TOWELS, WASHCLOTHS, AND SHEETS** AS YOU DO AT HOME.

11
DRINK TAP WATER instead of bottled. You'll help keep water free of pollution from delivery trucks.

12
WATER YOUR LAWN OR GARDEN IN THE EARLY MORNING. Water doesn't evaporate as fast when the air is cool, so you won't need as much.

13
AVOID USING THE TOILET AS A TRASH CAN. Flushing things such as medicine may contaminate water sources. It also simply wastes water.

14
VOLUNTEER at a local aquarium.

15
COLLECT RAINWATER IN A BUCKET OR BARREL. Use it to water plants.

ER HERO

You can make a big difference when it comes to protecting the planet. These 20 tips help conserve water; keep pollution out of oceans, rivers, and streams; and protect the animals that live there. You're being blue to be green!

16
KEEP YOUR DOG ON A LEASH at rivers, lakes, or beaches. Loose dogs can scare or harm creatures that live there.

17
Don't release pets such as fish or snakes into rivers, lakes, or streams. Non-native animals can totally mess up the ecosystem.

18
RECYCLE so your trash doesn't end up in water sources.

19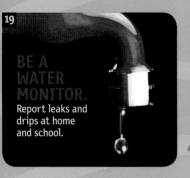
BE A WATER MONITOR. Report leaks and drips at home and school.

20
DON'T FEED WATER ANIMALS. They need to find their own food to keep themselves—and their environment—healthy.

10 Tips to Save EARTH

1 Use cloth towels. Instead of reaching for paper towels in the kitchen, use a hand towel. In public bathrooms, use the air dryer or limit yourself to one paper towel.

2 Close your blinds or curtains to block out the heat from the sun. If each home in the United States cut the use of air-conditioning by 10 percent annually, the energy savings could power 1.6 million homes for a year.

3 Think before you flush. By avoiding just one flush a day, you could save about 4.5 gallons (17 l) of water. That's as much water as the average person in Africa uses to bathe, drink, clean, and cook for an entire day.

4 Collect cans. Just one recycled can saves enough energy to run a small radio for more than ten hours.

5 Drink from one cup a day. The less your family runs the dishwasher, the more energy you'll save.

6 Replace one regular lightbulb. Put an energy-efficient compact fluorescent bulb in at least one lamp at home. If everyone did, it would be like taking 800,000 cars off the road for a year.

7 Use recycled paper. It takes less than half the energy to make notebook paper from recycled paper as it does to make new paper from trees.

8 Ride your bike or walk. You'll keep car emissions out of the atmosphere and you'll get some healthy exercise.

9 Do one less load of laundry a week. You can save as much as 2,000 gallons (7,500 l) of water a year.

10 Compact your trash. Reducing the volume of things like milk jugs and cereal boxes by stepping on them cuts down the number of garbage bags your family uses. Check to see if an item can be recycled before you stomp.

DID YOU KNOW that you will throw away enough trash to fill up about five garbage trucks in your lifetime?

CREATE A ZERO-WASTE LUNCH

Many schools and offices are going green by reducing their waste. Join in! Pick a reusable lunch box or bag. Take plastic containers that can be washed each night instead of sandwich bags that are used only once. Carry a cloth napkin, washable tableware, and a reusable bottle for your drink. Challenge your family to bring home their lunch waste for one week. At the end of the week see who has created the least trash.

Try This!

Global Warming

Feeling the Heat?

In the past century average temperatures rose 1°F (.56°C). That may not seem like a lot, but evidence shows that it is enough to change weather patterns and shift the directions of ocean currents. All of this is an effect of global warming. The heat is melting glaciers and polar ice sheets, causing sea levels to rise and habitats to shrink. This makes survival for many animals a big challenge. Warming also means flooding along the coasts and drought for inland areas.

The world's climate changes naturally, but now people are speeding up the process. Everyday activities, such as driving cars that use gasoline and burning fossil fuels, contribute to global warming. These kinds of activities produce greenhouse gases, which seep into the atmosphere and trap heat. Scientists predict that temperatures may continue to rise by as much as 10°F (5.6°C) over the next hundred years.

Summers in the ARCTIC could be nearly ice-free by 2037.

A GLACIER in GREENLAND loses 20 million tons (18 million t) of ice per day—that's equal to the amount of water NEW YORK CITY uses in a year.

A World at RISK

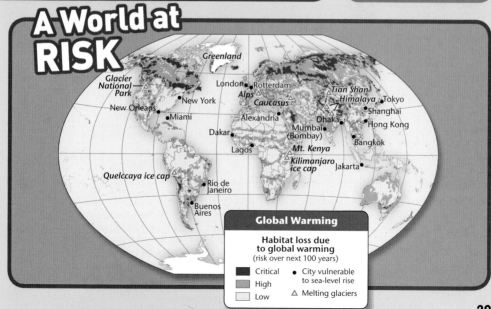

Greenland

Glacier National Park
London • Rotterdam
Alps
New York
New Orleans
Miami
Alexandria
Dakar
Lagos
Quelccaya ice cap
Rio de Janeiro
Buenos Aires
Caucasus
Tian Shan
Himalaya • Tokyo
Shanghai
Dhaka
Mumbai (Bombay)
Hong Kong
Bangkok
Mt. Kenya
Kilimanjaro ice cap
Jakarta

Global Warming

Habitat loss due to global warming
(risk over next 100 years)

- ■ Critical
- ■ High
- □ Low
- • City vulnerable to sea-level rise
- △ Melting glaciers

Pollution
Cleaning Up Our Act

So what's the big deal about a little dirt on the planet? Pollution can affect animals, plants, and people. In fact, some studies show that more people die every year from diseases linked to air pollution than from car accidents. And right now more than one billion of the world's people don't have access to clean drinking water.

A LITTLE POLLUTION=BIG PROBLEMS

You can probably clean your room in a couple of hours. (At least we hope you can!) But you can't shove air and water pollution under your bed or cram them into the closet. Once released into the environment, pollution—whether it's oil leaking from a boat or chemicals spewing from a factory's smokestack—can have a lasting environmental impact.

KEEP IT CLEAN

It's easy to blame things like big factories for pollution problems. But some of the mess comes from everyday activities. Exhaust fumes from cars and garbage in landfills can seriously trash the Earth's health. We all need to pitch in and do some housecleaning. It may mean bicycling more and riding in cars less. Or not dumping water-polluting oil or household cleaners down the drain. Look at it this way: Just as with your room, it's always better not to let Earth get messed up in the first place.

Too Much Light!

Seattle, Washington, U.S.A., at night

Bright lights threaten more than stargazing.
For some wildlife it's a matter of "light" or death. Light pollution, which is excessive or obtrusive artificial light, can affect ecosystems in many ways. For example, it blocks bugs from navigating their way, disorients birds, and misdirects turtles and frogs.

Declining Biodiversity

Saving All Creatures Great and Small

Earth is home to such a huge mix of plants and animals—perhaps 100 million species—and scientists have officially identified and named only about 1.9 million so far! Scientists call this healthy mix biodiversity.

THE BALANCING ACT

The bad news is that half of the planet's plant and animal species may be on the path to extinction, mainly because of human activity. People cut down trees, build roads and houses, pollute rivers, overfish, and overhunt. The good news is that many people care. Scientists and volunteers race against the clock every day, working to save wildlife before time runs out. By building birdhouses, planting trees, and following the rules for hunting and fishing, you can be a positive force for preserving biodiversity, too. Every time you do something to help a species survive, you help Earth keep thriving.

WILDLIFE BIODIVERSITY

Insects, Centipedes, and Millipedes

Other Animals

Mammals

A whitetip reef shark swims along a coral reef.

Habitat Destruction

Living on the Edge

Even though tropical rain forests cover only about 7 percent of the planet's total land surface, they are home to half of all known species of plants and animals. Because people cut down so many trees for lumber and firewood and clear so much land for farms, hundreds of thousands of acres disappear every year.

SHARING THE LAND

Wetlands are also important feeding and breeding grounds. People have drained many wetlands, turning them into farm fields or sites for industries. More than half the world's wetlands have disappeared within the past century, squeezing wildlife out. Balancing the needs of humans and animals is the key to lessening habitat destruction.

jaguar

31

World Energy & Minerals

Almost everything people do—from cooking to powering the International Space Station—requires energy. But energy comes in different forms. Traditional energy sources, still used by many people in the developing world, include burning dried animal dung and wood. Industrialized countries and urban centers around the world rely on coal, oil, and natural gas—called fossil fuels because they formed from decayed plant and animal material accumulated from long ago. Fossil fuel deposits, either in the ground or under the ocean floor, are unevenly distributed on Earth, and only some countries can afford to buy them. Fossil fuels are also not renewable, meaning they will run out one day. And unless we find other ways to create energy, we'll be stuck. Without energy we won't be able to drive cars, use lights, or send emails to friends.

TAKING A TOLL

Environmentally speaking, burning fossil fuels isn't necessarily the best choice either—carbon dioxide from the burning of fossil fuels, as well as other emissions, are contributing to global warming. Concerned scientists are looking at new ways to harness renewable, alternative sources of energy, such as water, wind, and sun.

COOL CLICK

To learn more about global trends, go online.
national geographic.com/ earthpulse

OIL, GAS, AND COAL

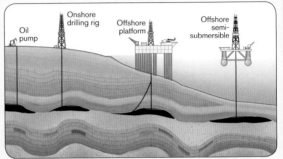

This illustration shows some of the different kinds of onshore and offshore drilling equipment. The type of drilling equipment depends on whether oil or natural gas is in the ground or under the ocean.

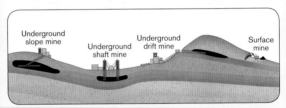

The mining of coal made the industrial revolution possible, and coal still provides a major energy source. Work that was once done by people using picks and shovels now relies heavily on mechanized equipment. This diagram shows some of the various kinds of mines currently in use.

WORLD PRIMARY ENERGY SUPPLY

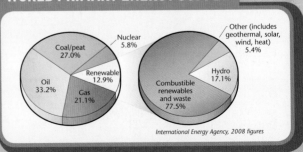

Coal/peat 27.0%
Nuclear 5.8%
Renewable 12.9%
Oil 33.2%
Gas 21.1%

Other (includes geothermal, solar, wind, heat) 5.4%
Hydro 17.1%
Combustible renewables and waste 77.5%

International Energy Agency, 2008 figures

Alternative Power

WIND

Strong winds blowing through California's mountains spin windmill blades on an energy farm, powering giant turbines that generate electricity for the state.

HYDROELECTRIC

Hydroelectric plants, such as Santiago del Estero in Argentina, use dams to harness running water to generate clean, renewable energy.

GEOTHERMAL

Geothermal power, from ground-water heated by molten rock, provides energy for this power plant in Iceland. Swimmers enjoy the warm waters of a lake created by the power plant.

SOLAR

Solar panels on Samso Island in Denmark capture and store energy from the sun, an environmentally friendly alternative to fossil fuels.

BIODIESEL

The superfast Die Moto bike runs on man-made fuel made mainly from vegetable oil, called biodiesel. Biodiesel is cleaner and emits fewer pollutants into the air.

CHANGE THE WORLD!

Just like rivers and trails, community parks need people like you to care about them so that everyone has a nice place to play. Here are some fun ideas to get you started.

LITTER PATROL

Hand out trash bags and latex gloves to friends, and get that garbage off the ground. Use separate bags for paper, plastic, and aluminum cans so you can recycle.

PARTY IN THE PARK

Throw a bash with your family and friends in your favorite park. Pick a theme—Earth Day, Summer Vacation, Global Safari—and come up with games, activities, and a menu to match your theme.

SPEAK UP!

If your local parks are run-down or dreary, tell someone. Get in touch with your mayor, city council, or parks and recreation department to ask them to make parks a priority.

PAINT PALS

Spiff up your park by painting a mural on a wall, games like hopscotch on the blacktop. You can even paint benches crazy colors. Make sure to first get permission from whoever is responsible for the park. (Start with your city's parks and recreation department.)

 Want to create your own place to play? Team up with an adult and check out KaBOOM!, an organization that provides support to help people design and build playgrounds in their communities. Learn more online. **kaboom.org**

Try This!

Need another reason to ride your bike? It's good for the planet! By ditching the car and cycling to your friend's house or soccer practice instead, you'll keep pollutants from being emitted into the atmosphere—3.6 pounds (1.6 kg) for every mile you ride! Sit down with your parents and map out safe routes you can cycle together. Then, spiff up your ride with these wheely—er—*really* fun bike license plates using items found around your house.

YOU WILL NEED

- cardboard
- pencil
- ruler
- scissors
- scrap construction paper or leftover wrapping paper
- glue
- hole punch
- markers, stickers, magazine cutouts
- ribbon or string

WHAT TO DO

1. Draw a 9-inch (23-cm) oval on the cardboard. Cut it out.

2. Trace the cardboard oval onto the paper, and cut it out as well.

3. Glue the paper to the cardboard.

4. Use a hole punch to make two holes on opposite sides of the oval.

5. Write a license plate message like "Born 2 Bike" or "Reduce, reuse, reCYCLE" in the center of the paper. Then decorate it with markers, stickers, and magazine cutouts.

6. Thread some ribbon or string through the holes and tie it tightly around the handlebars. Trim the ends.

HIT THE ROAD!

Encourage your family to use bikes more and the car less.

Ten bikes can park in the space used by one car.

By cleaning your bike parts, you'll make your bike last longer and help keep it out of the landfill. Be sure to use eco-friendly cleaning supplies.

BORN 2 BIKE EXPLORE

Write a Letter That Gets Results

Knowing how to write a good letter is a useful skill. It will come in handy anytime you want to persuade someone to understand your point of view. Whether you're emailing your congressman, or writing a letter for a school project or to your grandma, a great letter will help you get your message across. Most important, a well-written letter leaves a good impression.

Check out the example below for the elements of a good letter.

Your address

Date

Salutation
Always use "Dear" followed by the person's name; use Mr. or Mrs. or Dr. as appropriate.

Introductory paragraph
Give the reason you're writing the letter.

Body
The longest part of the letter, which provides evidence that supports your position. Be persuasive!

Closing paragraph
Sum up your argument.

Complimentary closing
Sign off with "Sincerely" or "Thank you."

Your Signature

Sadie Donnelly
1128 Albermarle Street
Los Angeles, CA 90045

March 31, 2012

Dear Mr. School Superintendent,

I am writing to you about all the trash I see at our school at lunchtime and to offer a solution.

I see the trash on the ground, blowing around the yard, getting stuck on the fences, and sometimes overflowing the trash cans. Usually, there are also plastic bags, paper bags, food containers, water bottles, and juice boxes from student and teacher lunches.

I am suggesting that one day a week the whole school have a No Trash Lunch Day. My idea is to have students and teachers bring their food and drinks in reusable containers. We would take the containers home to clean and use again another day.

Above all, I think our school could help the environment and cut back on how much of this trash goes to the landfills and pollutes the ocean. Let's see No Trash Lunch Day at our school soon. Thank you.

Sincerely,

Sadie Donnelly

COMMONLY USED COMPLIMENTARY CLOSINGS

Sincerely,
Sincerely yours,
Thank you,
Regards,
Best wishes,
Respectfully,

YOU CAN MAKE A DIFFERENCE!

Want to do more to make the world a better place? Have a question or an opinion? Do something about it. Turn your passion for a cause into meaningful action.

DIG DEEPER! Look to newspaper or magazine articles, books, the Internet, and anything else you can get your hands on. Learn about the issue or organization that most inspires you.

GET INVOLVED! The following organizations can connect you to opportunities so you can make a difference:
dosomething.org
volunteermatch.org
globalvolunteers.org

MAKE YOUR VOICE HEARD!
Email, call, or write to politicians or government officials:
congress.org

GO ONLINE TO HELP CARE FOR THE EARTH.
Learn more about environmental issues:
earthday.net
ecokids.ca/pub/kids_home.cfm
treepeople.org
meetthegreens.org
kidsplanet.org/defendit/new/

Collect pennies to help save wild species and wild places:
togethergreen.org/p4p

Start an environmental club at your school:
greenguideforkids.blogspot.com/
search/label/activities

Learn how to start a kitchen compost bin:
meetthegreens.org/episode4/kitchen-composting.html

Reduce paper waste by receiving fewer catalogs:
catalogchoice.org

Learn how to green your school:
nrdc.org/greensquad

LETTER-WRITING TIPS

Before you start writing, think about what you would like to write about.

Use your own words.

Use stationery that is appropriate for the recipient; for example, plain, nice paper for a congressman and maybe a pretty card for your grandma.

When handwriting, make sure you write neatly.

Follow the elements of a well-written letter at left.

Be creative!

Before you send the letter, read it again and check for spelling errors.

Write neatly on the envelope so that the postal worker can read it easily.

Don't forget the stamp for snail mail.

Want to find out more about how to help look after the planet? See these websites:
epa.gov/kids
childrenoftheearth.org

COOL CLICKS

GO GREEN!
Save paper and send your letter by email. If you have to print it out, try to use recycled paper.

Amazing Animals

Hanging out. A mother orangutan and two baby orangutans in Indonesia.

WHAT IS
Taxonomy?

Since there are billions and billions of living things, called organisms, on the planet, people need a way of classifying them. Scientists created a system called **taxonomy**, which helps to classify all living things into ordered groups. By putting organisms into categories we are able to better understand how they are the same and how they are different. There are seven levels of taxonomic classification, beginning with the broadest group, called a domain, down to the most specific group, called a species.

Biologists divide life based on evolutionary history and place organisms in three domains depending on their genetic structure: Archaea, Bacteria, and Eukarya. (See p. 135 for "The Three Domains of Life.")

Where do animals come in?

Animals are a part of the Eukarya domain, which means they are organisms made of cells with nuclei. There are more than one million species named, including humans. Like all living things, animals can be divided into smaller groups, called phyla. Most scientists believe there are more than 30 phyla into which animals can be grouped based on certain scientific criteria, such as body type or whether or not the animal has a backbone. It can be pretty complicated, so there is another less complicated system that groups animals into two categories: vertebrates and invertebrates.

Chinese stripe-necked turtle

SAMPLE CLASSIFICATION
MEERKAT

Domain:	Eukarya
Phylum:	Chordata
Class:	Mammalia
Order:	Carnivora
Family:	Viverridae
Genus:	*Suricata*
Species:	*S. suricatta*

TIP
Here's a sentence to help you remember the classification order:
Dear **P**hilip **C**ame **O**ver **F**or **G**ood **S**oup.

Bet you didn't know

THE LONGEST worms can grow to 100 FEET (30 m)

ABOUT 95 PERCENT of all ANIMALS ARE INVERTEBRATES

Vertebrates Animals WITH Backbones

Fish are cold-blooded and live in water. They breathe with gills, lay eggs, and usually have scales.

Amphibians are cold-blooded. Their young live in water and breathe with gills. Adults live on land and breathe with lungs.

Reptiles are cold-blooded and breathe with lungs. They live on both land and water.

Birds are warm-blooded and have feathers and wings. They lay eggs, breathe with lungs, and usually are able to fly. Some birds live on land, some in water, and some on both.

Mammals are warm-blooded and feed on their mothers' milk. They also have skin that is usually covered with hair. Mammals live on both land and water.

Bird:
White-faced owl

Fish:
Gray reef
shark

Invertebrates Animals WITHOUT Backbones

Sponges are a very basic form of animal life. They live in water and do not move on their own.

Echinoderms have external skeletons and live in seawater.

Mollusks have soft bodies and can live either in or out of shells, on land or in water.

Arthropods are the largest group of animals. They have external skeletons, called exoskeletons, and segmented bodies with appendages. Arthropods live in water and on land.

Worms are soft-bodied animals with no true legs. Worms live in soil.

Cnidaria live in water and have mouths surrounded by tentacles.

Worm:
Earthworms

Sponge:
Brown tube
sponges

Arthropod:
Red-kneed tarantula

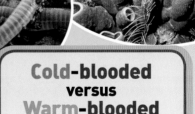

Cold-blooded versus Warm-blooded

Cold-blooded animals, also called ectotherms, get their heat from outside their bodies.

Warm-blooded animals, also called endotherms, keep their body temperature level regardless of the temperature of their environments.

41

Who's Smarter...

Cats or Dogs?

CATS FLUSH

Russ and Sandy Asbury were alone in their home when they suddenly heard the toilet flush. "My husband's eyes got huge," says Sandy. "Did we have ghosts?"

Nope. Their cats just like to play with toilets. Boots, a Maine coon cat, taught himself to push on the handle that flushes. Then his copycat brother, Bandit, followed. "It's kind of eerie," Sandy admits. "Bandit follows me into the bathroom and flushes for me—sometimes even before I'm finished!"

Now the cats use the stunt to get attention. They go into a flushing frenzy if supper's late!

These cats just play in the bathroom, but some cats can be trained to use the toilet instead of a litter box. For their lucky owners, cleanup is just a flush (instead of a scoop) away. Meanwhile, Fido's just *drinking* from the toilet.

DOGS "GO" ON CUE

To housebreak a pup, take him outside and watch closely. When he starts to urinate, say the same phrase, such as "right there," each time. Within weeks, he'll associate the phrase with the action.

Buffy, a keeshond belonging to Wade Newman of Turin, New York, has never had an "accident" in the house. In fact, the smart dog sometimes plans ahead. Once, called in for the night, she came running. "But suddenly she stopped, cocked her head, and took off in the other direction," Newman says. "I was kind of annoyed." But it turned out Buffy was simply getting ready for bed—by "going" first, after which she obediently ran back to Newman. Now, *that's* thinking ahead!

CATS LISTEN

When a small plane crash-landed in the ocean, a cargo vessel steamed over to help but found no survivors. They were just about to give up hope when suddenly, the crew's mascot, a cat, howled and started racing around on the front of the ship. The startled sailors shined searchlights on the water and found a woman floating in the water 100 yards (91 m) away—the length of a football field. The cat heard her, alerted the crew, and became a feline hero. It just goes to show that even when you think cats are asleep, they're listening!

DOGS PREDICT SEIZURES

Carol Folwell has epilepsy, a brain disorder. She used to fall during seizures, banging her head or breaking her arm. Then she got Lindsay, a golden retriever, who accompanies her everywhere and warns her of an impending seizure by bumping against her leg. How can a dog tell when a seizure is coming? She may notice some chemical or electrical change or a tiny shift in body language. Nobody knows for sure. But one thing is for certain: Dogs that can predict seizures have a very valuable talent.

DOGS PLAY THE PIANO

Forget "sit" and "shake." Chanda-Leah, a toy poodle who died in 2006 at the age of 12, used to settle down at a computerized keyboard and plunk out "Twinkle, Twinkle, Little Star." Flashing red lights under the white keys told her which notes to hit.

"She loved to show off," says owner Sharon Robinson, who says the secret to training is practice and patience. That must be true, because Chanda knew a record-breaking number of tricks! She's the trickiest canine ever listed in *The Guinness Book of World Records.*

CATS WALK TIGHTROPES

Animal trainers of cats that appear in movies and TV commercials train the feline actors to walk on tightropes, wave at crowds, and open doors.

"Cats can do a lot, like jump through hoops, retrieve toys, and give high fives," says Bonnie Beaver, a veterinarian at Texas A&M University. But unlike dogs, they won't work for praise. "Cats are motivated by food," she says, "and it's got to be yummy."

NAUGHTY PETS

WHERE'S MY ASSISTANT? I NEED MY SUNGLASSES.

NAME Sabacca

FAVORITE ACTIVITY
Watching humans perform tricks in the pool

FAVORITE TOY
Pool raft

PET PEEVE
Not being allowed to drink the pool water

So, which *is* smarter... a CAT or a DOG?

Actually, this is a trick question, and there's no simple answer.
Dogs and cats have different abilities. Each species knows what it needs to know in order to survive. "For that reason, we can't design a test that is equal for both animals," says Beaver. "When people ask me which is smarter, I say it's whichever one you own!"

WHAT TO NAME YOUR PET?

Just got a pet? Congrats! Maybe the instant you locked eyes with the fuzzy, cuddly creature, a name naturally came to you. Or maybe you're at a complete loss as to what to call your newest constant companion. Here are some tips for coming up with the perfect pet name.

- Keep it short. Animals respond better to one- or two-syllable names.

- Consider your cat or dog's breed, heritage, or where it was born as inspiration for a possible name.

- Avoid anything that you'd feel silly calling out in public. ("Chubby Hubby" may be cute at home, but maybe not so much at the park!)

- For dogs, try to steer clear of anything that sounds like a standard command (no, stay, sit, come, down, or fetch). For example, calling a dog "Joe," which sounds similar to "No," may confuse a poor pooch.

- Play with your pet for a couple of days to get a better grip on its personality. "Cuddly" may not be the best name for a standoffish cat. Same goes for a name that an animal might grow out of, such as "Tiny" or "Baby."

Q Do fish SLEEP?

A A goldfish could beat you in a staring contest in its sleep—literally! Most fish don't have eyelids, so they catch a few winks with their eyes wide open. Instead of snoozing deeply like people do, many fish just slow down to a resting state. As soon as prey or predators swim by, a fish gets an instant wake-up call. So they don't really sleep, but you could say that fish take catnaps.

PET PERKS

Why should cats and dogs get all the attention? Here's what makes other pets so special. See if one of them is right for you.

HORSE

If you have the time and money, pick one for its behavior, not its breed. Horses can take you for a ride!

GUINEA PIG

Guinea pigs love to snuggle up and have you pet their soft fur.

PARAKEET

Parakeets can be trained to talk and will perch on your finger.

NauGHty PETS

I'M GONNA GET A TASTE OF THAT TUNA SANDWICH AS SOON AS THEY LOAD THE DISHWASHER.

NAME Kaji

FAVORITE ACTIVITY
Licking leftovers off plates and utensils

FAVORITE TOY
Scrubby brush

PET PEEVE
Rinsed dishes

PET PROJECT

Want to adopt a dog or cat? If you already have a pet, it may growl at the idea. To avoid a fur fight, try these tips:

 Choose an animal younger than your current pet.

 Introduce your new pet during a vacation, when you will be home.

 Separate the animals for a few days, then bring them together for a few minutes at a time.

 Give each its own sleeping space, litter box (for cats), and food dish.

 Keep your current pet's routine the same.

"THEY'RE SURPRISINGLY EASY TO TRAIN!"

Q Does it HURT when a lizard's TAIL FALLS OFF?

A Probably, but losing a tail can save a lizard's life. Predators often grab the reptiles' tails during the chase. But some lizards can tighten the muscles at the base of their tails, so they snap right off. Even disconnected, the tail keeps wiggling, which confuses the hunter. A replacement—though stubbier than the original—grows back in a few weeks.

A CHAMELEON'S TONGUE CAN STRETCH TO ONE AND A HALF TIMES ITS BODY LENGTH.

Does Your Pet L♥ve You?

More scientists are beginning to agree with what most pet owners already believe: Pets do love the people in their lives. Decide for yourself!

Rescue Dog

When two-year-old Daisy Smith wandered from her family's yard one day, she was lucky to have her family's Labrador retriever, Thunder, tagging along. After 13 hours, a search party finally found the little girl (right) sitting by a river a mile and a half (2.4 km) from her home, with Thunder by her side. There's no doubt that this hero dog loves his Daisy!

Fire Cat

Boo Boo the cat is living proof that animals are capable of unselfish love. One night, as Frances Morris and her husband were asleep in their bed, Boo Boo began meowing and howling. Sleepily, Morris tried to calm Boo Boo, but the cat kept meowing. Fully awake, Morris realized the bedroom was filling with smoke. The kitchen was on fire! Instead of escaping outside, Boo Boo had run upstairs to warn the Morrises, and everyone escaped safely.

Funny Bunny

Who needs jokes when you have a bunny? That's what 13-year-old Kenny Clessas discovered when his pet rabbit, Killer, got him giggling after a bad day. Noticing Kenny crying, Killer started head-butting and running circles around the boy. Kenny just had to laugh!

How affectionate is your pet?

①

When you arrive at home, your dog...

ⓐ hides under the couch.

ⓑ barely looks up from its nap

ⓒ runs to greet you.

②

Whenever you sit down on a chair or the floor, your cat...

ⓐ leaves the room.

ⓑ watches you from afar.

ⓒ cuddles up on your lap, purring.

③

If you reach into the cage, your gerbil...

ⓐ digs into its wood chips to hide.

ⓑ backs away unless coaxed with a treat.

ⓒ jumps onto your hand eagerly.

IF YOUR ANSWER IS a, your pet plays it cool. It decides when it's cuddle time. **b,** your pet thinks you're its buddy. It likes you to be around. **c,** your pet is head over heels in love with you. It would do anything to be close to you.

47

Lifestyles of the

Showing love for your pet doesn't have to cost a thing. Still, pet owners spend billions a year on their pets—including hundreds on just food and treats for each cat and dog. Here's a look at some very posh pets.

DIAMONDS ARE A CODDLED KITTY'S BEST FRIEND.

◀ GETTIN' WIGGY

When Romeo the Yorkshire terrier wants to step out in style, he slips on a hot-pink wig. Lenny the Cavalier King Charles spaniel dons dreadlocks when he cruises the park. The price of the $40 hairpieces may cause some people to, uh, wig out. "But some owners spare no expense to keep their pets posh," says Ruth Regina, founder of the doggie-wig company Wiggles. "The dogs and the owners love how much attention they get when they wear the wigs."

RICH and FURRY

THIS PAMPERED POOCH DOESN'T MIND BEING STALKED BY THE *PAW*-PARAZZI.

▼ HOLY "*MUTT*-RIMONY"

JAKE AND JILL MAKE A LOVE CONNECTION.

Flowers: $1,000. Satin bridal gown: $500. "*Pup*-cakes": $100. Watching two dogs get "married" at a fancy wedding? Priceless. At least that's what some owners think when they cough up major cash for a pet wedding. "It's a way to honor the puppy love and have fun," says pet party planner Alma Rose Middleton, who has "married" dogs such as Boo Boo and Mimi after they "fell in love" at a birthday party. The cost of a to-drool-for wedding? Up to $8,000!

▼ THE SUITE LIFE

DOGS PADDLE ALL THEY WANT IN THE BONE-SHAPED POOL AT PARADISE 4 PAWS.

A regular kennel just won't do for pets like Chloe the Mi-Ki dog. When her owners go out of town, they put her up at Paradise 4 Paws outside of Chicago, Illinois, one of many pet hotels opening around the United States. There, Chloe can watch *Soccer Dog: The Movie* on a flat-screen TV, or check out the scene at the bone-shaped splashing pool. "She's just as spoiled there as she is at home," says owner Renee Miastkowski. At the Barkley Pet Hotel in Orange Village, Ohio, guests ride in a stretch "*cat*-illac" limousine and indulge in "*paw*-dicures."

Bugs, Bugs, and More Bugs!

Those creepy crawlers are the most diverse group of the animal kingdom. From the phylum Arthropoda, insects are considered to be the most successful life-form on the planet! There are so many millions of insect species that scientists can't even agree on the number. They live everywhere—in every habitat—from the frozen tundra to the arid desert. They even live on you!

The most common characteristic among arthropods is that they have a hard outer shell, called an exoskeleton. They also have segmented bodies, which include three parts: **head**, **thorax**, and **abdomen**. There are two classes in the arthropod phylum: Hexapoda (insects) and Arachnida (spiders, ticks, mites, scorpions, and their relatives).

> The study of insects is called entomology.

abdomen

head

thorax

INSECTS Helping Out

Insects aren't just about bugging you. There are lots of ways they are beneficial to humans. Here are some of the most common ways insects help us.

FOOD: Some insects are eaten by people. Bees make honey.

PRODUCTS: Silk, dyes, and beeswax

POLLINATION: They pollinate plants so that humans can grow fruit and vegetable crops, making insects responsible for billions of dollars' worth of the food we eat.

AND THEY'RE PRETTY TO LOOK AT, TOO!

Bet you didn't know

Houseflies **BUZZ** in the key of **F.**

A male African **CICADA** can make a **SOUND** as **LOUD** as a **POWER LAWN MOWER.**

Bee Mystery

Millions of honeybees are vanishing, and their disappearing act has experts stumped.

Since 2007, 25 percent to 35 percent of honeybee colonies have been wiped out each winter, a much higher rate than before. Some of these losses are caused by an unsolved problem called colony collapse disorder.

These losses have people all over the world buzzing, especially since a lot of what we eat is directly or indirectly pollinated by honeybees, including apples and almonds.

So what is the cause of this bizarre *bee*-havior? No one knows for sure. But experts think that environmental factors—like pesticides and unusually cold weather—as well as parasites that feed on bee blood are to blame. The parasites, called varroa mites, also spread a flu-like infection, which bees have trouble fighting with their weak immune systems.

There may not be a cure for colony collapse disorder yet, but experts are working hard to solve the puzzle. In fact, a British beekeeper named Ron Hoskins recently discovered a new strain of honeybees that may be resistant to varroa mites. How so? These bees "groom" one another to remove the mites, a move that could eventually save the hives.

Though Hoskins' research is still preliminary, it's a promising step in putting these busy bees back in business.

WHAT'S ALL THE BUZZ ABOUT?

Bees can be green, blue, or red.

Only female bees sting.

The average honeybee lives 30 days.

BY THE NUMBERS

- **5,000,000** flowers must be pollinated by bees to make one average-size jar of honey.
- **40,000** bees can live in one hive.

51

5 COOL THINGS ABOUT Butterflies

1

SOME **butterflies** shimmer.

2

BLUE MORPHO

Like all butterflies, the blue morpho butterfly has microscopic scales on its wings. Its scales make this brilliant blue insect iridescent. When you look at it from different angles, it appears to change color from light blue to purple—or even neon blue.

VICEROY

Butterflies ARE COPYCATS.

The orange-and-black viceroy, like many species of butterflies, has evolved to outsmart its hungry predators by mimicking the appearance of the poisonous monarch. Animals won't eat the viceroy for fear of a nasty stomachache.

Butterflies LIVE ALMOST EVERYWHERE.

3

Butterflies live on all continents except Antarctica. Lepidopterists, or scientists who specialize in butterfly biology, estimate that there are about 20,000 species of butterflies worldwide.

5

SOME **butterflies** ARE tiny.

The grass blue holds the Guinness World Record as the smallest butterfly. It's about the size of a penny.

4

SOME **butterflies** ARE world TRAVELERS.

RED ADMIRAL

The red admiral is found on several continents. It makes a remarkable round-trip journey between Africa and Europe. Monarch butterflies migrate from Canada to Mexico.

BACKYARD SAFARI

Want to find out what kinds of cool critters are living in your backyard? Conduct a BioBlitz! This is a quick and easy way to identify as many species as possible living in an environment. With about two million species living on Earth, who knows what you'll find?

WHAT TO DO

1 **GO EXPLORE.**
When searching for what's living outside your window, use your senses. In a notebook, jot notes of the size, color, sound, and smell of every plant and animal you find. Add photos or drawings.

2 **TAKE A CLOSER LOOK.**
Figure out what species you've spotted by studying its color and markings. For help identifying species, consult a nature guide or encyclopedia.

3 **X MARKS THE SPOT.**
Create a map—it'll help you remember where things are. Plus, a map will give you a better understanding of the relationships between plants and animals, and why they need each other to survive.

4 **COUNT IT.**
Add up the number of species you identify to get an idea of the habitat's biodiversity. It'll be helpful to put things into categories, such as mammals or insects.

More **BEETLES** live on Earth than any other creature.

Amazing Animal Friends

I KID YOU NOT: THIS GIRL IS MY BEST FRIEND.

Like humans, animals take care of each other. Sometimes it doesn't matter if they're different species. These stories prove that friendship comes in all shapes and sizes.

DOG PROTECTS GOAT

Buckfastleigh, England

When Lilly the goat arrived at Pennywell Farm after her mother abandoned her, humans weren't the only ones who cared for her. Billy the boxer did, too. Like an adoptive dad, Billy made sure Lilly kept her coat and muzzle clean by softly licking the milk the goat spilled on herself during bottle-feedings. Later, after the two playfully chased each other and it was time to go inside, Billy would gently nudge Lilly's bottom if she dawdled. When Billy leaped onto the sofa to watch TV, Lilly sprang up right next to him. "It's like Lilly has her own personal watchdog," owner Chris Murray says.

RABBIT BUILDS BED FOR DEER

Niedersachsen, Germany

After her mother was struck by a car, Finchen the fawn was brought to live on a farm. One day as she grazed, a wild rabbit appeared, and it's been by Finchen's side ever since. "I've watched them alert each other to hazards or predators so they can flee to safety," says Tanja Askani, who photographed the pair. But Finchen and her rabbit friend seem to be more than each other's bodyguard. The rabbit must have realized that Finchen was too big to sleep underground, because the bunny built a grassy nest that was big enough for them both to curl up in. They're like a real-life Bambi and Thumper.

I SEE YOU GOT THE EMAIL TO WEAR BROWN TODAY.

The word "orangutan" comes from two words in the Malay language: *orang*, meaning "man," and *utan*, meaning "of the forest."

ORANGUTAN KEEPS PET CAT

Panama City Beach, Florida

Tonda the orangutan was sad when her mate went away. She even lost interest in painting, one of her favorite hobbies. Then her keepers introduced her to a cat named T.K.—and suddenly the ape was back to her old self. "Tonda carried T.K. all over the place," says Stephanie Willard of ZooWorld. "She gave him food, stroked him, and dangled toys for him to play with." The orangutan even covered T.K.'s eyes when the ape got her shots so the cat wouldn't be afraid. Tonda wouldn't come into her enclosure at night until T.K. was there, too. The cat even inspired Tonda to start painting again.

Animal Talk

Talking to animals is not just for Dr. Dolittle—most people can learn to do it. How? Sometimes, you can teach them actual words, symbols, sounds, or gestures. Other times, you can read an animal's body language. Here are three surprising stories about how humans and animals communicate.

1 Fish Fry

Josephine the bottlenose dolphin likes her fish frozen. And by pressing a paddle whenever she hears a certain sound, she earns 25 treats in a row. But one day, Josephine simply stopped responding to the sound. When her trainer checked on the machine dispensing the fish, she realized the snacks were sunbaked and about as appetizing as warm ice cream. Ewww!

Josephine watched as the warm fish were replaced with frozen. Then, when her trainer hit the sound button, she zoomed right over and pressed the paddle to get her frozen fish. Now that's one brilliant bottlenose!

In Touch 2

An alert dog "hears" what we say, even when our message is unspoken. Radio pet show host Harrison Forbes learned this lesson from his perceptive pooch, PJ. Whenever Forbes's mom walked the dog, PJ would pick a fight with a neighbor's Rottweiler. But if Forbes walked PJ along the same route, the two dogs would just sniff and play.

Turns out, Forbes's mom was terrified of Rottweilers and tensed every time she met one. PJ picked up on that fear. "Your feelings, whether of confidence or anxiety, travel straight to the dog," says Forbes. So if your dog misbehaves, maybe changing your own behavior could help.

3 Open Sesame!

WHO'S UP FOR A GAME OF HIDE-AND-SEEK?

When Shanthi, a young zoo elephant, wants to go out and play, she really lets you know! That's what behavioral biologist Karen Pryor discovered when she tried to train the elephant, who lives in a cage with bars that reach to the roof.

Though she can't talk, Shanthi was able to communicate her preference to play by poking her trunk out through the side of her enclosure. "She looked back and forth, from me to where the trunk is," says the biologist.

Pryor followed the elephant's gaze—and saw that her trunk was gripping the fist-size padlock that holds her in.

"Her message was clear," says Pryor. She unlocked the door, and the playful pachyderm happily bounded out into the yard.

An Art-Smart Ape

Of all the great apes—bonobos, gorillas, orangutans, and chimpanzees—bonobos are the most like humans. And no other bonobo in captivity has shown off its smarts more than Kanzi, who lives at the Great Ape Trust research facility in Des Moines, Iowa.

In the past, Kanzi has blown researchers away with his ability to drink from a glass, brush his teeth, use the toilet, and communicate through a series of symbols on a chart that represent words. He even learned to make campfires, collecting and piling up wood before borrowing a lighter to ignite the blaze. Now, Kanzi has begun to paint pictures—and even gives titles to his works of art, something almost unheard of!

A True Artist

How does Kanzi name his paintings? It all started one day at the Great Ape Trust as Kanzi was painting away while munching on some watermelon. As he painted and snacked, his caretakers noticed he only dipped his brush in the red, green, and white paints—the same colors as the watermelon. But just in case his caretakers couldn't tell what he was painting, the bonobo actually named the work "Watermelon" with his symbols! The painting was so impressive that it was eventually auctioned for $1,500.

Caretaker Susannah Maisel says Kanzi's creativity gives insight into intelligence. "It shows that his paintings are more than just colors on a canvas," Maisel says. "He really puts thought into what he's painting, just as a human artist would."

I THINK I'LL TRY SCULPTING NEXT.

KANZI DISPLAYS ONE OF HIS UNTITLED PAINTINGS.

"Watermelon" (shown at right) was auctioned for $1,500, which will go toward ape conservation.

BONOBOS are only found in the wild in AFRICA's Congo Basin, the world's SECOND-LARGEST RAIN FOREST.

ANIMAL MYTHS BUSTED

Animals do some pretty strange things. Giraffes clean their eyes and ears with their tongues. Snakes see through their eyelids. Some snails can hibernate for three years. But other weird animal tales are hogwash. Find out how some of these myths started—and why they're not true.

MYTH Touching a frog or toad will give you warts.

HOW IT STARTED Many frogs and toads have bumps on their skin that look like warts. Some people think the bumps are contagious.

WHY IT'S NOT TRUE "Warts are caused by a human virus, not frogs or toads," says dermatologist Jerry Litt. But the wartlike bumps behind a toad's ears *can* be dangerous. These parotoid glands contain a nasty poison that irritates the mouths of some predators and often the skin of humans. So toads may not cause warts, but they can cause other nasties. It's best not to handle these critters—warty or not!

PHEW! YOU NEED A BIRDBATH!

MYTH Mother birds will reject their babies if they've been touched by humans.

HOW IT STARTED Well-meaning humans who find a chick on the ground may want to return the baby bird to the nest. But the bird is probably learning to fly and shouldn't be disturbed. The tale may have been invented to keep people from handling young birds.

WHY IT'S NOT TRUE "Most birds have a poorly developed sense of smell," says Michael Mace, bird curator at San Diego Zoo's Wild Animal Park. "They won't notice a human scent." One exception: vultures, who sniff out dead animals for dinner. But you wouldn't want to mess with a vulture anyway!

MYTH Opossums hang by their tails.

HOW IT STARTED Opossums use their tails to grasp branches as they climb trees. So it's not surprising that people believe they also hang from branches.

WHY IT'S NOT TRUE A baby opossum can hang from its tail for a few seconds, but an adult is too heavy. "Besides, that wouldn't help them survive," says Paula Arms of the National Opossum Society. "Why would they just hang around? That skill isn't useful—there's no point."

5 COOL THINGS ABOUT ELEPHANTS

1 ELEPHANTS HAVE LONG MEMORIES

Elephants never forget. "They keep coming to places they like, no matter what," says wildlife photographer Frans Lanting. One elephant herd has been visiting the same tree every November for at least 25 years!

2 ELEPHANTS CHAT WITH FRIENDS

Elephants are always "talking" in some way. This is fine in the wild. But it's a problem when elephants join sightseers on safari through the jungle. Noisy elephants spook wildlife away. "We depended on quiet," says John Roberts, who managed elephants at a lodge in the Royal Chitwan National Park in Nepal, in Asia.

When pachyderm pals Chan Chun Kali and Bhirikuti Kali worked together, they were too chatty, so Roberts moved the elephants to separate camps, six miles (10 km) apart. This worked during the day. But every night the chatterboxes started up again. They didn't rumble softly like most elephants do when "talking" long-distance. "They shouted!" says Roberts. He wore earplugs to get some sleep.

3 ELEPHANTS HELP EACH OTHER

A retired circus elephant named Peggy might have drowned if another elephant hadn't come to her rescue! Peggy, an elephant with a partially paralyzed trunk, and her friend Betty Boop were bathing in a pond, when Peggy lay down on her side. Swimming elephants use their trunks as snorkels, but Peggy's was completely underwater. The elephant couldn't breathe or stand! Luckily Betty Boop rushed over and used her head to push Peggy back up on her feet and save her.

4 ELEPHANTS THINK FOR THEMSELVES

The wild and wacky sport of elephant polo is popular in Thailand. During one game, a player couldn't quite hit the ball—he just kept swinging and missing. Finally his quick-thinking elephant took matters into her own hands. She picked up the ball and handed it to the player!

5 ELEPHANTS HELP PEOPLE

Some animals are very helpful to humans, and elephants are no exception. The massive mammals can be trained to lift heavy logs in forests, move toppled trees after floods, pull cars from rivers, and clear weed-clogged waterways. One pack of pachyderms in Oregon even learned how to stomp grapes to make wine! And after a tsunami destroyed parts of southern Asia in 2004, elephants used their trunks to hoist motorcycles (left) and cars from the wreckage. More recently, three domesticated elephants took to the streets of Bangkok, Thailand, with baskets in their trunks, collecting more than $21,000 for victims of the 2010 earthquake in Haiti. Guess that makes these animals huge heroes!

THE Great Koala RESCUE

Frightened and helpless, a baby koala clings to a tree branch. Below, his mother screams. Searching for dinner, the mother has gotten her head stuck in a fence.

For Australians, spotting a koala isn't unusual, but finding one in distress is. Desperate to save the koala, a family who happened upon the scene calls the Queensland Parks and Wildlife Service. Koala rescuer Vicki Pender is sent to help.

Pender knows she must act quickly to save the terrified animal, which is frantically struggling to free herself. After giving the koala a tranquilizer to calm her down, Pender carefully cuts away the fence with bolt cutters.

CAUGHT IN HER TRACKS

Just as she is about to rush to the animal hospital, a yipping sound stops Pender in her tracks. High in a nearby tree, the baby calls for its mother. The rescuer tries to coax him from the tree, but he scampers away. Knowing the baby will not survive alone, Pender needs to act fast.

Quick action, experience, and a little luck help the rescuer nab the confused baby before he gets far. At the hospital veterinarians check both koalas for injuries.

Every day, rescuers, scientists, and citizens work to help save koalas. Not too long ago millions of koalas thrived in Australian forests. Then people moved in, cutting down trees to build roads, houses, factories, and malls.

A DANGEROUS LIFE

Koalas stay in the trees as much as possible, preferring to spend little time on the ground. A koala's life consists mainly of sleeping during the day and devouring up to two pounds (907 g) of eucalyptus leaves at night. Now there are fewer trees, and koalas face more dangers as they walk greater distances to go from tree to tree. They must walk through yards, across streets, and often into danger to reach eucalyptus. On the ground koalas can be hit by cars or attacked by dogs.

Because koalas are also sensitive to stress and unable to adapt to the changing environment, their numbers have dropped drastically.

What are people doing to help save koalas? They're keeping pets in at night and planting trees for koalas to feed on. Warning signs remind drivers to watch out for koalas crossing roads. Most important, citizens continue to work hard to pass laws that protect koalas' remaining forests.

Luckily, the rescued koala and mother survived. After a short hospital stay, the rescuers released the healthy animals back into the wild.

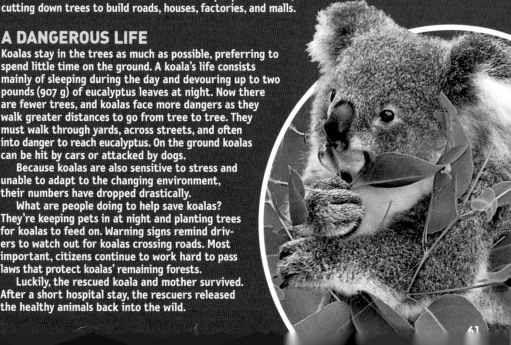

Wolf Speak

Understanding the secret language of a wolf pack

I f you want to understand wolf speak, you need to use your ears, eyes, and even your nose. Wolves talk to each other using their voices, body language, and, yes, body odor.

Wolves live in packs. Their survival depends on working as a team to find food, protect pack members, and raise pups. Being able to clearly read and express each wolf's rank is a matter of great importance.

Read My Lips and Ears and Shoulders

From head to tail, wolves express information through subtle and obvious body language. Facial expressions and how high a tail is held reveal a wolf's confidence level or where it fits within the pack. The higher a wolf ranks, the higher it stands and holds its head, ears, and tail. The lower it ranks, the lower it drops everything, even flopping to the ground belly side up. Wolves also puff up their fur or flatten it to express themselves.

From Growl to Howl

Yips, yaps, barks, and squeaks are all wolf sounds. Wolves usually use vocals when interacting with each other. Scientists have trouble eavesdropping on these shy animals, so little is known about wolves' private conversations. But they're sure vocalizations are important. Even a three-week-old puppy can mimic almost all the adult sounds.

The howl is a wolf's long-distance call. In a forest, a howl might be heard six miles (10 km)

Calling all pack members! Meet us over here **to go hunt!**

To all who can hear: If you're not in our pack, **stay off our turf.**

It's all good. **C'mon, let's go.**

away. On the tundra it can be heard up to ten miles (16 km) away. A wolf may howl to locate its pack. Or it may be announcing its availability to join or form a new pack. Packs howl together in a chorus to strengthen the team, warn other wolves away from their territory, or coordinate movements of packs.

Talk to the Paw

A wolf's sense of smell is a hundred times better than a human's, so it's no wonder scent is an important part of wolf communication. Wolves

intentionally leave their scent by marking trees and bushes with urine. They also secrete messages with scent glands in their feet and other body parts.

These odors aren't generally obvious to humans, but for wolves, sniffing tells all: the identity of an animal, its social status, whether it's an adult or a youth, how healthy it is, what it's been eating, if it's ready to breed, and much more.

As scientists keep learning how to understand wolf speak, they use their best tools—sniffing, spying, and eavesdropping.

GRAY WOLVES

You Are Here

CONTINENTS: EUROPE AND ASIA

COUNTRY: RUSSIA

SIZE: WORLD'S LARGEST COUNTRY, FOLLOWED BY CANADA, THE UNITED STATES, AND CHINA

LOCATION: NORTHWESTERN COUNTRYSIDE

Your plane lands in northern Russia. As you approach wolf territory, you hear them first. *Ow-oooo! Grrrr!* Then you spot the pack of wolves. Wrestling and playing, they look like they're celebrating. They're actually psyching themselves up for a hunt. One of wolves' preferred prey is moose. One moose can weigh twice as much as the entire pack. Confidence and teamwork mean survival. Only about one in ten attacks on a moose is successful.

Packs are led by the dominant male and female,

sometimes called the alpha wolves. Your heart pounds when you see the alpha female lunge toward a younger wolf in the pack. It falls down, exposing its neck to show submission. Growling, the alpha holds the young wolf down by its throat. Even from a distance, you understand the conversation. She's reminding the juvenile that she's in charge. The pup's submissive response means, "Yes, ma'am!" Communication and leadership help the pack survive.

You notice that the alpha pair really seem to like each other. The power couple nuzzles and cuddles; they're likely to remain lifelong partners. The two leaders rally the pack, and all but one adult trot off to hunt. Left behind: the pups and an adult babysitter. You watch as the wolves, working as a team, successfully bring down a moose. They eat their fill in about half an hour. Then they return home, and the pups nip at their snouts, begging for dinner. The adults immediately regurgitate undigested meat for the pups and babysitter to eat. Happy that a more appetizing meal is waiting for you on the plane, you slip away to begin your next adventure.

BY THE NUMBERS

1 litter of pups is born each year in a typical pack.

3 times bigger than a coyote, the gray wolf is the largest wild member of the dog family.

13 years is the average life span of a gray wolf in the wild.

22 pounds (10 kg) of meat may be wolfed down at one meal.

40 miles per hour (64 kph) is a wolf's top running speed.

100 times stronger sense of smell than a human's lets a gray wolf sense the presence of an animal up to three days after it's gone and smell prey more than a mile (1.6 km) away.

Where Bears Live

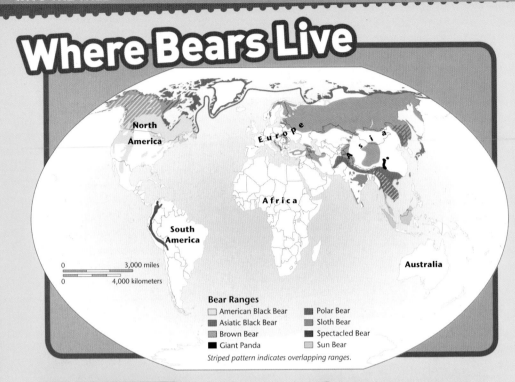

North America

Europe

Asia

Africa

South America

Australia

0   3,000 miles

0   4,000 kilometers

Bear Ranges

- American Black Bear
- Asiatic Black Bear
- Brown Bear
- Giant Panda
- Polar Bear
- Sloth Bear
- Spectacled Bear
- Sun Bear

Striped pattern indicates overlapping ranges.

BROWN BEARS

CLOSE-UP

Look, Ma. No Hands!

Open wide! Fish—it's what's for dinner. This salmon did not look before it leaped, so it's about to end up as brown bear food. Salmon by the thousands leave the ocean and head upstream to mate and lay eggs every fall. Attracted by the fish feast, brown bears by the dozens gather along the banks of Brooks Falls in Katmai National Park in Alaska to fatten up before their long winter hibernation. Timing, luck, and patience helped photographer Joel Sartore catch this fish—just before the bear did.

BEAR NECESSITIES

How Polar Bears Survive the Deep Freeze

In a polar bear's Arctic home, winter temperatures get unbelievably cold. But imagine running around outside in a heavy down jacket. Even if it's cold out, you might start to feel too warm. Much like you in that jacket, a polar bear is so well insulated that it can easily become overheated. Sometimes it cools off with a mouthful of snow or by lying flat to expose its belly directly to the snow. To keep from overheating, a polar bear usually moves slowly and doesn't run much.

So what keeps the polar bear so toasty? The most visible protection is its thick fur coat. The coat has two layers: an outer layer of long, dense guard hairs and an undercoat of short woolly hairs. A polar bear may look white, but underneath its hair its skin is black, which absorbs heat.

Another way a polar bear copes with the cold is with built-in insulation: a layer of blubber under its skin that can be more than four inches (10 cm) thick.

Many polar bears spend the winter living on slippery sea ice. Luckily, their paws are perfect for getting around on a slick, cold surface. Rough pads give them a nonslip grip, and thick fur between the pads keeps their feet warm. Sharp, curved claws act like hooks to climb and dig in the ice.

So bring on the snow, wind, and icy water. Because when it comes to keeping warm, a polar bear's got it covered!

KEY: WHERE POLAR BEARS LIVE

The Bear Facts

ICY HOME: Polar bears live in the far north, on sea ice and on land. Scientists estimate that some 20,000 to 25,000 polar bears roam the Arctic.

HANDY PAWS: Partially webbed front paws help polar bears swim. The bears may use their back paws like rudders— to steer.

SEA BEAR: Polar bears, seen swimming as far as 150 miles (241 km) offshore, are the only bears considered to be marine mammals.

BIG BOYS: Polar bears usually bear twins. A newborn weighs about a pound (450 g); an adult male, about 1,400 pounds (635 kg).

SNACKING: When a polar bear hunts, it looks for baby seals resting in dens under the snow near the water's edge.

SNOW BABIES

Baby polar bear cubs are born in mid- to late December inside a snow den built by their mother. She usually has one or two cubs. The den is about the size of a refrigerator, and so is mom, so it's not roomy.

As newborns, cubs are about the same size as a loaf of bread and weigh about a pound (.5 kg). They have no teeth, their eyes are closed, and their fur is not thick. They need their mother's warmth and protection 24/7.

By early April, when cubs leave the den for the first time, they weigh 20 to 30 pounds (9 to 14 kg). By two years old the cubs have learned all the bear lessons they'll need for their 30-year life span. Then the young bears find their own territory and start preparing for having their own cubs.

Meerkat CITY

Meerkats always have something to do. These mongoose relatives live in a busy community, with no time to sit around being bored. In their family groups of up to 40 members, everyone pitches in to get all the jobs done.

A SENTINEL KEEPS WATCH.

Guards

Meerkats are very territorial. Guards, called sentinels, are always on the lookout for rival meerkats that try to move in on their territory. If a sentinel (left) spots any intruding meerkats, it sends out an alarm call. The whole group gathers together and stands tall to try to scare away the rivals. If that doesn't work, meerkats quickly decide whether to fight or retreat.

Predators such as eagles or jackals rate a different warning call. If a sentinel spots the predator first, it lets out an alarm call that sends all the meerkats scurrying into the nearest bolt hole—an underground safety den where the eagle can't follow.

Babysitters

Within a meerkat group, the alpha, or leader, female and the alpha male are usually the only ones that have babies. When their babies are too young to follow along while they search for food, meerkat parents have to go without them. So they leave their pups with babysitters—other adult meerkats in the group. The pups stay inside their family's underground burrow for the first three weeks of life, protected and cared for by the babysitters.

Diggers

Picture yourself looking for a tasty bug to eat (below) when suddenly you hear the alarm call for "eagle." You dash left, you dash right, and you finally find a bolt hole.

Bolt holes provide fast getaways for meerkats in danger. Members of the group cooperate to make sure bolt holes are properly dug out, that nothing is blocking the entry, and that there are enough bolt holes in every area.

Meerkats are built to be superdiggers. All four of their paws have long, sturdy claws that they use like rakes. They dig to find food, such as lizards and other small reptiles, insects and their larvae, and scorpions.

HOME SWEET BURROW

DIGGING FOR FOOD

5 COOL REASONS TO LOVE BATS

1 FLIP, FLAP, AND FLY
Bats are the only mammals that can truly fly. A bat's wings are basically folds of skin stretched between extra-long finger and hand bones.

2 VALUABLE DROPPINGS
Bat droppings, called guano, are super-rich in nitrogen, a main ingredient in plant food. The ancient Inca of South America protected bats as a valuable source of fertilizer for their crops. Guano is still used in farming today.

3 MARVELOUS MOSQUITO MUNCHERS
Many bats are born bug-eaters, filling their bellies with moths, mosquitoes, and other winged insects. The brown bat gulps down as many as a thousand mosquito-size insects in an hour. Each night the bats from one Texas cave consume about 200 tons (181 t) of bugs, many of them crop-eating pests. That's about the weight of six fully loaded cement trucks.

4 EXTREME FLIGHT
Hoary bats migrate up to 1,000 miles (1,609 km) south from Canada each fall. Mexican free-tailed bats often fly up to 3 miles (5 km) high, where tailwinds help speed them along at more than 60 miles an hour (97 kph).

5 SUPERMOM STRENGTH
A newborn bat may weigh as much as one-third of its mother's weight, yet the mom can hold her baby while clinging by her toes to a crack in a cave's ceiling.

Going Batty

LITTLE BROWN BAT
"Little" is right—a brown bat weighs about as much as two small coins!

SHORT-TAILED FRUIT BAT
After just one night of dining, this bat can scatter up to 60,000 undigested seeds—crucial to rain forest plant growth.

COMMON VAMPIRE BAT
Vampires' main diet is the blood of cows and horses. Rarely do they take a bite out of humans.

WHITE TENT BATS
These fruit-eaters often create "tents" to roost in. They make bites in a large leaf so it folds over itself. Then the bats snuggle under.

FLYING FOX
There are about 60 species of bats called flying foxes (above). This kind sometimes roosts in a "camp" of up to a million individuals.

VELVETY FREE-TAILED BAT
This bat fills its cheek pouches with insects in midair, then chews and swallows them later.

PALLID BAT
Using big ears to listen for rustlings, a pallid bat locates and grabs its prey from the ground.

DESERT LONG-EARED BAT
Sonar emitted by this kind of bat echoes off prey, signaling where its meal lies.

OLD WORLD LEAF-NOSED BAT
Complex nose structures for hunting gave this bat its name.

Bet you didn't know

Bat Spit May Save Lives
A substance in the saliva of vampire bats could help victims of strokes survive, according to researchers at the University of Monash in Melbourne, Australia. Strokes happen when a blood clot blocks blood flow to the brain. An anticlotting substance in bat spit makes blood flow freely, so a bat can continue to feed. The researchers think the same substance may be able to dissolve blood clots in stroke patients. Fortunately the substance would be contained in medicine, and bats would not be required to bite patients!

Albino Animals

THESE ANIMALS FACE DANGER IN THE WILD

From mottled gray-and-white koalas to brilliantly hued reef fish, an animal's color serves a purpose. Color helps some species blend with their surroundings so they can hide from predators or sneak up on prey. The bright colors of some animals warn predators that they're poisonous, while others help attract a mate.

An animal's color comes from a pigment called melanin. Pigment cells color eyes, skin, fur, feathers, and scales. The specific colors the cells produce are determined by genes. Genes are a body's instructions on how to build the animal from head to toe, inside and out, down to the last detail.

But what happens if an animal's pigment cells cannot produce melanin? Animals without pigment have inherited a condition called albinism. In albinos, altered genes prevent pigment cells from making color. Albino animals are all white with pink or blue eyes. Many animal species can have the rare genes that cause albinism.

Albino animals face challenges in the wild. They stand out, which makes them targets for predators. Albino animals also may have trouble finding mates. Some birds, for example, reject albino partners. The reason may be that albinos lack the colors and patterns the birds rely on to choose a mate.

Below are two examples of rare albino animals. Many albino animals, like those shown below, live in captivity, where they are protected and live longer than they would in the wild.

Alligator

Wallaby

BEST PERFORMANCE BY AN ANIMAL...

If animals got Grammy Awards, male humpback whales would win trophies for their long and varied songs. Here are a few more animal acts that might take home Grammys for their sensational singing skills.

LOUDEST VOCALIST

The winner is the blue whale. Its low-frequency rumblings can reach 188 decibels. That's louder than a jet airplane. The howler monkey is a close runner-up. Its booming voice can carry a distance of three miles (5 km).

BEST SAMPLER

Let's hear it for the mockingbird, famous for copying the songs of other birds. Many talented mockingbirds can belt out the calls and songs of at least 30 other kinds of birds in just 10 minutes.

STRANGEST SINGER

Give it up for the male grasshopper mouse! When threatened, this five-inch (13-cm) -long rodent rears up on its hind legs, points its nose to the sky, and howls like a wolf. Each shrill cry can be heard across the length of a football field.

HORSE? ZEBRA? BOTH!

The name Eclyse (ee-KLEEZ) is a combination of her parents' names: mom Eclipse and dad Ulysses.

Schloss Holte-Stukenbrock, Germany

When Eclyse was about to be born, people figured the animal would be a zebra. After all, that's what the mother was. But the newborn's mix of stripe patterns and solid hair told a different story: Her father was a horse! Eclyse is a zorse: half horse, half zebra. How did this happen? In the wild, horses and zebras would never mate. But Eclyse's parents lived close together at a horse farm. The result was a rare, unintentional zorse.

Eclyse looks like two animals melded into one, but she behaves more like a horse. She eats hay, whinnies, and hangs out with Pedro the horse. "But she's a little wild like a zebra," says Susanna Stubbe of Zoo Safaripark Stukenbrock, where Eclyse now lives. "She's a bit jumpy, even if a fly lands on her back." Eclyse is definitely a horse of a different stripe!

PIG IN BOOTS!

A pig's funny-looking snout helps the animal dig.

Thirsk, England

Most pigs love wallowing in the mud. Not Cinders the pig. As a piglet, she refused to walk in mud, sometimes even shaking with fear if she couldn't find a way around a puddle. The solution? Boots!

Owner Andrew Keeble found that doll-size boots were a perfect fit for Cinders. Each day, she'd run to have them put on, then trot happily through the mud. The boots solved the problem but didn't explain her strange actions. Veterinarian Bruce Lawhorn of Texas A&M University thinks it might have been a behavioral response. "If Cinders had sore hoof pads while walking in mud, she might have associated the pain with the mud," he says.

Cinders has outgrown her boots and now braves the mud bare-hoofed. But she still doesn't roll around in it. Getting dirty just isn't this pig's idea of a good time.

WILD CAT
Family Reunion

There Are 37 Species of Wild Cats

Scientists have divided them into eight groups called lineages after studying their DNA. Here are representatives from each lineage. The domestic house cat comes from the lineage that includes the sand cat.

1

CHEETAH
(46 to 143 pounds: 21 to 65 kg)

- Often scans for prey from a high spot
- Can sprint up to 70 miles an hour (113 kph)
- From Puma lineage, which includes three species

2

CANADA LYNX
(11 to 38 pounds: 5 to 17 kg)

- Its main prey is the snowshoe hare
- Big paws act like snowshoes
- From Lynx lineage, which includes four species

3

OCELOT
(15 to 34 pounds: 7 to 15 kg)

- Most of an ocelot's prey is small
- Found from Texas to Argentina
- From Ocelot lineage, which includes seven species

4

TIGER
(165 to 716 pounds: 75 to 325 kg)

- Tigers are the only striped wild cats
- These big cats will hunt almost any mammal in their territory
- From Panthera lineage, which includes seven species, such as the lion and jaguar

5

SAND CAT (3 to 7.5 pounds: 1 to 3 kg)
- The sand cat lives in dry deserts of northern Africa and the Middle East
- Rarely drinks; gets water from food
- From Domestic Cat lineage, which includes six species of cat

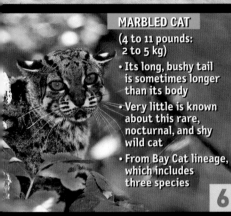

MARBLED CAT
(4 to 11 pounds: 2 to 5 kg)
- Its long, bushy tail is sometimes longer than its body
- Very little is known about this rare, nocturnal, and shy wild cat
- From Bay Cat lineage, which includes three species

6

7

SERVAL
(15 to 30 pounds: 7 to 14 kg)
- Longest legs, relative to its body, of any cat species
- Big ears used to listen for prey
- From Caracal lineage, which includes three species

FISHING CAT **8**
(11 to 35 pounds: 5 to 16 kg)
- A strong swimmer, it has slightly webbed feet
- Eats mainly fish
- From Leopard Cat lineage, which includes five species

How to tell a cat by its
SPOTS

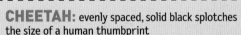

JAGUAR: little dots in the middle of larger rings (body); small black spots (head)
Home: mainly Mexico, Central and South America
Average Size: 80 to 350 pounds (36 to 159 kg)
Cat Fact: Third largest in the cat family after tigers and lions, the jaguar is the largest feline in the Western Hemisphere.

LEOPARD: rings without the jaguar's smaller dots inside
Home: much of Asia and Africa
Average Size: 62 to 200 pounds (28 to 91 kg)
Cat Fact: Some leopards are dark and look spotless. They're called black panthers.

CHEETAH: evenly spaced, solid black splotches the size of a human thumbprint
Home: parts of Africa
Average Size: 46 to 143 pounds (21 to 65 kg)
Cat Fact: On the fastest land animal, dark lines mark the face from the inner corner of each eye to the outer corners of its mouth.

SERVAL: usually a series of single black dots that can vary from the size of a freckle to one inch (2.54 cm) wide
Home: many parts of Africa
Average Size: 15 to 30 pounds (7 to 14 kg)
Cat Fact: A serval uses its huge ears to hunt by sound, surprising prey with a pounce.

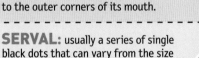

OCELOT: solid or open-centered dark spots that sometimes merge to look like links in a chain; fur in the center of open spots is often darker than background coat color.
Home: South, Central, and North America
Average Size: 15 to 34 pounds (7 to 15 kg)
Cat Fact: An ocelot's main prey is rodents.

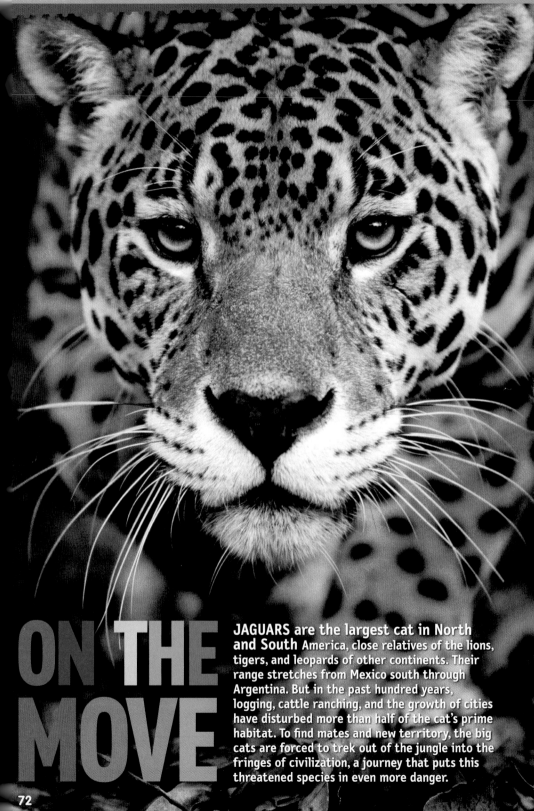

ON THE MOVE

JAGUARS are the largest cat in North and South America, close relatives of the lions, tigers, and leopards of other continents. Their range stretches from Mexico south through Argentina. But in the past hundred years, logging, cattle ranching, and the growth of cities have disturbed more than half of the cat's prime habitat. To find mates and new territory, the big cats are forced to trek out of the jungle into the fringes of civilization, a journey that puts this threatened species in even more danger.

PROTECTING THEIR PATH

As jaguars cross into human territory, obstacles like factories, highways, and river dams force them off-track—and into dangerous confrontations with cars zooming by or ranchers guarding their cattle. "A jaguar, unlike a human, is not stopped by many things," says scientist Alan Rabinowitz, president of the Panthera Foundation, an organization devoted to saving wild cats. "It's not stopped by a river or even a snowcapped mountain." But they are stopped by human development. That's why Rabinowitz began an international project called Path of the Jaguar, which works to protect the pathways jaguars use to travel between isolated habitats.

JAGUARS WILL DEFEND THEIR TERRITORIES AGAINST INTRUDERS.

> " **A jaguar,** unlike a human, is not stopped by many things. "

THE FINISH LINE

These protected corridors are not continuous stretches of jungle—plantations and ranches make up much of the land between jaguar populations. But what used to be deadly territory for jaguars, like the outskirts of a village that raises pigs for food, is now much safer. While villagers would shoot the cats to protect their livestock, Rabinowitz taught them to pen up their pigs to keep them safe from roaming jaguars. That way, the jaguars can prowl safely past the village and continue their journey deeper into the jungle.

A JAGUAR CUB USUALLY HAS AT LEAST ONE BROTHER OR SISTER.

A FEW JAGUARS HAVE BEEN SPOTTED RECENTLY IN THE UNITED STATES NEAR THE MEXICAN BORDER.

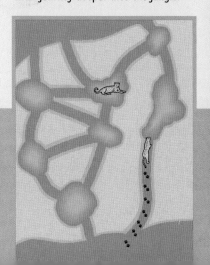

PATH OF THE JAGUAR

☐ Existing jaguar populations

☐ Jaguar travel corridor (forest or farmland)

☐ Rest area pocket for traveling jaguar

With a stocky, muscular build, jaguars pack more per-pound crushing power in their jaws than any other big cat.

LEOPARDS
Nature's
SUPERCATS

POWERFUL PROWLERS

No big cat is more at home in a tree than a leopard. It's in the trees that leopards often reveal their trademark strength. Thanks to muscular necks and stocky legs, these cats are made for pouncing and climbing. Plus, their massive heads pack powerful jaws that let leopards haul prey that's twice their weight up the trunks of trees two stories high. That would be like climbing a ladder while carrying your dad or big brother—with your teeth! The cats scramble skyward not only to hide prey from scavengers or escape from lions, but also to mount attacks from tree limbs, pouncing on unsuspecting prey below.

Tjololo the leopard is playing tug-of-war in a tree, and he's in no mood to lose. His opponents: two hyenas that had darted out of the night to swipe Tjololo's freshly killed impala. Not about to let the hyenas steal his meal, Tjololo (pronounced cha-LO-lo) did what leopards do best: He grasped the impala in his powerful jaws and carried it straight up the tree.

ADAPTABLE FELINE

Not all leopards spend their lives in trees, though. The cats are also perfectly happy hiding their dinners in the brush. This ability to adapt has helped the leopard become the most widespread member of the cat species. Leopards also adapt their diet to whatever prey is plentiful. They'll go after crocodiles, zebras, and other big animals. But they also snack on smaller prey, like rodents, lizards, and hares—no meal is too tiny for this wild cat.

THE MYSTERY OF THE BLACK PANTHER

Are you superstitious?
Do you think it's bad luck if
a black cat crosses your path?

Many people once believed that black cats part-nered with the devil. They show up regularly in comic books, posters, and movies. But in real life they are as rare as parents who allow kids to eat dessert before dinner. What are these mysterious black cats and where do they live?

"Black panthers are simply leopards with dark coats," says scientist John Seidensticker. "If you look closely, you can see the faint outline of spots in the dark fur," he adds.

Biologists used to think that black panthers were a separate species of leopard. The fierce black cats had a reputation of being more aggressive than spotted leopards, the way dark-maned lions are more aggressive than those with lighter manes. But zookeepers noticed that normal spotted leopards and black leopards can sometimes be born in the same litter (see below)—just as kids in the same family can have blue eyes or brown eyes.

BLENDING IN

Overall, black leopards are extremely rare in the wild. They are almost never seen in the leopard's range in Africa, and only occasionally in India. But surprisingly, these black cats are the only leopards known in the forests of Malaysia, in Southeast Asia. Black leopards are so much more common there that the local forest people don't even have a word in their vocabulary for *spotted* leopards.

Scientists don't really know why black leopards are the norm in Malaysia. One theory is that animals living in dark, humid forests like those in Malaysia tend to have darker fur for camou-flage. African leopards spend most of their lives in grasslands and forests, where spots may be the best disguise.

The black cats are not evil creatures of witches and devils. They are cats at their best— evolving to blend with their habitat.

75

White Lions

THE TRUTH ABOUT WHITE LIONS

White lions are beloved by many people around the world. But they're quite controversial, too. These beautiful beasts are not a separate species from the typical tawny-colored lions, but the result of a rare color gene mutation. When both a male and female lion carry the same white genes, there is a good chance that one or more of their cubs will be born with white fur.

Not many lions carry the white mutation. In nature, it's rare. But because breeders know how to create them, there are about 500 white lions living in captivity around the world. Creating white lions as moneymaking attractions—and the push to release these animals into the wild—has created serious concern and debate.

CAUSE FOR ALARM

White lions continue to exist only because people inbreed close relatives—fathers and daughters, sisters and brothers. White tigers are also bred this way, which has caused plenty of problems among the big cats, like distorted spines, cleft palates, bulging crossed eyes, and mental impairments. This has scientists worrying that the mutation will cause health issues for white lions, too.

INTO THE WILD?

Another concern is that people want to release captive-bred white lions into the wild in South Africa. But not everyone agrees this is a good idea. Some experts say that because so many of today's white lions are inbred, it could spread health problems. If they breed with wild lions, they'll pass on the genetic problems to the wild population.

ROARRR!
On a still night, the sound of lions roaring can carry for five miles (8 km). Roaring often is used to tell other lions, "This is my piece of land."

A SAFER OPTION

Some experts think that instead of releasing captive-bred white lions, we should just focus on protecting all wild lions. This would ensure the safety of the wild population of lions, which may produce healthy white cubs in the future.

BY THE NUMBERS

3 is the number of cubs in a typical litter of lions.

5 miles (8 km) is the distance the sound of a lion's roar can carry.

15 pounds (7 kg) of meat is a typical meal for an adult male lion.

36 miles an hour (58 kph) is a lion's top running speed.

2,200 pounds (998 kg) is the top weight of prey a pride can kill.

YOU CAN HELP SAVE THIS LEMUR'S HABITAT!

Anything you do to preserve the planet helps all living things, including the ring-tailed lemurs that live in the African island nation of Madagascar. And yes—just one kid, like you, can make a difference. Here are ideas for five small, easy things you can do.

1 CUT TRASH, NOT TREES.
In your kitchen, reach for a cloth towel instead of paper towels to dry your hands. In public bathrooms, use the air dryer or limit yourself to one paper towel. Changing daily habits can reduce the number of trees that are cut down each year and can help save important habitats for animals such as lemurs.

2 USE FISHY WATER.
When you clean out your fish tank, dump the water into your garden instead of down the drain. You'll cut water waste and the nutrients from the fishy water will fertilize your plants.

3 KEEP OUT THE HEAT.
On hot, sunny days close your blinds or curtains to block out the heat from the sun. If each home in the United States cut the use of air-conditioning by 10 percent annually, the energy savings could power 1.6 million homes for a year.

4 COLLECT CANS.
The next time you're at a friend's party or barbecue, ask if you can collect the aluminum soda cans to recycle. Just one recycled can saves enough energy to run a small radio for more than ten hours.

5 USE FEWER CUPS.
Instead of using several glasses a day, pick your favorite and use it all day. If you use fewer dishes, you will reduce the number of times your family runs the dishwasher. You'll save energy and about 100 glasses of water for each load of dishes you and your family eliminate.

COOL CLICK
For more about helping Earth, go online. preserveourplanet.com

Will the RED PANDA survive?

A mask marks one of the cutest faces in the forest. The red panda looks a little like a raccoon, a bit like a fox, and somewhat like a puppy. Soft, cuddly reddish fur blankets its body, which is a tad larger than a big house cat's. These harmless creatures live in the high mountain forests of the Himalaya in southeastern Asia. But their numbers in the wild are dwindling.

As loggers and firewood collectors chop down trees, and ranchers allow overgrazing by domestic livestock, the fragile mountain habitat of the red panda erodes.

SPECIALIZED DIET

The diet of the red panda also makes it vulnerable, because it is one of just a few mammal species in the world that eat mainly bamboo. It's not the most nutritious stuff. This giant grass has tough stems and leaves that make it difficult to chew and digest. A bamboo diet doesn't give red pandas much energy, so they have to conserve as much as possible.

SLOW-MOVING SLEEPYHEADS

Red pandas save energy simply by keeping activity to a minimum. They spend six to eight hours a day moving around and eating. The rest of their time is spent resting and sleeping. Their bodies are built to conserve energy. When the weather is cold, the pandas curl into a tight ball on a tree branch and go into a very deep sleep. This reduces their metabolism, or the amount of energy they use. When red pandas wake up, their metabolism returns to normal. But as soon as they go back to sleep their metabolism drops again, saving energy.

SAVING THE BLUE IGUANA

Found only on the Caribbean island of Grand Cayman, in the Cayman Islands, the blue iguana is one of the most endangered species of lizards in the world. It can't protect itself against threats such as the construction of houses and roads, or predators such as snakes, cats, and dogs. When the number of these wild, dragonlike creatures dropped to fewer than 25several years ago, experts took action. They began breeding them in captivity. The program has been so successful that more than 250 blue iguanas now live wild on the island. Luckily, it may be blue skies ahead for these living "dragons."

COOL CLICK

BY THE NUMBERS

There are 9,618 vulnerable or endangered animal species in the world. The list includes:

- **1,131 mammals**, such as the snow leopard, the polar bear, and the fishing cat.

- **1,240 birds**, including the Steller's sea eagle and the Madagascar plover.

- **1,851 fish**, such as the Mekong giant catfish.

- **594 reptiles**, including the American crocodile.

- **733 insects**, including the Macedonian grayling.

- **1,898 amphibians**, such as the Round Island day gecko.

- **And more**, including 19 arachnids, 596 crustaceans, 235 corals, 115 bivalves, and 1,173 snails and slugs.

For more information about the status of threatened species around the world, check out the IUCN Red List. iucnredlist.org

5 HARP SEALS

COOL THINGS ABOUT

With their irresistible faces and fluffy fur, harp seals are some of the cutest animals around. But their snow-white pelts and icy habitat make harp seals especially vulnerable to hunters, global warming, and other environmental threats. Here's more about harp seals—and why it's extra-important to protect these adorable animals.

1 6,000-MILE JOURNEY

Each year, harp seals migrate more than 6,000 miles (9,600 km), spending summers feeding in northern Arctic coastal waters and heading back south in the fall to breed. They migrate in small groups of up to 20 individuals. By late February, harp seals gather in large herds. As many as one million form an enormous herd found on the floating mass of pack ice in the Gulf of St. Lawrence in Canada. Once breeding season is over, the seals travel back north for the summer.

2 SEE-THROUGH COAT

When a harp seal pup is born, its coat has a yellow tint. But it turns completely white within a couple of days. The fine, silky fur is almost transparent. This allows the pup's skin to absorb the sun's rays, which helps it stay warm. The whitecoats, as they are called, look like this only for about two weeks. Then they molt, or shed, their white fur. Their new coats are gray.

3 HEART TRICK

When a young harp seal sees a polar bear, instinct takes over. The pup can't escape the predator by running away, so it hides—in plain sight. The ball of white fur plays possum. The seal lies motionless with its head tucked into its chubby neck, looking like a heap of snow (below). The pup's heart rate slows from about 80 to 90 beats a minute to only 20 to 30 beats. If the trick works, the bear doesn't see the harp seal and moves on. Then the seal can stretch out and relax. Whew!

4 DEEP DIVERS

It's not unusual for a harp seal to hold its breath for 5 minutes. But when it needs to, the seal can stay underwater for as long as 20 minutes and dive more than 800 feet (244 m) down. That's six times deeper than a scuba diver can go safely. Harp seals can get places fast, too—100 feet (30 m) down in 15 seconds. As the seals zip through the water hunting for fish, they also stay alert for orcas and sharks that might eat *them*.

5 QUICK-CHANGE ARTISTS

By the time a harp seal is 14 months old, it's changed coats—and nicknames—five times. A whitecoat at first, it then becomes a graycoat, a ragged jacket, a beater, and finally a bedlamer. At four years old a harp seal has a silvery gray coat with a few spots—and it's called a spotted harp. Some females look like that the rest of their lives. But males, as well as many females, develop a distinctive black pattern that is shaped like a harp, which explains the name of the species.

> **DID YOU KNOW?**
> Harp seals are known as "earless" seals because they don't have external earflaps.

PANDAMONIUM

Like a toddler at snack time, a giant panda sits with its legs stretched out in front of it and munches on bamboo. The tough bamboo is no match for the panda's powerful jaws and the crushing force of its huge molars. In one day, it'll polish off 20 to 40 pounds (9 to 18 kg) of bamboo!

Bamboo—a grass that grows tall like a tree—sprouts so fast you can actually watch it grow. Even so, nearly 138 giant pandas starved to death in the mid-1970s. Today, there are between 1,000 and 3,000 pandas left in the wild. Another loss would devastate the endangered population.

BLOOMING BAMBOO

For pandas, bamboo is the perfect food and shelter. Ninety-nine percent of a panda's diet is bamboo. Stems, shoots, leaves—pandas devour it all. That is, until the bamboo begins to flower. Even the hungriest panda isn't likely to eat it at that stage, because bamboo is not nutritious or appetizing as it flowers.

One blooming plant wouldn't be a big deal, but bamboo is peculiar. Unlike most plants, when one bamboo flowers, all of the bamboo plants of the same species do, too. After flowering, bamboo drops its seeds to the forest floor. Then the plant dies. If a majority of a forest is the same species of bamboo, then pandas are suddenly out of food.

FINDING FOOD

You would think that a panda would be able to hunker down and wait out the flowering by surviving on other plants and small animals. But many species of bamboo sprouts aren't big enough to be edible for at least five to seven years. That means a small area—or an entire forest—goes from a bamboo buffet to starvation-central practically overnight—and stays that way.

Scientists know very little about the bamboo flowering process because it happens so infrequently. Some haven't flowered in 120 years—when your great-grandparents or maybe even great-great-grandparents were still in diapers.

In the past, pandas would just search for other sources of bamboo. Today there's a short supply of dining digs because roads, farms, cities, logging, and mining isolate forests. The pandas can't get to a suitable new forest because their homes are surrounded by human activities.

LOOKING AHEAD

To halt habitat destruction, China has stopped most logging. The government also created some 50 nature reserves for pandas. And scientists are working with zoos worldwide to create an extensive panda breeding program with a goal of rebuilding the wild population. All this support gives giant pandas—and their bamboo habitat—a green future.

Rhino

Animal

Maalim the baby rhinoceros had been abandoned by its mother. Left with no one to nurture and protect him, Maalim was helpless against hungry predators on the African savanna. Luckily a group of government rangers found him before it was too late. They picked up the rhino and took him back to their base, where they called a specialist to assess the ailing animal.

Starving and sickly, Maalim was treated with a special milk formula and antibiotics. He was then transferred to an animal nursery, where he received round-the-clock care from concerned keepers. They bottle-fed him every four hours, took him on long walks, and even slept beside him in his stable.

After two months at the nursery, Maalim gained enough weight to be released back into the national park where he was found. With the added protection of the rangers who patrol the park, Maalim received his second chance to roam free as a wild rhino.

GROWING STEADILY

Bats

GETTING A BATH

FEEDING TIME

Rescues

Greyhound

GREYHOUNDS CAN BE MANY DIFFERENT COLORS AND PATTERNS.

When a female racing greyhound took a nasty fall during a race at a dog track near Orlando, Florida, she snapped two bones in her front leg. Although the injury wasn't life threatening, she was in grave danger. The dog's trainer took her to a veterinary clinic after the accident, but he had no intention of getting the leg fixed. He wanted the dog euthanized, or put to sleep.

Luckily for the greyhound with the broken leg, vets at the clinic couldn't stand to euthanize an otherwise healthy two-year-old dog. They splinted her leg and called Marilyn Varnberg, who runs Greyhound Adoptions of Florida. Determined that this greyhound would be adopted, she named the dog Mariah and went to work.

GREYHOUNDS CAN RUN UP TO 40 MILES PER HOUR (64 KPH).

Varnberg arranged for a donation to cover the expensive surgery Mariah needed to fix her leg. After three months in a cast and almost a year living with other rescued greyhounds at Varnberg's farm, Mariah met the Ubert family. The Uberts had already adopted one greyhound, but wanted another. Ending up with the Uberts made Mariah a lucky winner after all.

In eastern Australia, hundreds of baby bats were in trouble. The gray-headed flying foxes—who had not yet learned to fly—clung to their mothers, hanging high in a tree. But as a violent storm intensified, the wind knocked the babies from the shelter of their mothers' wings, and they fell to the ground. Wildlife volunteers rushed to the scene and discovered dozens of baby flying foxes lying helpless on the ground, 30 feet (9 m) below the tree.

The situation was scary, but after three long days, more than 350 little flying foxes were gently transported to a clinic. Bones were set, and antibiotics were given. Volunteers bottle-fed milk formula to the newborns every three hours. Soon, they graduated from bottles to solid foods, chowing down on chopped apples. They also learned to lap up nectar and finally figured out how to fly. After two and a half months at the clinic, the bats moved into an outside enclosure and eventually began to explore the wild, where they continued to thrive within the forest.

Secret Life of

U ntil recently, scientists knew almost nothing about how sea turtles spend their time underwater. But with the help of a really cool underwater camera, they've gotten a peek into the turtles' private lives—and a better idea of how to protect these endangered animals.

When strapped to a Crittercam, a specially designed camera that attaches to the turtle's shell, sea turtles show scientists life from their point of view. A suction cup holds the camera in place, then releases it after a few hours. The camera floats to the surface, where scientists can recover it and see what it recorded.

JELLYFISH

Must-Sea TV

And what has the Crittercam captured? Plenty! As in any great reality TV show, there are surprises around every corner with sea turtles. When the cameras started rolling, scientists saw just how surprisingly social turtles are. They even have staring contests, locking eyes on each other for a few minutes before one of the turtles swims away (scientists aren't sure about the purpose of this game, but found it pretty funny!).

CRITTERCAM SHOT

GREEN SEA TURTLE

SEA SPONGE

Scrub-A-Dub

The Crittercam also helped scientists discover why sea turtles have relatively clean shells, unlike the barnacle-encrusted loggerheads. Green sea turtles were seen taking sponge baths, rubbing against living sea sponges to clean their heads, flippers, and belly. Turtles even chase others away from the best rubbing spots!

Snack Surprise

When it came to food, scientists were surprised to find out that green sea turtles didn't munch on sea grass as suspected, but instead gobbled up nearly every bite-size jellyfish that floats into view (shown above). Before Crittercam, these turtles were thought to be vegetarians. But the jellyfish diet made sense: Why choose salad when there's jelly to snack on?

After all of these amazing observations, scientists are hoping to reveal even more secrets about this unique creature using the Crittercam. After all, the more scientists learn about the life of sea turtles, the more everyone can do to help ensure the reptiles' future.

Sea Turtles

DID YOU KNOW?
All seven species of sea turtles are endangered.

DID YOU KNOW?
One of the largest green sea turtles ever recorded has lived in California's San Diego Bay for about 40 years. Affectionately called Wrinklebutt due to a shell deformity, she weighs about 550 pounds (250 kg).

WRINKLEBUTT'S UNUSUAL SHELL SHAPE

COOL CLICK

To see Crittercam in action visit online at animals.nationalgeographic.com/animals/crittercam-wildcam/

GREAT WHITE SHARKS

You Are Here

CONTINENT AND COUNTRY: AUSTRALIA

LOCATION: SPENCER GULF OFF THE COAST OF SOUTH AUSTRALIA

UNIQUE: ONLY COUNTRY THAT IS ALSO A CONTINENT

"We've located a great white shark," the captain tells you on the deck of the research vessel. You're off the coast of South Australia, near Spencer Gulf. The captain points to the shark cage tied to the boat's stern. "Hop in!" he tells you. "This is an opportunity you won't want to miss."

You check your snorkeling gear and then slip down feet-first into the cage. (A shark cage is built to keep great white sharks out. The cage's metal bars protect divers like you.) Slowly you're lowered, inside the cage, to just below the ocean surface. Soon you spot what you came to see. Your heart races as a six-foot (2-m) great white shark glides past the cage, turns, and swims by again. You are safe.

Great white sharks are the world's largest

meat-eating fish. Their sharp teeth and powerful jaws are built to cut and tear their prey. The longest confirmed great white was longer than 20 feet (6 m)—about the length of four bathtubs! Your six-footer is a young shark.

Suddenly you see the shark's impressive teeth. The predator you're watching speeds by again—this time following a school of large fish. The shark grabs one that lags a bit behind the rest. In two gulps, the fish is gone. The scientist on board told you that great white sharks also scavenge or eat dead animals they come across. They particularly like whales. Whale blubber, or fat, gives these large sharks an excellent source of calories. Now the captain hoists you out of the water because the time has come to head for dry land.

Steering Clear of
SHARK BITES

Shark attacks on people are extremely rare. In the U.S., seven times as many people are bitten by squirrels as sharks every year. Here are tips to help you stay safe:

1 Stay out of the ocean at dawn, dusk, and night—when some sharks swim into shallow water to feed.

2 Don't swim in the ocean if you're bleeding.

3 Swim and surf at beaches with lifeguards on duty. They can warn you about shark sightings.

COOL CLICK

Want to color a picture of a great white shark? nationalgeographic.com/coloringbook/sharks.html

6 COOL THINGS ABOUT SHARKS

1 TEETH TO SPARE

If great white sharks had tooth fairies, they'd be rich! A great white loses and replaces thousands of teeth during its lifetime. Its upper jaw is lined with 26 front-row teeth; its lower jaw has 24. Behind these razor-sharp points are many rows of replacement teeth. The "spares" move to the front whenever the shark loses a tooth.

2 BOX OFFICE BULLY

Great white sharks are superstars. Before the *Star Wars* series, the 1975 movie *Jaws* was Hollywood's biggest moneymaker. *Jaws*, about a great white on the prowl, cost $12 million to film but made $470 million worldwide. Not bad for a fish story!

3 SPEEDY SWIMMERS

Great white sharks can sprint through the water at speeds of 35 miles an hour (56 kph)—seven times faster than the best Olympic swimmer! Scientists on the California coast tracked one shark as it swam all the way to Hawaii—2,400 miles (3,862 km)—in only 40 days.

4 CHOW DOWN, TUNA BREATH!

Picky eaters they're not. While great white sharks prefer to eat seals, sea lions, and the occasional dolphin, they've been known to swallow lots of other things. Bottles, tin cans, a straw hat, lobster traps, and a cuckoo clock are among the items found inside the bellies of great white sharks.

5 EAR THAT?

Great white sharks have ears. You can't see them, because they don't open to the outside. The sharks use two small sensors in the skull to hear and, perhaps, to zero in on the splashing sounds of a wounded fish or a struggling seal!

6 HOT ON THE TRAIL

Unlike most fish, great white sharks' bodies are warmer than their surroundings. The sharks' bodies can be as much as 27°F (15°C) warmer than the water the fish swim in. A higher temperature helps the great white shark swim faster and digest its food more efficiently—very useful for an animal that's always on the go!

Sensitive Sharks

What's the secret weapon a great white shark or a black-tip reef shark uses to track its prey? Gel in the snout! The clear gel acts like a highly sensitive thermometer, registering changes in water temperature as slight as a thousandth of a degree, according to one scientist. Tiny changes in the ocean's temperature tend to occur in places where cold and warm water mix, feeding areas for smaller fish—a shark's next meal. Once the gel registers a change, it produces an electrical charge that causes nerves in the snout to send a message to the shark's brain that says, "Let's do lunch!"

BY THE NUMBERS

6 is about the number of weeks a shark can go without eating.

8 is the number of senses sharks have. Humans have only 5.

170 million years before dinosaurs, sharks lived on Earth.

375 different species of sharks are found in the world's oceans.

UNDER the ICE

Jellyfish (right) with 30-foot (9-m) -long tentacles... sponges the size of bears ... these are just a few of the surprises beneath the surface of Antarctica's frozen seas.

One such surprise is **sea spiders.** Found in oceans worldwide, they are less than an inch (2.54 cm) long. But in Antarctica they often reach the size of a human hand. Luckily, people aren't their chosen snack food. They prefer to chow down on coral, anemones, and sponges.

EMPEROR PENGUINS

1 Emperors are the largest of the 17 penguin species.

2 One colony can number as many as 60,000 penguins.

3 These penguins can live 20 years or more in the wild.

4 Emperors eat fish, squid, and shrimplike krill.

5 Parents feed chicks every three to four days.

Incredible Powers
of
the OCTOPUS!

POTIONS AND POISONS

Blue-ringed octopuses make one of the deadliest poisons in the world. They have enough poison in their saliva to kill a human, though these mollusks mostly use their venom to paralyze prey or to defend themselves from enemies.

TRICK ARMS

When faced with danger, some octopuses will break off an arm and scoot away. The arm keeps wriggling for hours, sometimes crawling all over an attacker and distracting it. The octopus grows a new arm out of the stump.

THE OCTOPUS IS THE TALLER LUMP ON HE RIGHT. THAT'S BRAIN CORAL ON THE LEFT.

ESCAPE ARTIST

To confuse attackers, an octopus will squirt a concentrated ink out of its backside that forms a smokelike cloud. This allows enough time for an octopus to escape.

MAGICAL MOVES

Octopuses can squeeze through tiny holes as if they were moving from room to room through keyholes. Some can even swim through the sand, sticking up an eye like a periscope to see if the coast is clear.

DOLPHINS IN DISGUISE

If you think *you* have a few odd relatives... imagine having a second cousin who's six times your size or an uncle covered in scars from a lifetime of fighting. Welcome to the dolphin family, made up of more than 30 species that inhabit every ocean—and even some rivers. You probably know the common bottlenose dolphin, seen frolicking in aquariums. Now meet its surprisingly diverse relatives.

HOURGLASS DOLPHINS

Dolphin data Sailors once called these small mammals "skunk dolphins," but not because they smelled bad. The dolphin's white markings are similar to a skunk's stripe.

Spinning in air Leaping out of the water, hourglass dolphins make spectacular midair spins. "No one knows for sure why they spin," says Mark Simmonds, a dolphin biologist. "Theories include that they do it for fun, as a form of communicating to others, or to help get rid of parasites."

Where they live Frigid waters in the Antarctic

Dolphin data With its stubby dorsal fin and permanent grin on its beakless head, the Irrawaddy dolphin looks like a bottlenose dolphin reflected in a fun house mirror—recognizable but oddly misshapen. These dolphins, found in coastal waters and some freshwater rivers, are experts at catching dinner. They spit streams of water to confuse fish, making them a cinch to snatch.

Perfect catch Fishermen in Myanmar, in Asia, appreciate the Irrawaddy dolphin's fishing skills, too. In a tradition passed down for generations, the fishermen signal the dolphins to drive schools of fish into nets. These special dolphins don't do it for free—they snap up fish that get away.

Where they live Along coasts of India and Southeast Asia, and in some Southeast Asian rivers

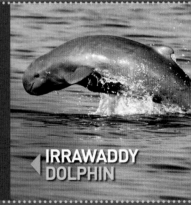

IRRAWADDY DOLPHIN

ORCA ▶

Dolphin data Don't let its titanic size or "killer whale" nickname fool you. A male orca may grow to the length of a school bus, but it is actually a dolphin. It's also the sea's top predator, using teamwork to hunt seals, sea lions, and other large prey—hence the killer alias. Researchers have even seen orcas gobbling up great white sharks!

Mother knows best Orcas love their moms. Elder females typically lead each family, or pod. Male orcas who wander off to mate in other pods return to their mothers' sides and never see their young. "It's unusual among mammals," says Val Veirs, who studies orcas. "This top predator gets all its marching orders from Mom."

Where they live Frigid coastal waters across the globe

BOTTLENOSE DOLPHINS

Dolphin data In the wild, these sleek swimmers can reach speeds of more than 18 miles an hour (29 kph). They surface often to breathe, doing so two or three times a minute.

Superstars They are well known as the intelligent and playful stars of many aquarium shows. Their curved mouths give the appearance of a friendly smile, and they can be trained to perform complex tricks.

Where they live In tropical oceans and other warm waters around the globe

Dolphin data Small and curious, the Commerson's dolphin is known for its playful nature and striking black-and-white coloring. These sleek swimmers look like they're wearing white capes!

Boat buds Many dolphin species enjoy playing with boats, but Commerson's seem especially excited to surf on a ship's wake and twirl in propeller turbulence. "One time two dolphins spent more than an hour playing with our research boat," says Vanesa Tossenberger, who studies Commerson's dolphins. "It certainly makes our work easier."

Where they live Off the southern tip of South America

COMMERSON'S DOLPHIN

HOW TO ID A DOLPHIN

Dolphins are part of a group of marine mammals called cetaceans, which also includes whales and porpoises. As you can see, dolphins come in many shapes, sizes, and colors. So what makes a dolphin ... a dolphin?

DENTAL CHECKUP

Dolphins are considered toothed whales. Their teeth are cone-shaped, unlike porpoises, which have spade-shaped teeth.

NOSE JOB

Most dolphins have a beak, called a rostrum, on their melon-shaped heads, although some family members, such as the orca, do not.

TEAM PLAYERS

"Of the toothed whales, the dolphin family is probably the most social and most diverse," says biologist Denise Herzing.

FINNED KIN

Many dolphins have a dorsal fin. The fin helps stabilize a dolphin as it swims and also helps regulate its body temperature.

Prehistoric
TIME LINE

HUMANS HAVE WALKED on Earth for some 200,000 years, a mere blip in Earth's 4.5-billion-year history. A lot has happened in that time. Earth formed, and oxygen levels rose in the millions of years of the Precambrian time. The productive Paleozoic era gave rise to hard-shelled organisms, vertebrates, amphibians, and reptiles. Dinosaurs ruled the Earth in the mighty Mesozoic. And 64 million years after dinosaurs became extinct, modern humans emerged in the Cenozoic era. From the first tiny mollusks to the dinosaur giants of the Jurassic and beyond, Earth has seen a lot of transformation.

THE PRECAMBRIAN TIME

4.5 billion to 542 million years ago

- The Earth (and other planets) formed from gas and dust left over from a giant cloud that collapsed to form the sun. The giant cloud's collapse was triggered when nearby stars exploded.
- Low levels of oxygen made Earth a suffocating place.
- Early life forms appeared.

THE PALEOZOIC ERA

542 million to 251 million years ago

- The first insects and other animals appeared on land.
- 450 million years ago (m.y.a.), the ancestors of sharks began to swim in the oceans.
- 430 m.y.a., plants began to take root on land.
- More than 360 m.y.a., amphibians emerged from the water.
- Slowly the major landmasses began to come together, creating Pangaea, a single supercontinent.
- By 300 m.y.a., reptiles had begun to dominate the land.

What Is a Dinosaur?

STRONG, HUGE, FIERCE—these are some words people generally associate with dinosaurs. But not all dinosaurs were big or mean; in fact, they had lots of different characteristics. One quality stands out about dinosaurs, though—they endured. With some standing as tall as a house and weighing up to 80 tons (72 t), dinosaurs were not only the largest animals, but also the biggest-brained and fastest of their time. While about 1,000 kinds of dinosaurs are known so far, there are probably thousands more species yet to be discovered.

DINO TIMES

THE MESOZOIC ERA

251 million to 65 million years ago

The Mesozoic era, or the age of the reptiles, consisted of three consecutive time periods (shown below). This is when the first dinosaurs began to appear. They would reign supreme for more than 150 million years.

TRIASSIC PERIOD

251 million to 199 million years ago

- Appearance of the first mammals. They were rodent-size.
- Appearance of the first dinosaur
- Ferns were the dominant plants on land.
- The giant supercontinent of Pangaea began breaking up toward the end of the Triassic.

JURASSIC PERIOD

199 million to 145 million years ago

- Giant dinosaurs dominated the land.
- Pangaea continued its breakup, and oceans formed in the spaces between the drifting landmasses, allowing for sea life, including sharks and marine crocodiles, to thrive.
- Conifer trees spread across the land.

CRETACEOUS PERIOD

145 million to 65 million years ago

- The modern continents developed.
- The largest dinosaurs developed.
- Flowering plants spread across the landscape.
- Mammals flourished and giant pterosaurs ruled the skies over the small birds.
- Temperatures grew more extreme. Dinosaurs lived in deserts, swamps, and forests from the Antarctic to the Arctic.

THE CENOZOIC ERA—TERTIARY PERIOD

65 million to 2.6 million years ago

- Following the dinosaur extinction, mammals rose as the dominant species.
- Birds continued to flourish.
- Volcanic activity was widespread.
- Temperatures began to cool, eventually ending in an ice age.
- The period ended with land bridges forming, which allowed plants and animals to spread to new areas.

Who Ate What?

Herbivores
- Primarily plant-eaters
- Weighed up to 100 tons (91 t)—the largest animals ever to walk on Earth
- Up to 1,000 blunt or flat teeth to grind vegetation
- Many had cheek pouches to store food.
- Examples: *Styracosaurus, Mamenchisaurus*

Carnivores
- Meat-eaters
- Long, strong legs to run faster than plant-eaters; ran up to 30 miles an hour (48 kph)
- Most had good eyesight, strong jaws, and sharp teeth.
- Scavengers and hunters; often hunted in packs

- Grew to 45 feet (14 m) long
- Examples: *Velociraptor, Gigantoraptor, Tyrannosaurus rex*

TYRANNOSAURUS REX

Dino Poo

You may wonder how we could possibly know what dinosaurs actually ate. Well, paleontologists search for coprolites, or fossilized waste. Yep, that's right, the poo of the prehistoric world has told us much of what we know about what dinosaurs ate. Coprolites contain digested plant and animal material, which can help us learn about a dinosaur's diet. Coprolites aren't the only things that can help scientists learn about the dinosaur diet—teeth, habitat, and plant and animal fossils also provide insight.

GIGANTORAPTOR

DID YOU KNOW?
More dinosaurs have been discovered in North America than anywhere else in the world. In the United States, Wyoming and Montana boast the largest number of fossils found in their soil, with bones from more than 50 types of dinosaurs.

VELOCIRAPTOR   **SINOSAUROPTERYX**

MAMENCHISAURUS

PARASAUROLOPHUS

ERKETU

Paleontologists learn about dinosaurs by studying fossils—plant and animal remains that have been preserved in rock.

Bet you **didn't know**

The biggest known **dinosaur SKULL** is longer than a racehorse's **BODY!**

TUOJIANGOSAURUS

STYRACOSAURUS

MONONYKUS

95

DINO Classification

Classifying dinosaurs and all other living things can be a complicated matter, so scientists have devised a system to help with the process. Dinosaurs are put into groups based on a very large range of characteristics.

Scientists put dinosaurs into two major groups: the bird-hipped ornithischians and the reptile-hipped saurischians.

Dinosaur Superlatives

Ornithischian

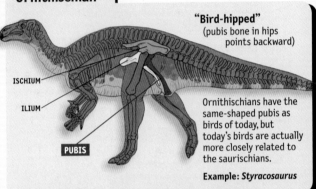

"Bird-hipped"
(pubis bone in hips points backward)

ISCHIUM

ILIUM

PUBIS

Ornithischians have the same-shaped pubis as birds of today, but today's birds are actually more closely related to the saurischians.

Example: *Styracosaurus*

Saurischian

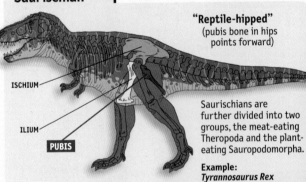

"Reptile-hipped"
(pubis bone in hips points forward)

ISCHIUM

ILIUM

PUBIS

Saurischians are further divided into two groups, the meat-eating Theropoda and the plant-eating Sauropodomorpha.

**Example:
*Tyrannosaurus Rex***

Within these two main divisions, dinosaurs are then separated into orders and then families, such as Stegosauria. Like other members of the Stegosauria, *Stegosaurus* had spines and plates along the back, neck, and tail.

COOL CLICK

What's the largest, most complete, best preserved *T. rex*? Learn about a fossil named Sue at the Field Museum.
fieldmuseum.org/sue

Smallest
Hesperonychus was a tiny dinosaur, reaching about 19 inches (48 cm) in length.

Tallest
Sauroposeidon was taller than a five-story building.

Loudest
The ***Parasaurolophus*** had extra-long nasal passages, allowing it to produce an ear-piercing honking noise from its nose.

Largest teeth
The ***Tyrannosaurus rex*** had thick, sharp teeth the size of bananas, set in jaws strong enough to smash bones and dent metal.

Dumbest
Stegosaurus was among the dumbest—it had a brain the size of a walnut!

Longest name
Micropachycephalosaurus (23 letters)

First dinosaur to be named
Megalosaurus was named in 1822 by the Reverend William Buckland.

16 DINOS YOU SHOULD KNOW

Dinosaur **(Group)** *Example*
What the name means
Length: XX ft (XX m)
Time Range: When they lived
Where: Where they are found

1 *Albertosaurus* **(Saurischian)**
Reptile from Alberta
Length: 28 ft (8 m)
Time Range: Late Cretaceous
Where: Canada (Alberta)

2 *Brachiosaurus* **(Saurischian)**
Arm lizard
Length: 98 ft (30 m)
Time Range: Late Jurassic
Where: U.S. (Colorado); Tanzania

5 *Lambeosaurus* (Ornithischian)
Lambe's lizard
Length: Up to 54 ft (16 m)
Time Range: Late Cretaceous
Where: U.S. (Montana); Canada (Alberta)

3 *Hypsilophodon* (Ornithischian)
High-ridged tooth
Length: 8 ft (2 m)
Time Range: Early Cretaceous
Where: England; Spain; Portugal

6 *Lesothosaurus* (Ornithischian)
Lesotho lizard
Length: 3 ft (1 m)
Time Range: Early Jurassic
Where: Lesotho

4 *Iguanodon* (Ornithischian)
Iguana tooth
Length: 33 ft (10 m)
Time Range: Early Cretaceous
Where: Europe

7 *Maiasaura* (Ornithischian)
Good-mother lizard
Length: 30 ft (9 m)
Time Range: Late Cretaceous
Where: U.S. (Montana)

8 *Pentaceratops* (Ornithischian)
Five-horned face
Length: 28 ft (8 m)
Time Range: Late Cretaceous
Where: U.S. (New Mexico)

9 *Oviraptor* (Saurischian)
Egg thief
Length: 8 ft (2 m)
Time Range: Late Cretaceous
Where: Mongolia

10 *Protoceratops* (Ornithischian)
First horned face
Length: 8 ft (2 m)
Time Range: Late Cretaceous
Where: Mongolia; China

11 *Stegosaurus* (Ornithischian)
Roofed reptile
Length: 30 ft (9 m)
Time Range: Late Jurassic
Where: U.S. (Colorado, Utah, Wyoming)

12 *Tarchia* (Ornithischian)
Brainy one
Length: 18 ft (5 m)
Time Range: Late Cretaceous
Where: Mongolia

13 *Therizinosaurus* (Saurischian)
Scythe lizard
Length: 36 ft (11 m)
Time Range: Late Cretaceous
Where: Mongolia

The *TROODON* may have been the SMARTEST DINOSAUR.

14

Troodon **(Saurischian)**

Wounding tooth

Length: 12 ft (4 m)

Time Range: Late Cretaceous

Where: U.S. (Alaska, Montana, Wyoming);
Canada (Alberta)

15

Tyrannosaurus rex **(Saurischian)**

Tyrant lizard

Length: 41 ft (12 m)

Time Range: Late Cretaceous

Where: U.S. (Western); Canada (Western)

16

Velociraptor **(Saurischian)**

Swift robber

Length: 7 ft (2 m)

Time Range: Late Cretaceous

Where: Mongolia; China

6 NEWLY DISCOVERED DINOS

Humans have been searching for—and discovering—dinosaur remains for hundreds of years. And in that time, almost 1,000 kinds of dinos have been found all over the world, with thousands more possibly still out there waiting to be unearthed. Here are some of the most exciting dino discoveries to date.

3 *Diamantinasaurus* **(Saurischian)**
Diamantina River lizard
Length: 50 ft (15 m)
Time Range: Early Cretaceous
Where: Australia

4 *Barrosasaurus* **(Saurischian)**
Lizard from Barrosa Hill
Length: 95 ft (29 m)
Time Range: Late Cretaceous
Where: Argentina

1 *Austroraptor* **(Saurischian)**
Southern thief
Length: 16 ft (5 m)
Time Range: Late Cretaceous
Where: Argentina

5 *Raptorrex* **(Saurischian)**
Robber king
Length: 10 ft (3 m)
Time Range: Early Cretaceous
Where: China

2 *Hesperonychus* **(Saurischian)**
West claw
Length: Less than 3 ft (1 m)
Time Range: Late Cretaceous
Where: Canada (Alberta)

6 *Fruitadens* **(Ornithischian)**
Fruita tooth
Length: 26–30 in (66–76 cm)
Time Range: Late Jurassic
Where: U.S. (Colorado)

SuperCroc ROCKED!

What's 40 feet (12 m) long, tips the scale at 10 tons (9 t), and eats dinosaurs for lunch? It's SuperCroc! National Geographic Explorer-in-Residence Paul Sereno dug up this bus-length, dino-era crocodilian's giant bones and teeth in Africa. We now know that about 110 million years ago, SuperCroc (aka *Sarcosuchus imperator*) was the toughest bully on the block. As if its six-foot (2-m) -long jaws weren't enough, this scaly, muscle-bound monster hid most of its bulk underwater while scoping out its next banquet-size dinosaur meal. Then, a sudden splash, the scramble of heavy footsteps, and...gulp! What's for dessert?

MEET THE NAT GEO EXPLORER

PAUL SERENO
A paleontologist at the University of Chicago, Paul has discovered more than two dozen new species of dinosaurs on five continents.

Famous Find: Aside from SuperCroc, Sereno unearthed the first dinosaurs to roam the Earth in the foothills of the Andes in Argentina.

Not Just Dinos: While searching for dinosaur fossils in the Sahara Desert, Sereno uncovered the largest known graveyard of Stone Age people. The remains were close to 5,000 years old!

Artistic Edge: Sereno began his career as an artist, a skill that helps him visualize a complete dinosaur skeleton from a pile of fragmented fossils.

Neat Nickname: Because of his adventurous lifestyle, many people call Sereno a modern-day "Indiana Jones."

Wise Words: Sereno's trick to finding big fossils? "You've got to be able to go where no one has gone before."

What Killed the Dinosaurs?

Sixty-five million years ago the last of the nonbird dinosaurs went extinct. So did the giant mosasaurs and plesiosaurs in the seas and the pterosaurs in the sky. Many kinds of plants died, too. Perhaps half of the world's species died in this mass extinction that marks the end of the Cretaceous and the beginning of the Paleocene period.

Why did so many animals die out while most mammals, turtles, crocodiles, salamanders, and frogs survived? Birds escaped extinction. So did many plants and insects. Scientists are searching for answers.

Asteroid or Volcano?

Scientists have a couple of theories: a huge impact, such as an asteroid or comet, or a massive bout of volcanic activity. Either of these might have choked the sky with debris that starved Earth of the sun's energy. Once the dust settled, greenhouse gases locked in the atmosphere may have caused the temperature to soar.

Regardless of what caused the extinction, it marked the end of *Tyrannosaurus rex*'s reign of terror and opened the door for mammals to take over.

Bet you didn't know

HUMANS have LIVED on Earth for about 200,000 years; DINOSAURS walked the planet for roughly 160,000,000 years.

Wildly Good Animal Reports

Velvety free-tailed bats in flight

Your teacher wants a written report on the velvety free-tailed bat. By Monday! Not to worry. Use the tools of good writing to organize your thoughts and research, and writing an animal report won't drive you batty.

STEPS TO SUCCESS Your report will follow the format of a descriptive or expository essay (see p. 228 for "How to Write a Perfect Essay") and should consist of a main idea, followed by supporting details, and a conclusion. Use this basic structure for each paragraph as well as the whole report, and you'll be on the right track.

1. Introduction
State your main idea.
The velvety free-tailed bat is a common and important species of bat.

2. Body
Provide **supporting points** for your main idea.
The velvety free-tailed bat eats insects and can have a large impact on insect populations.
Ranges from Mexico to Florida and South America.
Like other bats, its wings are built for fast, efficient flight.

Then **expand** on those points with further description, explanation, or discussion.
The velvety free-tailed bat eats insects and can have a large impact on insect populations.
Its diet consists primarily of mosquitoes and other airborne insects.
Ranges from Mexico to Florida and South America.
It is sometimes encountered in attics.
Like other bats, its wings are built for fast, efficient flight.
It has trouble, however, taking off from low or flat surfaces and must drop from a place high enough to gain speed to start flying.

3. Conclusion
Wrap it up with a summary of your whole paper.
Because of its large numbers, the velvety free-tailed bat holds an important position in the food chain.

KEY INFORMATION

Here are some things you should consider including in your report:

What does your animal look like?
To what other species is it related?
How does it move?
Where does it live?
What does it eat?
What are its predators?
How long does it live?
Is it endangered?
Why do you find it interesting?

FACT FROM FICTION: Your animal may have been featured in a movie or in myths and legends. Compare and contrast how the animal has been portrayed with how it behaves in reality. For example, penguins can't dance the way they do in *Happy Feet*.

PROOFREAD AND REVISE: As with any awesome essay, when you're finished, check for misspellings, grammatical mistakes, and punctuation errors. It often helps to have someone else proofread your work, too, as he or she may catch things you have missed. Also, look for ways to make your sentences and paragraphs even better. Add more descriptive language, choosing just the right verbs, adverbs, and adjectives to make your writing come alive.

BE CREATIVE: Use visual aids to make your report come to life. Include an animal photo file with interesting images found in magazines or printed from websites. Or draw your own! You can also build a miniature animal habitat diorama. Use creativity to help communicate your passion for the subject.

THE FINAL RESULT: Put it all together in one final, polished draft. Make it neat and clean, and remember to cite your references (see p. 257 for "Reveal Your Sources").

How to Observe ANIMALS

BOOKS, ARTICLES, and other second-hand sources are great for learning about animals, but there's another way to find out even more. Direct observation means watching, listening to, and smelling an animal yourself. To truly understand animals you need to see them in action.

VISIT

YOU CAN FIND ANIMALS in their natural habitats almost anywhere, even your own backyard. Or take a drive to a nearby mountain area, river, forest, wetland, or other ecosystem. There are animals to be seen in every natural setting you can visit. To observe more exotic varieties, plan a trip to a national park, aquarium, zoo, wildlife park, or aviary.

OBSERVE

GET NEAR ENOUGH to an animal to watch and study it, but do not disturb it. Be patient, as it may take a while to spot something interesting. And be safe. Don't take any risks; wild animals can be dangerous. Take notes, and write down every detail. Use all of your senses. How does it look? How does it act? What more can you learn?

RESEARCH

COMPARE YOUR own observations with those found in textbooks, encyclopedias, nonfiction books, Internet sources, and nature documentaries. (See p. 160 for "Research Like a Pro.") And check out exciting animal encounters in National Geographic's book series *Face to Face with Animals.*

COOL CLICK

Love to watch animals? Check out these amazing animal and pet videos.
video.kids.nationalgeographic.com/video/player/kids/index.html

TIP:
Binoculars are a good way to get up close and personal with wild animals while still keeping a safe distance.

Culture Connection

These color-splashed kids are celebrating Holi, an annual festival in India commemorating spring. Each year, the country comes alive with color as people say goodbye to winter by dousing the streets—and each other—with buckets of brightly hued water and powder.

CELEBRATE! World Holidays 2012

1 CHINESE NEW YEAR
January 23
Also called Lunar New Year, this holiday marks the new year according to the lunar calendar. Families celebrate the occasion with parades, feasts, and fireworks. Young people may receive gifts of money in red envelopes.

2 NIRVANA DAY
February 15
Celebrated by Mahayana Buddhists, this holiday commemorates the anniversary of Buddha's death. It's not a sad day, but a day to reflect on life and celebrate.

3 HOLI
March 8
This festival in India celebrates spring and marks the triumph of good over evil. People cover one another with powdered paint, called *gulal,* and douse one another with buckets of colored water. (See photograph on pp. 106-107.)

4 EASTER
April 8
A Christian holiday that celebrates the resurrection of Jesus Christ, Easter is celebrated by giving baskets filled with gifts or candy to children.

5 PASSOVER
April 7 – 13
A Jewish holiday that commemorates the exodus of the Jews from Egypt and their liberation from slavery, Passover is a seven-day holiday during which observers have seders, or ritual feasts, and abstain from eating leavened bread.

6 VICTORIA DAY
May 21
A Canadian celebration of Queen Victoria's birthday, this holiday is observed on a Monday and is Canada's unofficial start to summer. Born in 1819, Queen Victoria reigned over Canada—in addition to the U.K.

7 RAMADAN AND EID AL-FITR
July 20 – August 19
A Muslim religious holiday, Ramadan is a month long, ending in the Eid Al-Fitr celebration. Observers fast during this month—eating only after sunset—and do good deeds. Muslims pray for forgiveness and hope to purify themselves through observance.

8 ROSH HASHANAH AND YOM KIPPUR
September 17 – 18 and September 26
A Jewish religious holiday marking the beginning of a new year on the Hebrew calendar, Rosh Hashanah is celebrated with prayer, ritual foods, and a day of rest. Yom Kippur, known as the "Day of Atonement," is the most solemn of all Jewish holidays. It is observed with fasting and prayer, and is marked by a feast at sundown.

9 DAY OF THE DEAD
November 1 – 2
Known as *Día de los Muertos,* this Mexican holiday is a joyful time that honors the deceased. Festivities include parties in graveyards, where families feast, sing songs, clean tombstones, and talk to their buried ancestors.

10 HANUKKAH
December 9 – 16
This Jewish holiday is eight days long. It commemorates the rededication of the Temple in Jerusalem. It is observed with celebrations, the lighting of a menorah, and the exchange of gifts.

11 CHRISTMAS DAY
December 25
A Christian holiday marking the birth of Jesus Christ, Christmas is usually celebrated by decorating trees, exchanging presents, and having festive gatherings.

ANNIVERSARIES

Annual	1 year
Biennial	2 years
Triennial	3 years
Quadrennial	4 years
Quinquennial	5 years
Sexennial	6 years
Septennial	7 years
Octennial	8 years
Novennial	9 years
Decennial	10 years
Undecennial	11 years
Duodecennial	12 years
Tredecennial	13 years
Quattuordecennial	14 years
Quindecennial	15 years
Vigintennial or vicennial	20 years
Semicentennial or quinquagenary	50 years
Semisesquicentennial	75 years
Centennial	100 years
Quasquicentennial	125 years
Sesquicentennial	150 years
Demisemiseptcentennial or quartoseptcentennial	175 years
Bicentennial	200 years
Semiquincentennial	250 years
Tercentennial or tricentennial	300 years
Semiseptcentennial	350 years
Quadricentennial or quatercentenary	400 years
Quincentennial	500 years
Sexcentennial	600 years
Septicentennial or septuacentennial	700 years
Octocentennial	800 years
Nonacentennial	900 years
Millennial	1,000 years
Bimillennial	2,000 years

2012 CALENDAR

JANUARY
S	M	T	W	T	F	S
1	2	3	4	5	6	7
8	9	10	11	12	13	14
15	16	17	18	19	20	21
22	23	24	25	26	27	28
29	30	31				

FEBRUARY
S	M	T	W	T	F	S
			1	2	3	4
5	6	7	8	9	10	11
12	13	14	15	16	17	18
19	20	21	22	23	24	25
26	27	28	29			

MARCH
S	M	T	W	T	F	S
				1	2	3
4	5	6	7	8	9	10
11	12	13	14	15	16	17
18	19	20	21	22	23	24
25	26	27	28	29	30	31

APRIL
S	M	T	W	T	F	S
1	2	3	4	5	6	7
8	9	10	11	12	13	14
15	16	17	18	19	20	21
22	23	24	25	26	27	28
29	30					

MAY
S	M	T	W	T	F	S
		1	2	3	4	5
6	7	8	9	10	11	12
13	14	15	16	17	18	19
20	21	22	23	24	25	26
27	28	29	30	31		

JUNE
S	M	T	W	T	F	S
					1	2
3	4	5	6	7	8	9
10	11	12	13	14	15	16
17	18	19	20	21	22	23
24	25	26	27	28	29	30

JULY
S	M	T	W	T	F	S
1	2	3	4	5	6	7
8	9	10	11	12	13	14
15	16	17	18	19	20	21
22	23	24	25	26	27	28
29	30	31				

AUGUST
S	M	T	W	T	F	S
			1	2	3	4
5	6	7	8	9	10	11
12	13	14	15	16	17	18
19	20	21	22	23	24	25
26	27	28	29	30	31	

SEPTEMBER
S	M	T	W	T	F	S
						1
2	3	4	5	6	7	8
9	10	11	12	13	14	15
16	17	18	19	20	21	22
23	24	25	26	27	28	29
30						

OCTOBER
S	M	T	W	T	F	S
	1	2	3	4	5	6
7	8	9	10	11	12	13
14	15	16	17	18	19	20
21	22	23	24	25	26	27
28	29	30	31			

NOVEMBER
S	M	T	W	T	F	S
				1	2	3
4	5	6	7	8	9	10
11	12	13	14	15	16	17
18	19	20	21	22	23	24
25	26	27	28	29	30	

DECEMBER
S	M	T	W	T	F	S
						1
2	3	4	5	6	7	8
9	10	11	12	13	14	15
16	17	18	19	20	21	22
23	24	25	26	27	28	29
30	31					

DIWALI

FLAMES FROM OIL LAMPS flicker as families gather together to share music, food, and gifts in the spirit of Diwali, often called the "Festival of Lights." This Hindu holiday, celebrating the triumph of good over evil and the lifting of spiritual darkness, is actually a series of festivals: Each of the five days of Diwali honors a different tradition. Diwali customs include cleaning and decorating houses and wearing new clothes.

Women in Chandigarh, India, light lamps on the eve of Diwali.

Carnival celebration in Salvador, Brazil

CARNIVAL

COLORFUL COSTUMES, festive music, parades, and parties for days—sounds fun, huh? One of the biggest bashes around the world, Carnival originated as a way for Catholics to mark the last days before Lent, the period of fasting before Easter. Thousands of partiers also take to the streets each spring, especially in the Caribbean country of Trinidad and Tobago and throughout South America. The hottest place to celebrate at Carnival time? Salvador, Brazil, considered one of the biggest street parties on the planet!

What's Your Chinese Horoscope?
Locate your birth year to find out.

In Chinese astrology the zodiac runs on a 12-year cycle, based on the lunar calendar. Each year corresponds to one of twelve animals, each representing one of twelve personality types. Read on to find out which animal year you were born in and what that might say about you.

RAT
1972, '84, '96, 2008
Say cheese! You're attractive, charming, and creative. When you get mad, you can really have sharp teeth!

RABBIT
1975, '87, '99, 2011
Your ambition and talent make you jump at opportunity. You also keep your ears open for gossip.

HORSE
1966, '78, '90, 2002
Being happy is your "mane" goal. And while you're smart and hardworking, your teacher may ride you for talking too much.

ROOSTER
1969, '81, '93, 2005
You crow about your adventures, but inside you're really shy. You're thoughtful, capable, brave, and talented.

OX
1973, '85, '97, 2009
You're smart, patient, and as strong as an ... well, you know what. Though you're a leader, you never brag.

DRAGON
1976, '88, 2000, '12
You're on fire! Health, energy, honesty, and bravery make you a living legend.

SHEEP
1967, '79, '91, 2003
Gentle as a lamb, you're also artistic, compassionate, and wise. You're often shy.

DOG
1970, '82, '94, 2006
Often the leader of the pack, you're loyal and honest. You can also keep a secret.

TIGER
1974, '86, '98, 2010
You may be a nice person, but no one should ever enter your room without asking—you might attack!

SNAKE
1977, '89, 2001, '13
You may not speak often, but you're very smart. You always seem to have a stash of cash.

MONKEY
1968, '80, '92, 2004
No "monkey see, monkey do" for you. You're a clever problem-solver with an excellent memory.

PIG
1971, '83, '95, 2007
Even though you're courageous, honest, and kind, you never hog all the attention.

World Religions

A round the world, religion takes many forms. Some belief systems, such as Christianity, Islam, and Judaism, are monotheistic, meaning that followers believe in just one supreme being. Others, like Hinduism, Shintoism, and most native belief systems, are polytheistic, meaning that many of their followers believe in multiple gods.

All of the major religions have their origins in Asia, but they have spread around the world. Christianity, with the largest number of followers, has three divisions—Roman Catholic, Eastern Orthodox, and Protestant. Islam, with about one-fifth of all believers, has two main divisions—Sunni and Shiite. Hinduism and Buddhism account for almost another one-fifth of believers. Judaism, dating back some 4,000 years, is the oldest of all the major monotheistic religions.

CHRISTIANITY

Based on the teachings of Jesus Christ, a Jew born some 2,000 years ago in the area of modern-day Israel, Christianity has spread worldwide and actively seeks converts. Followers in Switzerland (above) participate in a procession with lanterns and crosses.

BUDDHISM

Founded about 2,400 years ago in northern India by the Hindu prince Gautama Buddha, Buddhism spread throughout East and Southeast Asia. Buddhist temples have statues, such as the Mihintale Buddha (above) in Sri Lanka.

HINDUISM

Dating back more than 4,000 years, Hinduism is practiced mainly in India. Hindus follow sacred texts known as the Vedas and believe in reincarnation. During the festival of Navratri, which honors the goddess Durga, the Garba dance is performed (above).

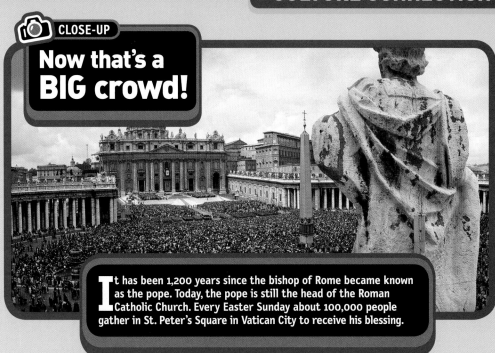

CLOSE-UP

Now that's a BIG crowd!

It has been 1,200 years since the bishop of Rome became known as the pope. Today, the pope is still the head of the Roman Catholic Church. Every Easter Sunday about 100,000 people gather in St. Peter's Square in Vatican City to receive his blessing.

COOL CLICK

To learn more about ancient and medieval religions, go online.
historyforkids.org/learn/religion

ISLAM

Muslims believe that the Koran, Islam's sacred book, records the words of Allah (God) as revealed to the Prophet Muhammad around A.D. 610. Believers (above) circle the Kabah in the Haram Mosque in Mecca, Saudi Arabia, the spiritual center of the faith.

JUDAISM

The traditions, laws, and beliefs of Judaism date back to Abraham (the Patriarch) and the Torah (the first five books of the Old Testament). Followers pray before the Western Wall (above), which stands below Islam's Dome of the Rock in Jerusalem.

MYTHOLOGY

GREEK

EGYPTIAN

The ancient Greeks believed that many gods and goddesses ruled the universe. According to this mythology, the Olympians lived high atop Greece's Mount Olympus. Each of these 12 principal gods and goddesses had a unique personality that corresponded to particular aspects of life, such as love or death.

Egyptian mythology is based on a creation myth that tells of an egg that appeared on the ocean. When the egg hatched, out came Ra, the sun god. As a result, ancient Egyptians became worshippers of the sun and the nine original deities, most of which were the children and grandchildren of Ra.

THE OLYMPIANS

Aphrodite was the goddess of love and beauty.

Apollo, Zeus's son, was the god of the sun, music, and healing. Artemis was his twin.

Ares, Zeus's son, was the god of war.

Artemis, Zeus's daughter and Apollo's twin, was the goddess of the hunt and childbirth.

Athena, born from the forehead of Zeus, was the goddess of wisdom and crafts.

Demeter was the goddess of fertility and nature.

Hades, Zeus's brother, was the god of the underworld and the dead.

Hephaestus, the son of Hera, was the god of fire.

Hera, the wife and older sister of Zeus, was the goddess of women and marriage.

Hermes, Zeus's son, was the messenger of the gods.

Poseidon, the brother of Zeus, was the god of the sea and earthquakes.

Zeus was the most powerful of the gods and the top Olympian. He wielded a thunderbolt and was god of the sky and thunder.

THE NINE DEITIES

Geb, son of Shu and Tefnut, was the god of the Earth.

Isis, daughter of Geb and Nut, was the goddess of fertility and motherhood.

Nephthys, daughter of Geb and Nut, was protector of the dead.

Nut, daughter of Shu and Tefnut, was the goddess of the sky.

Osiris, son of Geb and Nut, was the god of the afterlife.

Ra (Re), the sun god, is generally viewed as the creator. He represents life and health.

Seth, son of Geb and Nut, was the god of the desert and chaos.

Shu, son of Ra, was the god of air.

Tefnut, daughter of Ra, was the goddess of rain.

All cultures around the world have unique legends and traditions that have been passed down over generations. Many myths refer to gods or supernatural heroes who are responsible for occurrences in the world. For example, Norse mythology tells of the red-bearded Thor, the God of Thunder, who is responsible for creating lightning and thunderstorms. And many creation myths, especially from some of North America's native cultures, tell of an earth-diver represented as an animal that brings a piece of sand or mud up from the deep sea. From this tiny piece of earth, the entire world takes shape.

NORSE

ROMAN

Norse mythology originated in Scandinavia, in northern Europe. It was complete with gods and goddesses who lived in a heavenly place called Asgard that could be reached only by crossing a rainbow bridge.

While Norse mythology is lesser known, we use it every day. Most days of the week are named after Norse gods, including some of these major deities.

NORSE GODS

Balder was the god of light and beauty.

Freya was the goddess of love, beauty, and fertility.

Frigg, for whom Friday was named, was the queen of Asgard. She was the goddess of marriage, motherhood, and the home.

Heimdall was the watchman of the rainbow bridge and the guardian of the gods.

Hel, the daughter of Loki, was the goddess of death.

Loki, a shape-shifter, was a trickster who helped the gods—and caused them problems.

Thor, for whom Thursday was named, was the god of thunder and lightning.

Tyr, for whom Tuesday was named, was the god of the sky and war.

Skadi was the goddess of winter and of the hunt. She is often represented as "The Snow Queen."

Wodan, for whom Wednesday was named, was the god of war, wisdom, death, and magic.

Much of Roman mythology was adopted from Greek mythology, but the Romans also developed a lot of original myths as well. The gods of Roman mythology lived everywhere and each had a role to play. There were thousands of Roman gods, but here are a few of the stars of Roman myths.

ANCIENT ROMAN GODS

Ceres was the goddess of the harvest and motherly love.

Diana, daughter of Jupiter, was the goddess of hunting and the moon.

Juno, Jupiter's wife, was the goddess of women and fertility.

Jupiter, the patron of Rome and master of the gods, was the god of the sky.

Mars, the son of Jupiter and Juno, was the god of war.

Mercury, the son of Jupiter, was the messenger of the gods and the god of travelers.

Minerva was the goddess of wisdom, learning, and the arts and crafts.

Neptune, the brother of Jupiter, was the god of the sea.

Venus was the goddess of love and beauty.

Vesta was the goddess of fire and the hearth. She was one of the most important of the Roman deities.

THE OLYMPICS

LEGEND HAS IT THAT the Olympic Games were founded in ancient times by Heracles, a son of the Greek god Zeus. Unfortunately, that can't really be proven. The first Olympic Games for which there are still written records took place in 776 B.C. There was only one event: a running race called the stade. From then on, the Olympics were held every four years until they were abolished in A.D. 393.

It wasn't until more than 1,500 years later that the Olympics were resurrected. The modern Olympic Games were held for the first time in 1896 and have continued around the world ever since.

Summer Olympic Games Sites

1896	Athens, Greece
1900	Paris, France
1904	St. Louis, Missouri, U.S.A.
1906	Athens, Greece
1908	London, England, U.K.
1912	Stockholm, Sweden
1920	Antwerp, Belgium
1924	Paris, France
1928	Amsterdam, Netherlands
1932	Los Angeles, California, U.S.A.
1936	Berlin, Germany
1948	London, England, U.K.
1952	Helsinki, Finland
1956	Melbourne, Australia
1960	Rome, Italy
1964	Tokyo, Japan
1968	Mexico City, Mexico
1972	Munich, West Germany (now Germany)
1976	Montreal, Canada
1980	Moscow, U.S.S.R. (now Russia)
1984	Los Angeles, California, U.S.A.
1988	Seoul, South Korea
1992	Barcelona, Spain
1996	Atlanta, Georgia, U.S.A.
2000	Sydney, Australia
2004	Athens, Greece
2008	Beijing, China
2012	London, England, U.K.
2016	Rio de Janeiro, Brazil

Winter Olympic Games Sites

1924	Chamonix, France
1928	St. Moritz, Switzerland
1932	Lake Placid, New York, U.S.A.
1936	Garmisch-Partenkirchen, Germany
1948	St. Moritz, Switzerland
1952	Oslo, Norway
1956	Cortina d'Ampezzo, Italy
1960	Squaw Valley, California, U.S.A.
1964	Innsbruck, Austria
1968	Grenoble, France
1972	Sapporo, Japan
1976	Innsbruck, Austria
1980	Lake Placid, New York, U.S.A.
1984	Sarajevo, Yugoslavia
1988	Calgary, Alberta, Canada
1992	Albertville, France
1994	Lillehammer, Norway
1998	Nagano, Japan
2002	Salt Lake City, Utah, U.S.A.
2006	Torino (Turin), Italy
2010	Vancouver, British Columbia, Canada
2014	Sochi, Russia

Note: Due to World Wars I and II, the 1916 Summer Olympics and both the summer and winter games of 1940 and 1944 were not held.

Strange Olympic Sports of the Past & Future

Some sports that were once played in the Olympics no longer make an appearance. Here are a few that you won't see in the Olympics this year: Tug-of-War • Croquet • Lacrosse • Golf • Powerboating

The following are among a long list of sports that aren't currently played at the games but are recognized as International Sports Federations by the Olympic Committee. So who knows, maybe one day you can win a gold medal in: Billiards • Bridge • Chess • Lifesaving • Netball • Orienteering • Roller Sports • Waterskiing

1912 Summer Olympics Tug-of-War

STRAIGHT TALK

Would you hate someone just because he or she looks different?

Unfortunately, a lot of people judge other people on the way they look, what they eat, or what they wear. But that's not fair. It's not right to judge people. It doesn't matter where you are from, what your culture is, what religion you practice, or what you look like. We're all people, and everyone should be accepted as an individual. After all, we're all the same on the inside.

DIFFERENT IS GOOD!

Accepting differences is like eating a burrito—without all the different meats, veggies, and cheeses, all you get is a boring tortilla. "And when I chew all the ingredients together, it's good!" says Deborah Crockett, a school psychologist in Atlanta, Georgia. Sometimes it's hard to keep an open mind about things—or people—you don't understand. So to really enjoy your next "cultural burrito," use Crockett's tips below.

COMMON GROUND. Everyone's different. But everyone also has things in common. Do you wear a baseball cap, a Jewish yarmulke, or a Muslim hijab? Yeah, they're from different cultures. But the point is, they're all head coverings.

CULTURE CLUB. Learning about other groups of people helps you understand them. Try eating foods from another culture. Or teach yourself words in another language.

BLAME GAME. Has your entire class ever had to stay in from recess because one kid couldn't keep his mouth shut? That's not fair! It's also not fair to blame an entire group of people for the actions of a few individuals.

TIME-OUT

TYPECAST. It's normal to make assumptions; we all do it. But the key is to be aware that you've done it—then try to be more open-minded the next time around.

Languages and Literacy

Every 14 days a language dies. By 2100, more than half of the more than 7,000 languages spoken on Earth—many of them not yet recorded— may disappear, taking with them a wealth of knowledge about history, culture, and the environment.

Earth's seven billion people live in 194 independent countries and speak more than 7,000 languages. Some countries, such as Japan, have one official language. Others have many languages: India has 22 official languages. Experts believe that humans may once have spoken as many as 10,000 languages, but that number has dropped by one-third and is still declining.

Language defines a culture, through the people who speak it and what it allows speakers to say. Throughout human history, the languages of powerful groups have spread while the languages of smaller cultures have become extinct.

LITERACY is the ability to read and write in one's native language. Eighty-three percent of the people in the world (ages 15 and over) are literate.

Literacy rates vary greatly from country to country and region to region. Many factors play a role in whether people are literate; some of those factors are wealth, gender, educational availability, and locale.

There are 796 million illiterate adults (those who cannot read and write) in the world. Two-thirds of those are women, generally because women in less-developed countries often lack access to education.

COOL CLICK

To read more about preserving languages, go online.
nationalgeographic.com/
mission/enduringvoices

LEADING LANGUAGES

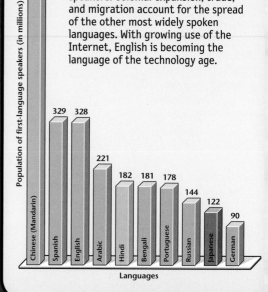

Some languages have only a few hundred speakers, but 23 languages stand out with more than 50 million speakers each. Earth's population giant, China, has 845 million speakers of Mandarin, more than double the next-largest group of language speakers. Colonial expansion, trade, and migration account for the spread of the other most widely spoken languages. With growing use of the Internet, English is becoming the language of the technology age.

Population of first-language speakers (in millions)

Language	Speakers
Chinese (Mandarin)	845
Spanish	329
English	328
Arabic	221
Hindi	182
Bengali	181
Portuguese	178
Russian	144
Japanese	122
German	90

Languages

BRAILLE

Braille is an alphabet system used by blind people to read and write using touch. It consists of groups of dots arranged in various ways to designate certain letters, numbers, words, and punctuation to form sentences. Each character is made up of six dots within a Braille cell. The dots can be raised or not raised, creating the Braille codes. The blind can read Braille by running their fingers over the text and feeling the dot arrangements.

Braille can be adapted to languages that do not use the Latin alphabet. In this case, the codes are usually assigned to the new alphabet in relation to how it is translated into the Latin alphabet.

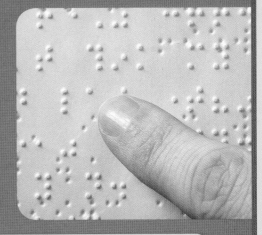

To learn more about Braille, go online. brailler.com/braille.htm

FINGER SPELLING

The manipulation of the fingers and hands to form the letters of a written language is called finger spelling. These manual alphabets are used in deaf education and generally form the basis for sign languages around the world.

It is interesting to know, though, that finger spelling is not the same around the world. For example, in languages with a Latin alphabet, there are both one-handed (American Sign Language and Irish Sign Language) and two-handed (Turkish Sign Language and British Manual Alphabet) manual alphabets. And languages with non-Latin alphabets, such as Japanese, use hand shapes to represent the written characters.

American Sign Language

A B C D

See more information on deaf culture.
pbs.org/wnet/soundandfury/culture/index.html

Currency Around

Australia—Australian Dollar (AUD)
Australia was the first country to issue plastic currency.

Egypt—Egyptian Pound (EGP)
The Qaitbay Mosque appears on the one-pound note.

Canada—Canadian Dollar (CAD)
Canada once released an orange 50-dollar bill.

European Union—Euro
There is a 500-euro bill.

Colombia—Colombian Peso (COP)
The official symbol of the peso is $.

India—Indian Rupee (INR)
"Rupee" comes from the Sanskrit word for "silver."

Cuba—Cuban Peso (CUP) & Convertible Peso (CUC)
Cuba has two official currencies.

Israel—Shekel (ILS)
The plural of shekel is shekalim.

the World

Japan—Japanese Yen (JPY)
The yen is based on ancient Chinese coins called "yuan."

South Africa—South African Rand (ZAR)
Rand banknotes feature the "Big Five" animals.

United Kingdom—British Pound (GBP)
The pound is the world's oldest currency still in use.

United States—United States Dollar (USD)
Most one-dollar bills circulate for almost two years.

HIDDEN TREASURE

THE TREASURE: ANCIENT ROMAN COINS

FOUND: IN A FIELD

NOW WORTH: £320,250 ($497,041)

David Crisp was hoping to find something interesting when he set out on a walk with his metal detector in a field in the English countryside. But little did he know he'd discover a true treasure buried beneath the dirt—a collection of coins dating back to the third century A.D. The 52,503 bronze and silver coins were contained in a two-foot (61-cm) pot about a foot (30 cm) below the surface. Knowing he'd found something special, Crisp called on a team of archaeologists to unearth the treasure, and they concluded the coins were buried about 1,700 years ago. The collection may be valued at £320,250 ($497,041), but Crisp will get only a portion of the profits: He'll have to split his share with the farmer who owns the field.

SALT HAS BEEN USED AS MONEY.

BUILD A SNOW

This snow carving of King Kong could eat Frosty the Snowman for dinner! Create a smaller version in your backyard by following these tips from Don Berg, head of the United States National Snow Sculpting Competition.

YOU WILL NEED

Ask for permission to use these supplies and be sure to return them clean and dry.

- SNOW SHOVEL
- GARBAGE CAN
- PLASTIC PAIL
- SQUARE AND V-SHAPED CHISELS
- GARDEN TROWEL
- SMALL PUTTY KNIFE
- TRY METAL KITCHEN UTENSILS OR OTHER HOUSE-HOLD TOOLS IF YOU DON'T HAVE THESE ITEMS.

TIPS FOR GETTING STARTED

BEGIN WITH A PICTURE for reference of the subject you want to snow-sculpt.

CARVE FROM THE TOP DOWN to make sure the bottom will support the top.

PATCH UP MISTAKES by adding slightly melted snow to your sculpture.

BUNDLE UP! The ideal temperature for carving is about 20°F to 32°F (-7°C to 0°C).

Ask for a parent's help and permission before you start this project. Be sure to wear waterproof gloves and boots.

MAKE A SNOW PILE

Shovel snow into a garbage can or pail. Stomp on the snow frequently or press hard to pack it down. Turn the can or pail upside down and lift up to release the block of snow.

START SCULPTING

1. Using a chisel, carve shallow lines to show where you want to remove snow. Slowly carve away a little snow at a time.

2. With a garden trowel, carve the gorilla's basic shape. Do not carve detailed features yet.

3. Make shallow lines where the gorilla's eyes, nose, and mouth will go. Then use the trowel to hollow them out.

4. Using a chisel, carve the lips, eyeballs, ears, and any other facial features. Use the V-shaped chisel to carve waves and layers in hair. Be careful not to dig too deep.

5. Use the putty knife to smooth out grooves or gouges.

6. Shovel away any excess snow from your work. Then watch the neighbors go ape over your creative sculpture!

SCULPTURE!

CHECK OUT OTHER COOL ANIMAL CARVINGS!

THE BIGGEST SNOW SCULPTURES IN THE WORLD, LIKE THIS ONE FROM THE SAPPORO FESTIVAL IN JAPAN, CAN WEIGH UP TO 100 TONS (90 T)— THAT'S MORE THAN 50 HIPPOS.

AT SNOW SCULPTURE COMPETITIONS, PEOPLE KNOWN AS "STOMPERS" HELP COMPRESS SNOW BY STOMPING ON IT.

TO ADD COLOR, SPRAY WATER ON THE SCULPTURE, WHICH CREATES AN ICY LAYER. THEN APPLY NONTOXIC SPRAY BODY PAINT.

THIS ELEPHANT WAS SCULPTED FROM AN EIGHT-FOOT (2.4-M) -TALL CUBE OF SNOW.

123

WILD RIDES

How creative minds turn ordinary cars into wacky works of art

Cross a regular four-wheeled vehicle with tons of imagination, and you might just get an art car. "When you see an art car, you're viewing someone's individuality," says art car builder Harrod Blank. Some can be driven on the streets; others are just for show. But all of them are head-turners. Check out these photos to see how *car*-tists express themselves on wheels.

QUILTING BUG

When his car got dinged, Ron Dolce tried to pretty it up with glued-on marbles. Then he kept going, adding thousands of pieces of stained glass. More than 10,000 marbles later, Dolce has pieced together a quiltlike, solid car: "Its glass skin protects it from sun, wind, or rain."

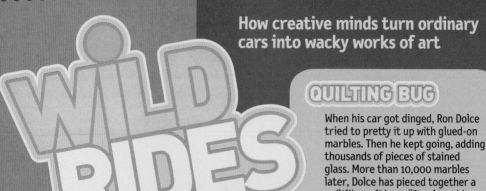

LOBSTERFEST

Art the Lobster was supposed to be a seafood delivery truck. But after six years of building it, sculptor A. J. Strasser couldn't give up his crustacean creation. Strasser carved the creature out of spray foam, covered it in a fiberglass shell, then painted it bright red. Art's tail sections are on hinges so they can open like a car trunk.

MUSIC MACHINE

It's a car! It's a band! It's Pico de Gallo, Blank's salute to Mexican mariachi music. Using brackets, bolts, and superstrong glue, he mounted guitars, drums, a trumpet, a saxophone, an accordion, 300 bells, and other instruments onto an old car. "When you hit a bump, there's a lot of jingling and jangling," Blank says.

DOUBLE TROUBLE

What do you do if you have an extra VW Beetle lying around? Dennis Clay created an art car. The upside-down car is just the car's shell welded around a big pipe. The legs sticking out are mannequins'. "It's only for parades," Clay says. "Above 30 miles an hour, it gets all wiggly."

ROAD SHOW

Wonder what Piet Mondrian, a modern artist, would have thought about this car, which was inspired by the Dutchman's distinctive style? Artist Emily Duffy painted the patterns on the vehicle, then made a matching roof sculpture and clothing. "I want to show people that nothing in life has to be boring," Duffy says.

MYTHS BUSTED!

WAA-HOO!

WHOA!

SWEET!

A wise man says, "Welcome to America!"

CHINA

THE MYTH

Chewing gum takes seven years to digest.

WHY IT'S NOT TRUE

Gum is made from a substance similar to rubber, so it's impossible for the acid in your stomach to break it down. But that doesn't mean the gum sticks around. It can't adhere to the slippery lining in your gut, so as long as you don't make meals out of it, gum will come out of your body with the rest of your waste. "In a couple days, it comes out looking pretty much the same as when it went in," says David E. Milov, a doctor at Nemours Children's Hospital in Orlando, Florida.

THE MYTH

Fortune cookies come from China.

WHY IT'S NOT TRUE

Fortune cookies aren't even found in China! "They most likely came from Japan," says Jennifer 8. Lee, author of *The Fortune Cookie Chronicles*. The proof: an 1878 Japanese book that shows a man baking fortune cookies. Chinese people weren't associated with the treats until at least 1907. "The cookies were brought to California by Japanese immigrants," Lee says. It's still a mystery why fortune cookies are now served mostly in Chinese restaurants.

Pop History

BUBBLE GUM IS MADE FROM SWEETENERS like sugar, a variety of different flavorings, and a chewy gum base. The gum base originally was made from a product called "chicle," which comes from *Manilkara chicle* trees.

Today, the gum base is sometimes made from a latex product or a type of rubber. But these products also come from trees. Think it's weird to chew gum from a tree? People have been doing it for centuries, ever since the ancient Maya of present-day Mexico and Central America chewed chicle thousands of years ago.

Interested in learning about other food history and fun facts?
foodfunandfacts.com/foodfun.htm

COOL CLICK

Snack Bandits BUSTED!

MINNESOTA, U.S.A.

Hansel and Gretel left a trail of bread crumbs to follow. These dumb crooks left a trail of cheese curls. Police investigating a shattered vending machine at a recreation center found the snacks missing, and a trail of orange cheese curls led them all the way to a nearby house. Officers found the stolen snacks in a closet and busted the crooks. These guys should have listened when their moms told them, "No snacking between meals."

Try This! VIVA Mexico!

Throw yourself a fun fiesta with some tasty treats from Mexico. These cheesy molletes topped with tangy pico de gallo are sure to make you say, "Olé."

MOLLETES (mo-YEH-tehs)

Ask an adult for help when you try these recipes.

YOU WILL NEED

French bread baguette
2 cups refried beans
12 ounces shredded cheddar cheese
pico de gallo

WHAT TO DO

Preheat oven to 400°F (200°C). Slice the baguette in half lengthwise, then cut it into thick pieces. Spread with the beans and top with cheese. Place on a baking sheet, and bake for about five minutes, or until the cheese melts and the beans are hot. Top with store-bought pico de gallo, or make your own.

PICO DE GALLO (pee-koh deh GUY-yo)

YOU WILL NEED

1/4 cup chopped fresh cilantro
2 1/2 cups chopped ripe tomatoes
1 chopped jalapeño, without seeds (optional)
1 medium diced onion
juice of 1 lime
salt to taste

WHAT TO DO

Mix all ingredients in a bowl and stir well.

Bet you didn't know

7 sweet facts about desserts

1 The **largest** **s'more** ever made used 40,000 marshmallows, **8,000** chocolate bars, and 55,000 graham crackers.

2 The oldest **chocolate** ever found was in a **2,600-year-old pot.**

3 A man once ate **49 glazed** doughnuts in 8 minutes.

4 The word **"cookie"** comes from the Dutch word *koekje,* which means **small cake.**

5 Some **astronauts** living on the *Mir* space station ate **Jell-O** every Sunday to help keep track of the days.

6 **Olive oil** ice cream is a popular **flavor** in several fancy restaurants.

7 **STRAWBERRIES** contain more **VITAMIN C** than **ORANGES.**

WE ALL SCREAM FOR ICE CREAM

People love ice cream. Funny thing, though—no one knows for sure who invented it. Get the *scoop* on the history and mystery behind this sweet treat.

Sweet Snow: A.D. 54 Roman emperor Nero knew how to throw a feast. For dessert, he served a one-of-a-kind treat: sweet snow. Nero's slaves would run up into the mountains and gather snow. Then they would sprint back to the kitchen, where cooks would flavor the snow with fruit, wine, or honey.

Cool Legend: 1295 Italian explorer Marco Polo returned home after 17 years in China. Among the strange things he saw was "milk dried into a kind of paste." Over time, that piece of the story grew into the legend that he brought home a recipe for ice cream. He didn't.

Rare Treat: 1660s Wealthy Europeans enjoyed a rare new treat—"water ices." Before long, creative cooks added cream to the mix. To make things really fancy, they used metal molds to form ice cream into all sorts of shapes.

Old World: 1700s At first, ice cream was mainly a treat for the rich and the royal. Before refrigeration, ice was rare and expensive. Making ice cream also took hours, so it helped to have servants.

Mighty Machine: 1843 Making ice cream took a lot of muscle—cooks had to stir the cream and shake the ice for hours. Things got much easier when the ice-cream machine was invented. Turning a crank stirred the ingredients and made the ice cream freeze smoothly. With the rise of factories in the 1800s, particularly in America, ice cream became a mass-produced treat. By 1900, almost anyone could afford it.

Sundaes: 1880s The sundae is probably named for the first day of the week. One popular tale is that many places banned selling sodas on Sunday. In response, a crafty merchant put just ice cream and syrup into a dish—a total hit.

First Cone? 1904 Countless visitors attended the World's Fair in St. Louis, Missouri. Many marveled at their first sight of an ice-cream cone. But just who invented it? Generally the glory goes to Ernest Hamwi, a Syrian immigrant who was selling thin, waffle-shaped cakes. Next to him was an ice-cream stand. When the ice-cream seller ran out of dishes, Hamwi quickly shaped his cakes into cones that could hold ice cream.

Funny Flavors: Some things about ice cream haven't changed. Back in the 1790s, a New York cookbook included recipes for parmesan, ginger, and brown bread ice cream. Today, people can try rose, ketchup, or potato chip. Ice cream is as flavorful as ever!

129

Explore a New Culture

You're a student, but you're also a citizen of the world. Writing a report on a foreign nation or your own country is a great way to better understand and appreciate how people in other parts of the world live. Pick the country of your ancestors, one that's been in the news, or one that you'd like to visit someday.

Passport to Success

A country report follows the format of an expository essay (see p. 228 for "How to Write a Perfect Essay") because you're "exposing" information about the country you choose.

Simple Steps

1. RESEARCH Gathering information is the most important step in writing a good country report. Look to Internet sources, encyclopedias, books, magazine and newspaper articles, and other sources to find important and interesting details about your subject.

2. ORGANIZE YOUR NOTES Put the information you gathered into a rough outline. For example, sort everything you found about the country's system of government, climate, etc.

3. WRITE IT UP Follow the basic structure of good writing: introduction, body, and conclusion. Remember that each paragraph should have a topic sentence that is supported by facts and details. Incorporate the information from your notes, but make sure it's in your own words. And make your writing flow with good transitions and descriptive language.

4. JAZZ IT UP Include maps, diagrams, photos, and other visual aids.

5. PROOFREAD AND REVISE Correct any mistakes, and polish your language. Do your best!

6. CITE YOUR SOURCES Be sure to keep a record of your sources (see p. 257 for "Reveal Your Sources").

TIP: Choose a country that's in the news. For example, think about the ongoing war efforts around the world, such as in Iraq or Afghanistan. These places would make ideal topics for your next country report.

Key Information

You may be assigned to write a report on a specific aspect of a country, such as its political system, or your report may be more general. In writing a broad survey, be sure to touch on the following areas:

GEOGRAPHY—the country's location, size, capital, major cities, topography, and other physical details

NATURE—the country's various climates, ecosystems (rain forest, desert, etc.), and unique wildlife

HISTORY—major events, wars, and other moments that affected the country and its people

GOVERNMENT—the country's political system (democracy, dictatorship, etc.) and the role of the individual citizen in the country's governance

ECONOMY / INDUSTRY—the country's economic system (capitalism, socialism, etc.), major industries and exports, and the country's place in the world economy

PEOPLE AND CULTURE—the country's major religions, spoken languages, unique foods, holidays, rituals, and traditions

GO BEYOND THE BASICS.

✔ Explain the history of the country's flag and the meaning of its colors and symbols. crwflags.com/fotw/flags

✔ Play the country's national anthem. Download the anthem, words, and sheet music. nationalanthems.info

✔ Convert the country's currency into currencies from around the world. xe.com/ucc

✔ Check the local weather. Go to the website below and enter the city or country's name in the bar marked "Find Weather." weather.com

✔ Figure out the time difference between the country you're studying and where you live. worldtimeserver.com

✔ Still want more information? Go to National Geographic's One-Stop Research site for maps, photos, art, games, and other information to make your report stand out. nationalgeographic.com/onestop

COOL CLICKS

Write With Power

Using good transitions makes any kind of writing read more smoothly. It gives organization and helps the reader to understand and improve connections between thoughts. Here are a few examples of good transitions you might want to use:

Addition
also, again, as well as, besides, coupled with, furthermore, in addition, likewise, moreover, similarly

Generalizing
as a rule, as usual, for the most part, generally, generally speaking, ordinarily, usually

Emphasis
above all, chiefly, with attention to, especially, particularly, singularly

Similarity
comparatively, coupled with, correspondingly, identically, likewise, similar, moreover, together with

Restatement
in essence, in other words, namely, that is, that is to say, in short, in brief, to put it differently

Contrast and Comparison
by the same token, conversely, instead, likewise, on one hand, on the other hand, on the contrary, rather, similarly, yet, but, however, still, nevertheless, in contrast

Super
Science

It's a bird...It's a plane...It's a submarine?! The *Deep Flight II* sub uses wings and thrusters to move up and down like an airplane—a unique design that helps it speed to the bottom of the ocean faster than other subs. It's just a prototype for now, but *Deep Flight II* may one day help scientists explore the 35,827-foot (10,972-m) -deep Mariana Trench—the deepest place on Earth!

WHAT IS LIFE?

This seems like such an easy question to answer. Everybody knows that singing birds are alive and rocks are not. But when we start studying bacteria and other microscopic creatures, things get more complicated.

SO WHAT EXACTLY IS LIFE?

Most scientists agree that something is alive if it has the following characteristics: It can reproduce, grow in size to become more complex in structure, take in nutrients to survive, give off waste products, and respond to external stimuli, such as increased sunlight or changes in temperature.

KINDS OF LIFE

Biologists classify living organisms by how they get their energy. Organisms such as algae, green plants, and some bacteria use sunlight as an energy source. Human beings, fungi, and some Archaea use chemicals to provide energy. When we eat food, chemical reactions within our digestive system turn our food into fuel.

Living things inhabit land, sea, and air. In fact, life also thrives deep beneath the oceans, embedded in rocks miles below the Earth's crust, in ice, and in other extreme environments. The life-forms that thrive in these challenging environments are called extremophiles. Some of these draw directly upon the chemicals surrounding them for energy. Since these are very different forms of life than what we're used to, we may not think of them as alive, but they are.

HOW IT ALL WORKS

To try and understand how a living organism works, it helps to look at one example of its simplest form—the single-celled bacterium called *Streptococcus*. There are many kinds of these tiny organisms, and some are responsible for human illnesses. What makes us sick or uncomfortable are the toxins the bacteria give off in our bodies.

A single *Streptococcus* bacterium is so small that at least 500 of them could fit on the dot above the letter *i*. These bacteria are some of the simplest forms of life we know. They have no moving parts, no lungs, no brain, no heart, no liver, no leaves or fruit. And yet this life-form reproduces, grows in size by producing long chain structures, takes in nutrients, and gives off waste products. This tiny life-form is alive, just as you are alive.

What makes something alive is a question scientists grapple with when they study viruses, such as the ones that cause the common cold and smallpox. They can grow and reproduce within host cells, such as those that make up your body. Because viruses lack cells and cannot metabolize nutrients for energy or reproduce without a host, scientists ask if they are indeed alive. And don't go looking for them without a strong microscope—viruses are a hundred times smaller than bacteria.

Scientists think life began on Earth some 3.9 to 4.1 billion years ago, but no fossils exist from that time. The earliest fossils ever found are from the primitive life that existed 3.6 billion years ago. Other life-forms, some of which are shown below, soon followed. Scientists continue to study how life evolved on Earth and whether or not it is possible that life exists on other planets.

MICROSCOPIC ORGANISMS

Common soil *Bacillus*

Flu virus

Recently discovered primitive virus

Cyanobacteria

Diatom

Paramecium

E. coli bacteria

Streptococcus bacteria

*organisms are not drawn to scale

PROGRESS OF LIFE ON EARTH

About 3.5 billion years ago
Earth was covered by one gigantic reddish ocean. The color came from hydrocarbons.

The first life-forms on Earth were Archaea that were able to live without oxygen. They released large amounts of methane gas into an atmosphere that would have been poisonous to us.

About 3 billion years ago
erupting volcanoes linked together to form larger landmasses. And a new form of life appeared—cyanobacteria, the first living things that used energy from the sun.

Some 2 billion years ago
the cyanobacteria algae filled the air with oxygen, killing off the methane-producing Archaea. Colored pools of greenish-brown plant life floated on the oceans. The oxygen revolution that would someday make human life possible was now under way.

About 530 million years ago
the Cambrian explosion occurred. It's called an explosion because it's the time when most major animal groups first appeared in our fossil records. Back then, Earth was made up of swamps, seas, a few active volcanoes, and oceans teeming with strange life.

More than 450 million years ago
life began moving from the oceans onto dry land. About 200 million years later dinosaurs began to appear. They would dominate life on Earth for more than 150 million years.

Black Holes

A black hole really seems like a hole in space. Most black holes form when the core of a massive star collapses, falling into oblivion. A black hole has a stronger gravitational pull than anything else in the known universe. It's like a bottomless pit, swallowing anything that gets close enough to it to be pulled in. It's black because it pulls in light. Black holes come in different sizes. The smallest known black hole has a mass about three times that of the sun. The biggest one scientists have found so far has a mass about three billion times greater than the sun's. Really big black holes at the centers of galaxies probably form by swallowing enormous amounts of gas over time. One of NASA's spacecraft has found thousands of possible black holes in the Milky Way, but there are probably more. The nearest one to Earth is about 1,600 light-years away.

What Is the Milky Way?

Our galaxy, the Milky Way, appears to be a band of stars in the sky, but it's actually a disk. Its 400 billion stars are clumped into lines called spiral arms because they spiral outward. When we look up at the night sky, we're seeing the edge of the disk, like the side of a Frisbee. It appears to us as a hazy band of white light.

Earth is located about halfway between the center of the Milky Way and its outer edge, in one of the spiral arms. Light from the galaxy's center takes 25,000 years to reach us.

Our solar system orbits the galactic center once every 250 million years. The last time we were on this side of the Milky Way, the earliest dinosaurs were just starting to emerge.

At the galaxy's center, frequent star explosions fry huge sections of space. Those explosions would wipe out any life on nearby planets. We're lucky that Earth is located where it is, far away from the center.

Solar System Glossary

ASTEROID
A rocky body, measuring from less than 1 mile (1.6 km) to 600 miles (966 km) in diameter, in orbit around the sun. Most asteroids are found between the orbits of Mars and Jupiter.

DWARF PLANET
Generally smaller than Mercury, a dwarf planet orbits the sun along with other objects near it. Its gravity has pulled it into a round (or nearly round) shape.

ECLIPSE
An event caused by the passage of one astronomical body in front of another astronomical body, briefly blocking light from the farthest one.

COMET
A body of rock, dust, and gaseous ice in an elongated orbit around the sun. Near the sun, heat diffuses gas and dust to form a streaming "tail" from the comet's nucleus.

PLANET
A planet orbits a star. Gravity has pulled it into a round (or nearly round) shape, and it has cleared its neighborhood of other objects.

THE SUN

The sun is a star that is about 4.6 billion years old. As the anchor that holds our solar system together, it provides the energy necessary for life to flourish on Earth. It accounts for 99 percent of the matter in the solar system. The rest of the planets, moons, asteroids, and comets added together amount to the remaining one percent.

Even though a million Earths could fit inside the sun, it is still considered an average-size star. Betelgeuse (BET-el-jooz), the star on the shoulder of the constellation known as Orion, is almost 400 times larger.

A BIG BALL OF GAS

Like other stars the sun is a giant ball of hydrogen gas radiating heat and light through nuclear fusion—a process by which the sun converts about four million tons (3,628,739 t) of matter to energy every second.

Also like other stars, the sun revolves around its galaxy. Located halfway out in one of the arms of the Milky Way galaxy, the sun takes 225 to 250 million years to complete one revolution around the galaxy.

The sun is composed of about 74 percent hydrogen, 25 percent helium, and one percent trace elements like iron, carbon, lead, and uranium. These trace elements provide us with amazing insight into the history of our star. They're the heavier elements that are produced when stars explode. Since these elements are relatively abundant in the sun, scientists know it was forged from materials that came together in two previous star explosions. All of the elements found in the sun, on Earth, and in our bodies were recycled from those two exploding stars.

OUR AMAZING SUN

When viewed from space by astronauts, the sun burns white in color. But when we see it from Earth, through our atmosphere, it looks yellow.

Solar flares—explosions of charged particles—sometimes erupt from the sun's surface. They create beautiful aurora displays on Earth, Jupiter, Saturn, and even distant Uranus and Neptune.

We know that the sun makes life possible here on Earth. We couldn't survive without it.

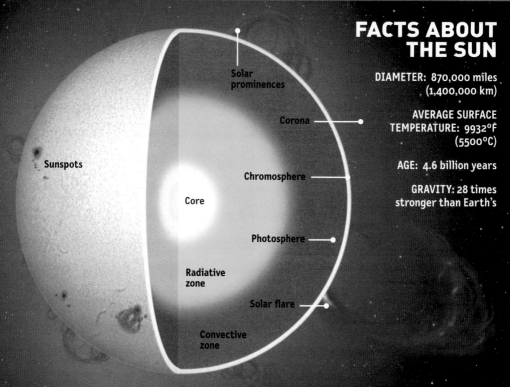

Solar prominences

Corona

Sunspots

Chromosphere

Core

Photosphere

Radiative zone

Solar flare

Convective zone

FACTS ABOUT THE SUN

DIAMETER: 870,000 miles (1,400,000 km)

AVERAGE SURFACE TEMPERATURE: 9932°F (5500°C)

AGE: 4.6 billion years

GRAVITY: 28 times stronger than Earth's

PLANETS

Mercury
Venus
Earth
Mars
Ceres
Jupiter
Sun

MERCURY
Average distance from the sun:
35,980,000 miles (57,900,000 km)
Position from the sun in orbit: first
Equatorial diameter: 3,030 miles (4,878 km)
Mass (Earth = 1): 0.055   Density (Water = 1): 5.43
Length of day: 58 Earth days
Length of year: 88 Earth days
Surface temperatures: -300°F (-184°C) to 800°F (427°C)
Known moons: 0

VENUS
Average distance from the sun:
67,230,000 miles (108,200,000 km)
Position from the sun in orbit: second
Equatorial diameter: 7,520 miles (12,100 km)
Mass (Earth = 1): 0.815   Density (Water = 1): 5.25
Length of day: 243 Earth days
Length of year: 225 Earth days
Average surface temperature: 864°F (462°C)
Known moons: 0

EARTH
Average distance from the sun:
93,000,000 miles (149,600,000 km)
Position from the sun in orbit: third
Equatorial diameter: 7,900 miles (12,750 km)
Mass (Earth = 1): 1   Density (Water = 1): 5.52
Length of day: 24 hours
Length of year: 365 days
Surface temperatures: -126°F (-88°C) to 136°F (58°C)
Known moons: 1

MARS
Average distance from the sun:
141,633,000 miles (227,936,000 km)
Position from the sun in orbit: fourth
Equatorial diameter: 4,333 miles (6,794 km)
Mass (Earth = 1): 0.107   Density (Water = 1): 3.93
Length of day: 25 Earth hours
Length of year: 1.88 Earth years
Surface temperatures: -270°F (-168°C) to 80°F (27°C)
Known moons: 2

CERES (DWARF PLANET)
Position from the sun in orbit: fifth
Length of day: 9.1 Earth hours
Length of year: 4.6 Earth years
Known moons: 0

JUPITER
Average distance from the sun:
483,682,000 miles (778,411,000 km)
Position from the sun in orbit: sixth
Equatorial diameter: 86,880 miles (139,820 km)
Mass (Earth = 1): 318   Density (Water = 1): 1.3
Length of day: 9.9 Earth hours
Length of year: 11.9 Earth years
Average surface temperature: -235°F (-148°C)
Known moons: at least 63

If you
TRAVELED
at the speed of
LIGHT,
you could reach
PLUTO in just
4 HOURS.

This artwork shows the 13 planets and dwarf planets that astronomers now recognize in our solar system. The relative sizes and positions of the planets are shown but not the relative distances between them. Many of the planets closest to Earth can be seen without a telescope in the night sky.

Saturn

Uranus

Neptune   Pluto

Haumea

Makemake   Eris

SATURN
Average distance from the sun:
886,526,000 miles (1,426,725,000 km)
Position from the sun in orbit: seventh
Equatorial diameter: 72,370 miles (116,460 km)
Mass (Earth = 1): 95   Density (Water = 1): 0.71
Length of day: 10 Earth hours
Length of year: 29.46 Earth years
Average surface temperature: -218°F (-139°C)
Known moons: at least 60

URANUS
Average distance from the sun:
1,784,000,000 miles (2,871,000 km)
Position from the sun in orbit: eighth
Equatorial diameter: 31,500 miles (50,694 km)
Mass (Earth = 1): 15   Density (Water = 1): 1.24
Length of day: 17.9 Earth hours
Length of year: 84 Earth years
Average surface temperature: -323°F (-197°C)
Known moons: 27

NEPTUNE
Average distance from the sun:
2,795,000,000 miles (4,498,116,000 km)
Position from the sun in orbit: ninth
Equatorial diameter: 30,775 miles (49,528 km)
Mass (Earth = 1): 17   Density (Water = 1): 1.67
Length of day: 19 Earth hours
Length of year: 164.8 Earth years
Average surface temperature: -353°F (-214°C)
Known moons: 13

PLUTO (DWARF PLANET)
Position from the sun in orbit: tenth
Length of day: 6.4 Earth days
Length of year: 248 Earth years
Known moons: 3

HAUMEA (DWARF PLANET)
Position from the sun in orbit: eleventh
Length of day: 4 Earth hours
Length of year: 284 Earth years
Known moons: 2

MAKEMAKE (DWARF PLANET)
Position from the sun in orbit: twelfth
Length of day: unknown
Length of year: 307 Earth years
Known moons: 0

ERIS (DWARF PLANET)
Position from the sun in orbit: thirteenth
Length of day: less than 8 Earth hours
Length of year: 557 Earth years
Known moons: 1

**FOR THE DEFINITIONS OF *PLANET*
AND *DWARF PLANET* SEE P. 138.**

Sky Calendar
2012

Horsehead Nebula

Leonid meteor shower

Milky Way

January 3–4 Quadrantids Meteor Shower Peak. View up to 40 meteors per hour.

March 3 Mars at Opposition. Mars is at its closest approach to Earth, making it the perfect time to view the red planet.

April 15 Saturn at Opposition. Saturn is at its closest approach to Earth.

May 20 Annular Solar Eclipse. A partial eclipse can be seen throughout most of North America and parts of eastern Asia. For more about annular solar eclipses, see p. 143.

June 4 Partial Lunar Eclipse. A partial lunar eclipse can be observed throughout the Americas, Australia, the Pacific Ocean, and most of Asia.

June 6 Transit of Venus across the Sun. June 5 in North America. A very rare event! Venus will appear as a small dark spot traveling across the sun. At least part of the transit can be viewed from everywhere except southern South America, western Africa, Portugal, and southern Spain. Remember: Never look directly at the sun.

July 27–29 Southern Delta Aquarids Meteor Shower Peak. View up to 20 meteors per hour.

August 12-14 Perseids Meteor Shower Peak. One of the best! Up to 60 meteors per hour.

October 21–22 Orionids Meteor Shower Peak. View up to 20 meteors per hour.

November 13 Total Solar Eclipse. Visible in northern Australia, southern South America, and the southern Pacific Ocean. Partial eclipse visible in eastern Australia and New Zealand. Remember: Never look directly at the sun.

November 17–18 Leonid Meteor Shower Peak. View up to 15 meteors per hour.

November 28 Lunar Eclipse. Visible in most of Europe, eastern Africa, Asia, Australia, the Pacific Ocean, and North America.

December 3 Jupiter at Opposition. December 2 in North America. Jupiter is at its closest approach to Earth.

December 13–14 Geminids Meteor Shower Peak. A spectacular show! Up to 60 multicolored meteors an hour.

Dates may vary slightly depending on your location. Check with a local planetarium for the best viewing time in your area.

SOLAR AND LUNAR ECLIPSES

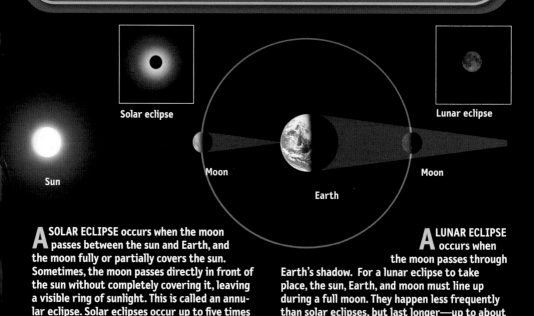

Solar eclipse

Lunar eclipse

Sun

Moon

Earth

Moon

ASOLAR ECLIPSE occurs when the moon passes between the sun and Earth, and the moon fully or partially covers the sun. Sometimes, the moon passes directly in front of the sun without completely covering it, leaving a visible ring of sunlight. This is called an annular eclipse. Solar eclipses occur up to five times each year and may last up to several minutes.

ALUNAR ECLIPSE occurs when the moon passes through Earth's shadow. For a lunar eclipse to take place, the sun, Earth, and moon must line up during a full moon. They happen less frequently than solar eclipses, but last longer—up to about a hundred minutes each.

The Big Dipper is part of the constellation commonly known as the Great Bear.

SKY DREAMS

LONG AGO, people looking at the sky noticed that some stars made shapes and patterns. By playing connect-the-dots, they imagined people and animals in the sky. Their legendary heroes and monsters were pictured in the stars.

Today, we call the star patterns identified by the ancient Greeks and Romans "constellations." There are 88 constellations in all. Some are only visible when you're north of the Equator, and some only when you're south of it.

European ocean voyagers named the constellations that are visible in the Southern Hemisphere, such as the Southern Cross. In the

16th-century age of exploration, their ships began visiting southern lands. Astronomers used the star observations of these navigators to fill in the blank spots on their celestial maps.

Constellations aren't fixed in the sky. The star arrangement that makes up each one would look different from another location in the universe. Constellations also change over time because every star we see is moving through space. Over thousands of years, the stars in the Big Dipper, which is part of the larger constellation Ursa Major (the Great Bear), will move so far apart that the dipper pattern will disappear.

CONSTELLATIONS

Nothing to do on a clear night? Look up! There's so much to see in that starry sky. The constellations you can see among the stars vary with the season. As the following maps show, some are more visible in the winter and spring, while others can be spotted in the summer and fall.

Looking for constellations in the Southern Hemisphere? Go online.
sydneyobservatory
.com.au/blog/?cat=10

COOL CLICK

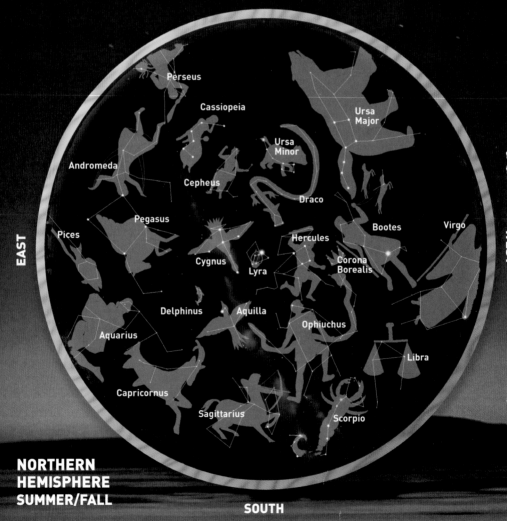

NORTH

Perseus
Cassiopeia
Ursa Major
Ursa Minor
Andromeda
Cepheus
Draco
Pegasus
Pices
Bootes
Virgo
Hercules
Cygnus
Corona Borealis
Lyra
Delphinus
Aquilla
Ophiuchus
Aquarius
Libra
Capricornus
Sagittarius
Scorpio

EAST

WEST

NORTHERN
HEMISPHERE
SUMMER/FALL

SOUTH

Planet or Star?

On a clear night, you'll see a sky filled with glittering lights. But not every bright spot is a star—you may be peeking at a planet, too. How to tell a star from a planet? While stars twinkle, planets shine more steadily and tend to be the brightest objects in the sky, other than the moon. Planets also move across the sky from night to night. If you think you've spotted one, keep checking on it as the week goes by. Has it moved closer or farther away from the moon? Then it's probably a planet.

TRY SEARCHING THE SKY with binoculars or a telescope and see if you can **SPOT SOME COOL STUFF,** such as **JUPITER'S MOONS.**

NORTH

EAST

WEST

SOUTH

Draco
Cepheus
Cassiopea
Ursa Minor
Bootes
Andromeda
Perseus
Ursa Major
Auriga
Aries
Virgo
Gemini
Taurus
Leo
Cancer
Canis Minor
Orion
Crater
Canis Major
Hydra

NORTHERN HEMISPHERE WINTER/SPRING

SPACE
GIANT LEAPS FORWARD

c. 150 Alexandria's Ptolemy tracks 48 constellations as well as the 5 planets visible to the naked eye—Mars, Venus, Mercury, Jupiter, and Saturn.

1609 Italian astronomer Galileo Galilei uses a telescope to observe the sun, moon, planets, and stars.

1687 English scientist Isaac Newton publishes the law of gravity.

1923 U.S. astronomer Edwin Hubble shows that spiral nebulas are galaxies—huge collections of stars distinct from the Milky Way.

1957 The first man-made satellite, the Soviet Union's Sputnik 1, is launched.

1961 Soviet cosmonaut Yuri Gagarin is the first person in space. Less than one month later, astronaut Alan Shepard is the first American in space.

1969 American Neil Armstrong of the Apollo 11 mission steps onto the lunar surface, becoming the first man on the moon.

1972 Charles Thomas Bolton proves the existence of a black hole in space.

1973 The first U.S. space station, Skylab, is launched.

1981 *Columbia*, the first space shuttle from the U.S. National Aeronautics and Space Administration (NASA), makes its maiden flight.

1986 The space shuttle *Challenger* explodes shortly after launch, halting U.S. space travel for almost three years.

2000 A crew of humans travels to the International Space Station for the first time. It has since been visited by hundreds of scientists. The football field-size research center, which orbits about 250 miles (400 km) above the Earth, is operated by space agencies from Canada, Russia, Japan, Europe, and the U.S.

2001 American businessman Dennis Tito becomes the first tourist to fly into space. He pays 20 million U.S. dollars to ride with a Russian space crew.

2003 NASA's Mars exploration rover mission sends two robotic rovers to the red planet with the primary goal of gathering information about the history of water on Mars.

2003 The space shuttle *Columbia* breaks up in the atmosphere while returning to the Earth. All seven-members of the crew are killed, and NASA once again grounds the entire space shuttle fleet until safety updates can be made.

2005 A small probe, called Huygens, lands on Saturn's largest moon, Titan. Huygens successfully sends a series of images of this alien moon back to Earth.

2006 NASA's Stardust mission lands after a seven-year journey in space, returning dust and particle samples from the comet Wild 2.

2015 Aerospace company Boeing plans to start sending tourists into space by selling off seats for a trip to the International Space Station.

mid-2030s NASA expects to send humans to orbit Mars.

Astronaut Buzz Aldrin walks on the moon during the 1969 Apollo 11 mission.

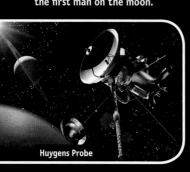

Huygens Probe

5 WAYS

You Use Satellites

Psst! Want in on a secret? Spaceships control our world! Well, not exactly. But much of the technology you use—TVs, telephones, email—relies on tons of satellites whizzing around Earth. Here's a look at five ways you use satellites.

1 TELEVISION

If you've watched TV, then you've used a satellite. Broadcast stations send images from Earth up to satellites as radio waves. The satellite bounces those signals, which can only travel straight, back down to a satellite dish at a point on Earth closer to your house. Satellite transmission works sort of like a shot in a game of pool when you ricochet your ball off the side of the pool table at an angle that sinks it into the right pocket.

2 WEATHER

News flash! A severe thunderstorm with dangerous lightning is approaching your town. How do weather forecasters know what's coming so they can warn the public? They use satellites equipped with cameras and infrared sensors to watch clouds. Computers use constantly changing satellite images to track the storm.

3 TELEPHONE

As you talk back and forth with a relative overseas on a landline, you might experience a delay of a quarter second—the time it takes for your voices to be relayed by a satellite bounce.

4 EMAIL

Satellites also bridge long distances over the Internet by transmitting emails. Communications satellites for phones and the Internet use a geostationary orbit. That means that a satellite's speed matches Earth's rotation exactly, keeping the satellite in the same spot above Earth.

5 GPS

Driving you to a party at a friend's house, your dad turns down the wrong street. You're lost. No problem if the car has a global positioning system (GPS) receiver. GPS is a network of satellites. The receiver collects information from the satellites and plots its distance from at least three of them. It can show where you are on a digital map. Thanks to satellites, you will make it to the party on time.

HOW A BASIC MOBILE CALL REACHES A FRIEND

You punch in a phone number and press SEND.

Your mobile (cell) phone sends a coded message—a radio signal—to a cellular tower, which transfers the radio signal to a landline wire. From there, the signal travels underground.

The underground signal reaches a switching center; there a computer figures out where the call needs to go next.

Through landlines the message reaches the cell tower nearest the call's destination.

Switched back to a radio signal, the call reaches the person you dialed. Let the talking begin!

WHAT IS THE "CELL" IN CELL PHONE?

A typical cellular, or mobile, tower serves a small area—about ten square miles (26 sq km). That area is called a cell. Whichever cell you are in when you make your call is the cell that picks up your data and sends it on.

YOUR AMAZING BODY!

The human body is a complicated mass of systems—nine systems, to be exact. Each system has a unique and critical purpose in the body, and we wouldn't be able to survive without all of them.

The **NERVOUS** system controls the body.

The **MUSCULAR** system makes movement possible.

The **SKELETAL** system supports the body.

The **CIRCULATORY** system moves blood throughout the body.

The **RESPIRATORY** system provides the body with oxygen.

The **DIGESTIVE** system breaks down food into nutrients and gets rid of waste.

The **IMMUNE** system protects the body against disease and infection.

The **ENDOCRINE** system regulates the body's functions.

The **REPRODUCTIVE** system enables people to produce offspring.

weird but true

MESSAGES FROM YOUR BRAIN TRAVEL ALONG YOUR NERVES AT UP TO 200 MILES AN HOUR (322 kph).

The smallest bone in the human body is shorter than a grain of rice.

You breathe in 2,000 gallons (7,570 l) of air a day.

YOUR AMAZING Heart!

YOUR HEART has the power to lift a 3,000-pound (1,360-kg) car, the strength to pump 2,000 gallons (7,570 L) of blood twice around the world in a day, and the stamina to never take a break. And, oh yeah, it keeps you alive, too!

Here are three more heart-pumping facts about this awesome organ.

Your heart beats 100,000 times daily. And each of these little pitter-patters you feel is actually your heart filling with blood, squeezing, then forcing the blood out and throughout your body. This is done with enough power to pump blood to every cell, delivering oxygen and removing carbon dioxide waste.

Thanks to your heart, blood constantly circulates throughout your body to keep you healthy. And every day, your heart pumps more than 2,000 gallons (7,570 L) of blood through 60,000 miles (96,000 km) of blood vessels—a distance greater than two trips around the world.

During its endless journeys to and from your heart, the several quarts of blood in your body travel through three types of vessels: arteries, veins, and capillaries. Most arteries carry oxygen-rich blood away from your heart. Veins deliver oxygen-depleted blood back toward your heart. And tiny capillaries connect arteries and veins, forming a vast network in your tissues and reaching every cell in your body. These fragile vessels are so narrow that the microscopic blood cells have to pass through them single file.

#1 One heartbeat is so powerful that it could shoot water six feet (1.8 m) into the air!

#2 Blood travels 60,000 miles (96,000 km) through your body every day.

#3 You have at least four quarts (3.8 L) of blood in your body.

Heart Parts

AORTA
PULMONARY ARTERY

RIGHT ATRIUM
LEFT ATRIUM
RIGHT VENTRICLE
LEFT VENTRICLE

COOL CLICK

To learn more about your heart and how it works, go online.
http://science.nationalgeographic.com/science/health-and-human-body/human-body/heart-article.html

Your Amazing
eyes

Discover the magic of your body's built-in cameras.

You carry around a pair of cameras in your head so incredible they can work in bright sunshine or at night. Only about an inch (2.5 cm) in diameter, they can bring you the image of a tiny ant or a twinkling star trillions of miles away. They can change focus almost instantly and stay focused even when you're shaking your head or jumping up and down. These cameras are your eyes.

A CRUCIAL PART OF YOUR EYE IS AS FLIMSY AS A WET TISSUE.

A dragonfly darts toward your head! Light bounces off the insect, enters your eye, passes through your pupil (the black circle in the middle of your iris), and goes to the lens. The lens focuses the light onto your retina—a thin lining on the back of your eye that is vital but as flimsy as a wet tissue. Your retina acts like film in a camera, capturing the picture of this dragonfly. The picture is sent to your brain, which instantly sends you a single command—*duck!*

YOU BLINK MORE THAN 10,000 TIMES A DAY.

Your body has many ways to protect and care for your eyes. Each eye sits on a cushion of fat, almost completely surrounded by protective bone. Your eyebrows help prevent sweat from dripping into your eyes. Your eyelashes help keep dust and other small particles out. Your eyelids act as built-in windshield wipers, spreading tear fluid with every blink to keep your eyes moist

and wash away bacteria and other particles. And if anything ever gets too close to your eyes, your eyelids slam shut with incredible speed—in $^2/_5$ of a second—to protect them!

YOUR EYES SEE EVERYTHING UPSIDE DOWN AND BACKWARD!

As amazing as your eyes are, the images they send your brain are a little quirky: They're upside down, backward, and two-dimensional! Your brain automatically flips the images from your retinas right side up and combines the images from each eye into a three-dimensional picture. There is a small area of each retina, called a blind spot, that can't record what you're seeing. Luckily your brain makes adjustments for this, too.

YOUR PUPILS CHANGE SIZE WHENEVER THE LIGHT CHANGES.

Your black pupils may be small, but they have an important job—they grow or shrink to let just the right amount of light enter your eyes to let you see.

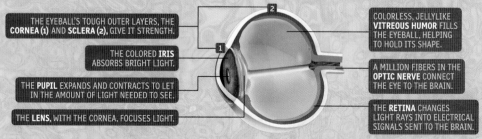

THE EYEBALL'S TOUGH OUTER LAYERS, THE **CORNEA (1)** AND **SCLERA (2)**, GIVE IT STRENGTH.

THE COLORED **IRIS** ABSORBS BRIGHT LIGHT.

THE **PUPIL** EXPANDS AND CONTRACTS TO LET IN THE AMOUNT OF LIGHT NEEDED TO SEE.

THE **LENS**, WITH THE CORNEA, FOCUSES LIGHT.

COLORLESS, JELLYLIKE **VITREOUS HUMOR** FILLS THE EYEBALL, HELPING TO HOLD ITS SHAPE.

A MILLION FIBERS IN THE **OPTIC NERVE** CONNECT THE EYE TO THE BRAIN.

THE **RETINA** CHANGES LIGHT RAYS INTO ELECTRICAL SIGNALS SENT TO THE BRAIN.

What Your FAVORITE COLOR Says About YOU

Your favorite color can say a lot about you. Researchers say that we have two basic responses to color: physical (red can make you hot) and emotional (yellow can make you happy). These responses, as well as what some colors represent historically, mean fave colors may reflect your personality. Just for fun, see how colors may affect your mood. Feeling blue? Maybe grab some yellow! *If these personality profiles don't match you, that's okay. These are just for fun!*

ORANGE
can represent energy and warmth. It can also make you hungry and boost your health.

IF YOU LIKE ORANGE, YOU ... are a nice person who's rarely sick. When you're not cooking or eating, you're outside enjoying the sun.

PINK
can represent health and love.

IF YOU LIKE PINK, YOU ... are cheerful and always look out for your friends. You have no problem speaking your mind, and you express your feelings well.

RED
can represent danger. It can also excite the senses and activate blood circulation.

IF YOU LIKE RED, YOU ... are energetic and like taking risks. Very aware of what's going on around you, you are a leader who's not afraid to speak up.

YELLOW
can represent victory. It can also help you be more organized and optimistic.

IF YOU LIKE YELLOW, YOU ... are a positive person who likes cheering people up. Your competitiveness and organizational skills help you succeed.

PURPLE
can represent wealth or royalty. It's also associated with art and music.

IF YOU LIKE PURPLE, YOU ... have great taste in anything from clothes to music to food, which you always share with your friends. You are also very creative.

BLUE
can represent peace and loyalty. It's also a universally popular color.

IF YOU LIKE BLUE, YOU ... are well liked by everyone. People come to you with their problems, and you do what you can to make sure everyone gets along.

GREEN
can represent nature and growth. It may also calm people down.

IF YOU LIKE GREEN, YOU ... spend a lot of time outside and like doing new things. You're very mellow and easygoing, never taking things too seriously.

Bet you didn't know

You **SEE** color **DIFFERENTLY** from the **PERSON** next to you.

There is a **CRAYON COLOR** called "**macaroni and cheese.**"

NO WORDS in the **DICTIONARY** rhyme with "**ORANGE.**"

Your Amazing
brain

Inside your body's supercomputer

You carry around a three-pound (1-kg) mass of wrinkly material in your head that controls every single thing you will ever do. From enabling you to think, learn, create, and feel emotions to control-ing every blink, breath, and heartbeat—this fantastic control center is your brain. It is a structure so amazing that a famous scientist once called it the "most complex thing we have yet discovered in our universe."

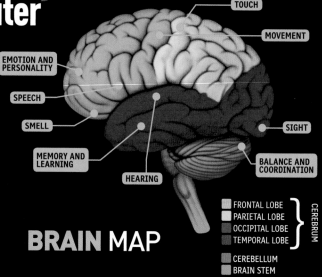

BRAIN MAP

TOUCH
MOVEMENT
EMOTION AND PERSONALITY
SPEECH
SMELL
SIGHT
MEMORY AND LEARNING
BALANCE AND COORDINATION
HEARING

FRONTAL LOBE
PARIETAL LOBE
OCCIPITAL LOBE
TEMPORAL LOBE

CEREBRUM

CEREBELLUM
BRAIN STEM

THE BIG QUESTION

WHAT TAKES UP TWO-THIRDS OF YOUR BRAIN'S WEIGHT AND ALLOWS YOU TO SWIM, EAT, AND SPEAK?

The huge hunk of your brain called the cerebrum. It's definitely the biggest part of the brain. It houses the centers for memory, the senses, movement, and emotion, among other things.

The cerebrum is made up of two hemispheres—the right and the left. Each side controls the muscles of the opposite side of the body.

How to Decode Your Dreams

YOUR BRAIN MAY BE TELLING YOU SOMETHING

How many times have you told someone, "I had the craziest dream last night"? Lots of times, huh? You can have up to six dreams a night. Some of them are sure to be wild!

Dreams are created by the part of your brain that stores memories, emotions, and thoughts. At night your brain blends what's stored in your mind with what you've been thinking about lately.

Dreams hardly ever become reality, but they may contain hints about what's going on in your life. "Dreams help us get in touch with our deeper feelings," says dream researcher Alan Siegel. "They can tell us a lot about ourselves and may even help us figure out problems."

Scientists have discovered that many dreams contain common themes that have meaning. Here are eight types of dreams that may tell you a lot about yourself and what's happening in your life!

THE THEME Being chased

WHAT IT MEANS The scary thing that's chasing you is probably a symbol of a real-life problem you don't want to deal with. But this dream is telling you it's time to stop running from the problem and start facing it.

THE THEME Showing up in pajamas

WHAT IT MEANS Your brain may be helping you recover from a real-life embarrassing moment. If no one's making a big deal about the pj's, chances are your friends think you're cool no matter what. If they *are* laughing? It may be time for some new friends.

THE THEME Flying

WHAT IT MEANS It's likely you're flying high in real life as well. Maybe your friends see you as a leader or your parents have given you more freedom.

THE THEME Being lost

WHAT IT MEANS You're probably feeling a little lost in life. Are you currently facing a tough decision? You might be afraid of making the wrong choice. Think carefully about your options to find your way out of this dilemma.

THE THEME Falling

WHAT IT MEANS You might have too much going on. It's time to slow down and take a break from whatever is stressing you out. And the soft landing? A sign that you'll soon get over this tough time.

THE THEME Not being able to move

WHAT IT MEANS You're probably feeling "stuck" in life. (Maybe your parents just grounded you.) You need to think about how you got into this sticky situation and then try to make smarter choices in the future.

THE THEME Losing something

WHAT IT MEANS You may be looking for an ego boost. Perhaps you want to try out a new sport or hobby, and you're not sure if you can do it. Search deep inside yourself for that confidence. It's there—you just have to find it!

THE THEME Being unprepared or late

WHAT IT MEANS You're worrying big-time about an upcoming event or project. If you're prepared, it's just a sign that you're nervous. That's normal. But if you've been slacking, take this dream as a hint and get to work!

ZZzz!

You'll spend about six years of your life dreaming.

A dream usually lasts from 10 to 40 minutes.

Your brain waves can be more active when you're dreaming than when you're awake.

Get Fit!

Try to work an hour of physical activity into each day. Whether you choose to play sports, go for a hike, or ride your bike, make your exercise exciting by switching things up and trying new ways to stay fit.

Exercise is awesome! Here's why:
• It makes you stronger and fitter.
• It makes you healthier.
• It makes you happier.

Ways to work out without even knowing it!

HOOF IT. Walk or bike short distances instead of riding in a car.

DO YARD WORK. Activities like gardening, mowing the lawn, and even shoveling snow are all great ways to burn calories—plus the fresh air is good for you!

STEP IT UP. Take the stairs instead of the elevators or escalators.

STICK TOGETHER. Get your friends and family together for a run, walk, or bike ride.

10 Tips for a Germ-Free School Year

Follow these tips and you might score a perfect attendance record this year!

1. **Wash your hands** with soap and water after you sneeze, cough, or use the bathroom. Count to 20 or sing a couple of rounds of "Row, Row, Row Your Boat" while you scrub!

2. **Use an alcohol-based hand sanitizer** if soap and water aren't available.

3. **Use a tissue** when you need to sneeze or cough. Throw your tissues in the trash.

4. **Take a multivitamin** every day.

5. **Don't share water bottles,** drinks, or even earbuds. That's a quick way to pick up bacteria from your friends.

6. **Stay home** from school, sports practice, and parties if you feel sick or have a fever.

7. **Eat lots of fruits** and vegetables. A healthy diet can help boost your immune system and help you fight off illnesses before they make you sick!

8. **Sleep eight or more hours** every night. A strong body will help you fend off infections.

9. **Blow kisses to your sick family** and friends instead of giving kisses and hugs.

10. **Get a flu shot** if your doctor or school recommends it.

All about YOU

105 CHINESE FOOD CARTONS FILLED WITH FORTUNE COOKIES

93 SANDWICH BAGS FILLED WITH CHEESE CURLS

1 SCOTTISH TERRIER

THREE-QUARTERS OF A KITCHEN TRASH BAG FILLED WITH MARSHMALLOWS

A **9-FOOT (2.7 m) TOWER OF APPLES**

ENOUGH CHEERIOS TO FILL A 20-GALLON AQUARIUM

16 SMALL JARS OF PEANUT BUTTER

ENOUGH POPPED POPCORN TO FILL ALMOST HALF A BATHTUB

A **male lion** weighs as much as the food it would take to feed **21** ten-year-old boys for a week.

A TRAIL OF PIZZA SLICES ALONG THE LENGTH OF MORE THAN 5 OLYMPIC-SIZE SWIMMING POOLS

*Based on the 20 pounds (9 kg) of food that an average ten-year-old boy eats in a week. All other numbers also based on averages.

WAVES OF THE FUTURE

It's 2035. You have a job, spouse, kids ... and guess what? It's a totally techno world full of amazing possibilities. Step into your future life and check out some cool things you might see there.

1 The kitchen is your personal shopper. All food packaging contains a **Radio Frequency Identification (RFID)** tag, a tiny electronic version of a bar code. Your kitchen reads RFIDs, so it knows whether the milk is about to go sour and when you ate the last cookie. It automatically adds them to your grocery list and even e-shops to have your favorite foods delivered.

2 Change your outfit without undressing! Interactive **smart clothes**, made of smart materials and RFIDs, change color, texture, pattern, and even smell. Tired of stripes? Turn your pants plaid. Have your shirt change patterns to match the beat of the music you're listening to. Going hiking? Wear a jacket that repels insects. Clothes can stretch, shrink, translate languages, play music, pay bills, find your keys, give you a massage, and even read your email aloud.

3 **Robots** make your life easier, often taking over tasks you find boring. They come in various forms and sizes. Robotics expert Reid Simmons envisions tiny dust-eating bugs that will work together to keep things clean. Other robots will slurp up spills, mow the lawn, or feed the dog. Will robots do your kid's homework? Maybe, but the teacher's grouchy robot may not accept it!

4 Need a little advice on what to wear? The **smart mirror** in your bathroom can help you. It will select a shirt in your closet that'll match the pants you've chosen and suggest the best clothes for the weather. A display in the mirror lets you read your email, watch TV, or check your schedule as you finish getting ready.

CLOTHING WITH RFID

HOLOCONSOLE

SMART MIRROR

SPILL
ALERT!

EXPIRED

SPACE VACATION

3 destinations that are out of this world

How far would you travel to play zero-gravity tag or go on safari to another planet? Here are three out-of-this-world vacations that scientists believe will someday be possible.

DESTINATION 1

The Space Elevator

Press the button for the millionth floor and ride in an elevator 22,000 miles (35,000 km) straight up into space! Propelled by magnetic forces, your elevator car races through the clouds at more than a 1,000 miles an hour (1,600 kph) while attached to an amazingly long cable—made of carbon nanotubes 100 times stronger than steel—anchored to a satellite in space. Earth disappears below as you're enveloped in the starry blackness of space. When your elevator ride is over, board a ship to the moon, where you can soar through the sky as you slam dunk a basketball, thanks to low levels of gravity.

DESTINATION 2

A Sightseeing Cruise

Have lots of zero-gravity fun while you cruise to the most fantastic sights in the solar system. Catch extraordinary views of Mars. Continue on to Jupiter, a planet so enormous that if it were hollow, a thousand Earths could fit inside. Stare at Saturn's stunning rings—actually a collection of massive quantities of particles, mostly ice crystals—orbiting the planet. And don't miss spectacular Io, one of Jupiter's many moons. It's covered by lakes and rivers of lava, massive mountains, and volcanoes that spew lava more than 150 miles (240 km) high. Stunning!

DESTINATION **3**

Extreme Martian Adventure

Welcome to the red planet, home to Olympus Mons, the highest mountain in the solar system. It's more than 14 miles (22 km) high. Hike down Valles Marineris, a system of canyons so vast and deep they could swallow several Grand Canyons. When you're ready for more, explore cave systems created by ancient volcanic eruptions. Or visit ice-covered poles on Mars for some unbelievable ski jumping. In the low gravity, you'll sail above the slope for so long you might just think you're flying.

A SOLAR SAIL LIKE THIS NASA CONCEPT MAY SOMEDAY POWER YOUR SPACE CRUISER.

COOL CLICK

To learn more about the future of space travel, go online to NASA's website. nasa.gov

Research Like a Pro

There is so much information on the Internet. How do you find what you need and make sure it's accurate?

Be Specific

To come up with the most effective keywords, write down what you're looking for in the form of a question, and then circle the most important words in that sentence. Those are the keywords to use in your search. And for best results use words that are specific rather than general.

Research

Research on the Internet involves "looking up" information using a search engine (see list below). Type one or two keywords—words that describe what you want to know more about—and the search engine will provide a list of websites that contain information pertinent to your topic.

Trustworthy Sources

When conducting Internet research, be sure the website you use is reliable and the information it provides can be trusted. Sites produced by well-known, established organizations, companies, publications, educational institutions, or the government are your best bet.

Don't Copy

Avoid Internet plagiarism. Take careful notes and cite the websites you use to conduct research (see p. 229 for "Don't Be A Copycat").

HELPFUL AND SAFE SEARCH ENGINES FOR KIDS

Google Safe Search	squirrelnet.com/search/Google_SafeSearch.asp
Yahooligans	yahooligans.com
Superkids	super-kids.com
Ask Kids	askkids.com
Kids Click	kidsclick.org
AOL Kids	kids.aol.com

COOL CLICKS

Looking for a good science fair project idea? Go online. sciencebuddies.org. Or read about a science fair success. kids.nationalgeographic.com/stories/spacescience/snowfences

ACE YOUR SCIENCE FAIR

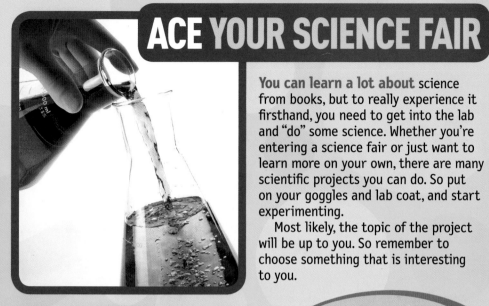

You can learn a lot about science from books, but to really experience it firsthand, you need to get into the lab and "do" some science. Whether you're entering a science fair or just want to learn more on your own, there are many scientific projects you can do. So put on your goggles and lab coat, and start experimenting.

Most likely, the topic of the project will be up to you. So remember to choose something that is interesting to you.

THE BASIS OF ALL SCIENTIFIC INVESTIGATION AND DISCOVERY IS THE SCIENTIFIC METHOD. CONDUCT THE EXPERIMENT USING THESE STEPS:

Observation/Research—Ask a question or identify a problem.

Hypothesis—Once you've asked a question, do some thinking and come up with some possible answers.

Experimentation—How can you determine if your hypothesis is correct? You test it. You perform an experiment. Make sure the experiment you design will produce an answer to your question.

Analysis—Gather your results, and use a consistent process to carefully measure the results.

Conclusion—Do the results support your hypothesis?

Report Your Findings—Communicate your results in the form of a paper that summarizes your entire experiment.

Bonus!

Take your project one step further. Your school may have an annual science fair, but there are also local, state, regional, and national science fair competitions. Compete with other students for awards, prizes, and scholarships!

EXPERIMENT DESIGN
There are three types of experiments you can do.

MODEL KIT—a display, such as an "erupting volcano" model. Simple and to the point.

DEMONSTRATION—shows the scientific principles in action, such as a tornado in a wind tunnel.

INVESTIGATION—the home run of science projects, and just the type of project for science fairs. This kind demonstrates proper scientific experimentation and uses the scientific method to reveal answers to questions.

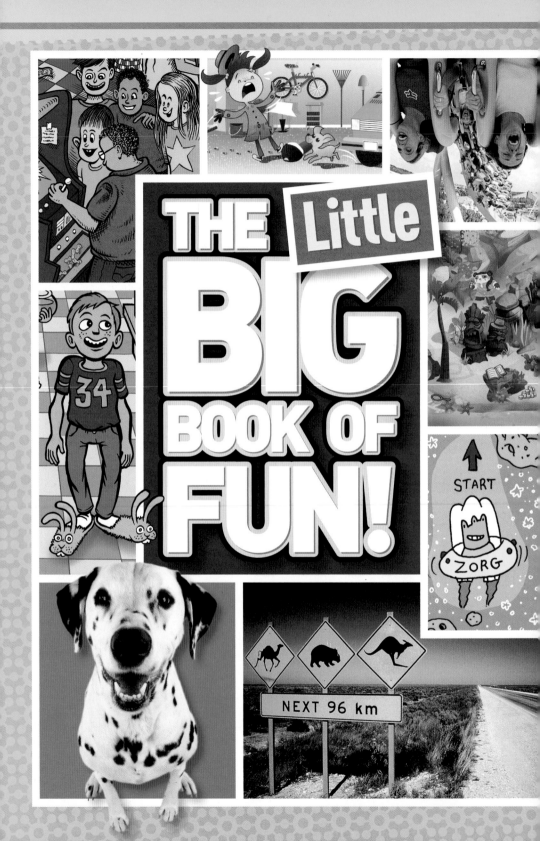

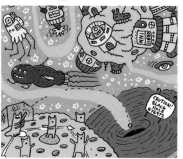

Boredom-Busting Games,
Jokes, Puzzles, Mazes,
and more **FunStuff**

Galaxy Quest

Help Zorg the alien find the starry path that leads back to the mother ship. ANSWER ON PAGE 338

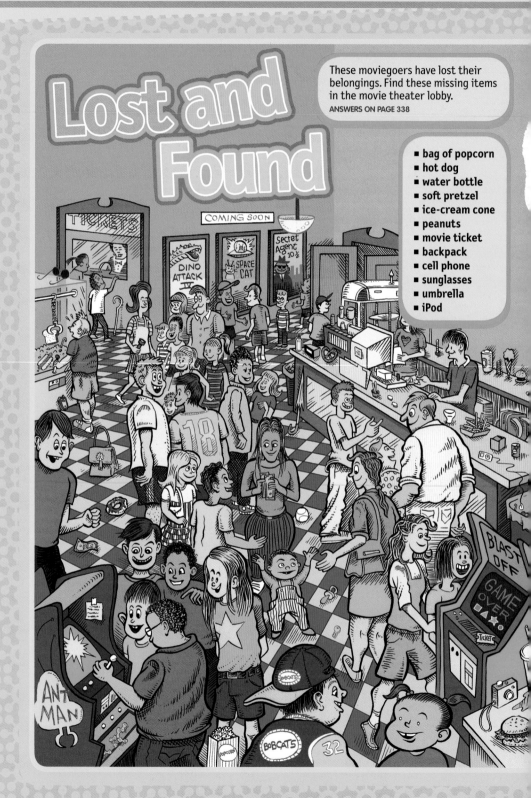

Lost and Found

These moviegoers have lost their belongings. Find these missing items in the movie theater lobby.
ANSWERS ON PAGE 338

- bag of popcorn
- hot dog
- water bottle
- soft pretzel
- ice-cream cone
- peanuts
- movie ticket
- backpack
- cell phone
- sunglasses
- umbrella
- iPod

FUNNY FILL-IN
On Safari

Ask a friend to give you words to fill in the blanks in this story without showing it to him or her. Then read out loud for a laugh.

You'll never believe what happened when my family went on a(n) _____ safari in
adjective

_____ . We were having a great time snapping photos of the _____
country _adjective_

wildlife. We saw _____ cubs, a(n) _____ -striped _____ that could run
animal _color_ _different animal_

faster than _____ , and a(n) _____ _____ in a tree.
famous athlete _different animal_ _verb ending in -ing_

Then our safari vehicle suddenly _____ to a stop. The wheels had become
past-tense verb

stuck in _____ inches of _____ . I turned around and saw a(n)
number _something gross_

_____ the size of _____ _____ toward us and making
different animal _movie monster_ _verb ending in -ing_

a sound like a(n) _____ . It was so close I could smell its _____
musical instrument _something that stinks_

-scented breath. I thought the animal was going to flatten us like _____ ;
breakfast food, plural

instead, it just _____ the vehicle out of the muck with its _____
past-tense verb _animal body part_

and _____ away. I couldn't wait to post these pictures on _____ .
past-tense verb _website_

That's when I realized that I was still holding my _____ , but I had not taken
electronic gadget

a single picture. No one at home will ever believe this _____ tale.
adjective

167

SIGNS
OF THE TIMES

Seeing isn't always believing. Two of these funny signs are not real. Can you figure out which two are fake?

ANSWERS ON PAGE 338

Mousetrap

A tiny mouse has sneaked into this restaurant and caused chaos. Find 20 things in the dining room that the mouse has nibbled on, and then find the mouse. We've circled one nibble for you.

ANSWERS ON PAGE 338

Play interactive "What in the World?" and other games online. kids.nationalgeographic.com

SEEING SPOTS!

These photographs are close-up views of things with spots or dots. Unscramble the letters to identify each picture. Feel like you're on the spot? ANSWERS ON PAGE 338

SWRTITE

_____

HERAFTE

_____

COGEK

_____

YAGBDLU

_____

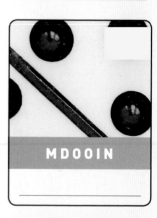

MDOOIN

_____

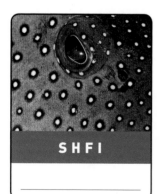

SHFI

_____

AYDNC TSBTONU

_____

UHRMOMOS

_____

STUMP
YOUR PARENTS

If your parents can't answer these questions, maybe *they* should go to school instead of you! ANSWERS ON PAGE 338

1 What was the R.M.S. *Titanic*'s final destination before it sank in 1912?
A. Boston, Massachusetts
B. New York City, New York
C. Halifax, Nova Scotia, in Canada
D. Philadelphia, Pennsylvania

2 If you were a gladiator in ancient Rome, who would you most likely fight?
A. professional fighter
B. criminal
C. slave
D. all of the above

3 Which of these was reclassified as a dwarf planet?
A. Mercury
B. Neptune
C. Saturn
D. Uranus
E. Jupiter
F. Pluto
G. Earth
H. Mars

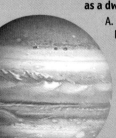

4 Which Springfield is where the Simpsons live?
A. Springfield, Massachusetts
B. Springfield, Missouri
C. Springfield, Illinois
D. none of the above

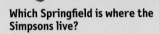

5 Which theme park does not have a site in Florida, in the U.S.A.?
A. Magic Kingdom
B. Six Flags
C. SeaWorld
D. Universal Studios

6 Which vacation destination is the oldest?
A. Grand Canyon, in the United States
B. Pyramids at Giza, in Egypt
C. London, England, in the United Kingdom
D. Great Wall of China

7 How many hours do lions nap each day?
A. 20
B. 18
C. 10
D. 8

A Piece of Cake

Find at least 25 items in this bakery that start with the letter *B*. ANSWERS ON PAGE 338

The Funnies

"DO YOU HAVE ANY IDEA HOW FAST YOU WERE GOING BACK THERE?"

WHEN TOMATOES RUN

"NOT EVERYONE'S A DOG PERSON!"

We Gave It a Swirl

Use the clues below to figure out which animals appear in these swirled pictures. ANSWERS ON PAGE 339

1

HINT! A movie starring this clown did swimmingly at the box office.

2

HINT! If this sprinter took off down a highway, it could run fast enough to get a speeding ticket.

3

HINT! Hey, who are you calling a quack?

4

HINT! Slowing down climate change can help protect animals like this Arctic giant.

5

HINT! This many-legged creature will go through a major transformation.

A Wintry Mix-Up

This snowy park seems picture-perfect. But look again! Find and circle at least 12 things wrong in this scene.

ANSWERS ON PAGE 339

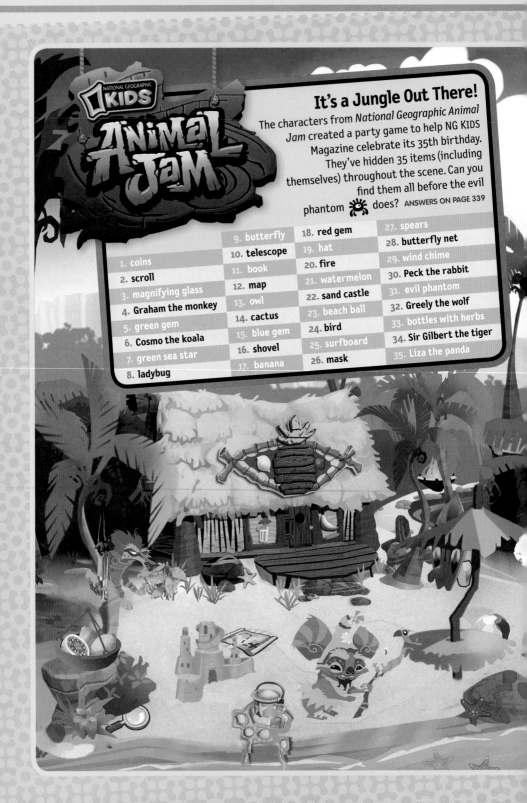

It's a Jungle Out There!

The characters from *National Geographic Animal Jam* created a party game to help NG KIDS Magazine celebrate its 35th birthday. They've hidden 35 items (including themselves) throughout the scene. Can you find them all before the evil phantom does? ANSWERS ON PAGE 339

1. coins
2. scroll
3. magnifying glass
4. Graham the monkey
5. green gem
6. Cosmo the koala
7. green sea star
8. ladybug
9. butterfly
10. telescope
11. book
12. map
13. owl
14. cactus
15. blue gem
16. shovel
17. banana
18. red gem
19. hat
20. fire
21. watermelon
22. sand castle
23. beach ball
24. bird
25. surfboard
26. mask
27. spears
28. butterfly net
29. wind chime
30. Peck the rabbit
31. evil phantom
32. Greely the wolf
33. bottles with herbs
34. Sir Gilbert the tiger
35. Liza the panda

EXPLORE!

NATIONAL GEOGRAPHIC KIDS'
new virtual world
online.
AnimalJam.com

*see special code below

NATIONAL GEOGRAPHIC

*Enter the special code
explore2012
for a bonus!
AnimalJam.com

Having a Blast!

These expressions describe guests at this barbecue—literally! Find and circle the people in the scene who match these descriptions.

ANSWERS ON PAGE 339

1. Joe is all ears.
2. Brittany is a barrel of laughs.
3. Gretchen bends over backward for her friends.
4. John is good at breaking the ice.
5. Jane is a backseat driver.
6. Peter just opened a can of worms.
7. Kaitlyn is getting married in two days and has cold feet.
8. Brandon is ready to hit the sack.
9. Emily is in the doghouse.
10. Jake just let the cat out of the bag.

Funny FILL-IN

Stop, Thief!

Ask a friend to give you words to fill in the blanks in this story without showing it to him or her. Then read out loud for a laugh.

Something fishy was going on. Lately things had been disappearing around my house, like my dad's _____ (household object), my mom's favorite _____ (famous singer) CD, and my little sister's _____ (adjective) _____ (type of toy). And just today my lucky _____ (type of clothing) vanished. Whoever the _____ (adjective) thief was, he wasn't going to get away with this. With a magnifying _____ (noun), I searched for suspicious _____ (body part) prints. I checked under the _____ (piece of furniture), behind the big-screen _____ (electronic gadget), and even inside the _____ (kitchen appliance). Then I heard a(n) _____ (loud noise) coming from the garage. Could the thief actually be here right now? As I _____ (past-tense verb) into the garage, a(n) _____ (adjective) figure darted behind the _____ (adjective) type of car. I yelled, "_____ (exclamation)!" and started to run away, when I heard a(n) _____ (animal noise). In a flash, my dog _____ (past-tense verb) out from behind the car with my _____ (same type of clothing) in his _____ (animal body part). And there, behind the _____ (yard tool), was a big pile of my family's missing possessions. This case is officially closed.

Double Take

See if you can spot 12 differences in the two pictures.   ANSWERS ON PAGE 339

A crowd of people and balloons fills a street on the Italian island of Sicily.

PET PROJECT

Ten people in this store will each take home a new pet today. Using clues in the picture, match the ten people to their future pets. Then draw lines connecting the pairs.

ANSWERS ON PAGE 339

The Great Fountain Geyser erupts in
Yellowstone National Park, Montana, U.S.A.

Wonders of Nature

Got a smart phone?
SCAN THIS to experience the powers of nature!
(See instructions inside the front cover.)

No smart phone? Go online.
kids.nationalgeographic.com/almanac-2012

WORLD WATER

Earth's most precious resource

More than two-thirds of Earth is covered by water, but fresh water, which many plants and animals —including humans—need to survive, makes up less than three percent of all the water on Earth. Much of this fresh water is trapped deep underground or frozen in ice sheets and glaciers. Of the small amount of water that is fresh, less than one percent is available for human use.

Unfortunately, human activity often puts great stress on vital watersheds. For example, Brazil has approved the construction of large dams on the Amazon River. This will alter the natural flow of water in this giant watershed and help provide water and electricity. In the United States, heavy use of chemical fertilizers and pesticides has created toxic runoff that threatens the health of the Mississippi River watershed.

Access to clean fresh water is critical for human health. But in many places, safe water is scarce due to population pressure and pollution.

Water Facts

Over the course of 100 years, a water molecule will spend an average of 98 years in the ocean. The rest of the time it's either ice, in lakes and rivers, or in the atmosphere.

If all the glaciers and ice sheets on Earth's surface melted, they would raise the level of Earth's oceans by about 230 feet (70 m). It is estimated that during the last ice age, when glaciers covered about one-third of the land, the sea level was 400 feet (122 m) lower than it is today.

Because of its ability to dissolve more substances than any other liquid, water is known as a "universal solvent." So wherever water goes—whether it's through the ground or through our bodies—it picks up valuable chemicals, minerals, and nutrients.

Water consists of two hydrogen atoms and one oxygen atom bonded together by an electrical charge.

If all the world's water were fit into a gallon jug, only about one tablespoon (0.5 fl oz) of it would be okay for us to drink.

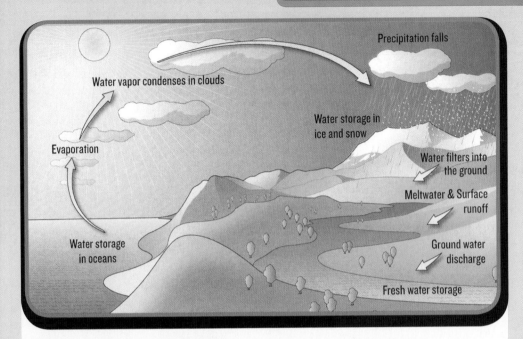

Precipitation falls

Water vapor condenses in clouds

Water storage in ice and snow

Evaporation

Water filters into the ground

Meltwater & Surface runoff

Water storage in oceans

Ground water discharge

Fresh water storage

WATER CYCLE

The amount of water on Earth is more or less constant—only the form changes. As the sun warms Earth's surface, liquid water is changed to water vapor in a process called **evaporation**. Plants lose water from the surface of leaves in a process called **transpiration**. As water vapor rises into the air, it cools and changes form again. This time it becomes clouds in a process called **condensation**. Water droplets fall from the clouds as **precipitation,** which then travels as groundwater or runoff back to the lakes, rivers, and oceans, where the cycle (shown above) starts all over again.

Bet you didn't know

97 PERCENT OF EARTH'S WATER IS SALT WATER.

COLD WATER weighs more than HOT WATER.

EARTH has the SAME AMOUNT of WATER today as it did 100 million years ago.

THE OC

PACIFIC OCEAN

STATS

Surface area
65,436,200 sq mi (169,479,000 sq km)

Earth's water area
47 percent

Greatest depth
**Challenger Deep
(in the Mariana Trench)
-35,827 ft (-10,920 m)**

Surface temperatures
**Summer high: 90°F (32°C)
Winter low: 28°F (-2°C)**

Tides
**Highest: 30 ft (9 m)
near Korean peninsula
Lowest: 1 ft (0.3 m)
near Midway Islands**

GEO WHIZ

The area of the Pacific Ocean is greater than all the land surfaces on Earth combined.

The ocean's name comes from the Latin *Mare Pacificum*, meaning "peaceful sea," but earthquakes and volcanic activity along its coasts occasionally generate powerful waves called tsunamis, which can cause death and destruction when they slam ashore.

The Pacific is home to the largest number of coral reefs, including Earth's longest: Australia's 1,429-mile (2,300-km)-long Great Barrier Reef.

It would take a stack of more than 24 Empire State Buildings to equal the depth of the Challenger Deep in the western Pacific, the deepest point among all of the oceans.

ATLANTIC OCEAN

STATS

Surface area
35,338,500 sq mi (91,526,300 sq km)

Earth's water area
25 percent

Greatest depth
**Puerto Rico Trench
-28,232 ft (-8,605 m)**

Surface temperatures
**Summer high: 90°F (32°C)
Winter low: 28°F (-2°C)**

Tides
**Highest: 52 ft (16 m)
Bay of Fundy, Canada
Lowest: 1.5 ft (0.5 m)
Gulf of Mexico and Mediterranean Sea**

GEO WHIZ

The Atlantic can be a dangerous place. Icebergs in the far northern Atlantic have wrecked many ships, including the R.M.S. *Titanic* in 1912. Treacherous currents and towering waves off the coast of Namibia in Africa have also caused countless shipwrecks.

The Atlantic Ocean is about half the size of the Pacific, but it's growing. Spreading along the Mid-Atlantic Ridge—an undersea mountain range—allows molten rock from Earth's interior to escape and form new ocean floor.

Of all of the world's oceans, the Atlantic is the youngest. It is thought to have been created about 150 million years ago.

Humans inhabited the Atlantic coast of Africa more than 100,000 years ago. Fossils from that time period show that people there hunted fish and penguins and gathered shellfish.

EANS

INDIAN OCEAN

STATS

Surface area
28,839,800 sq mi (74,694,800 sq km)

Earth's water area
21 percent

Greatest depth
**Java Trench
-23,376 ft (-7,125 m)**

Surface temperatures
**Summer high: 93°F (34°C)
Winter low: 28°F (-2°C)**

Tides
**Highest: 36 ft (11 m)
Lowest: 2 ft (0.6 m)
Both along Australia's west coast**

GEO WHIZ

Each day tankers carrying 17 million barrels of crude oil from the Persian Gulf enter the waters of the Indian Ocean, transporting their cargo for distribution around the world.

Some of the world's largest breeding grounds for humpback whales are in the Indian Ocean, the Arabian Sea, and off the east coast of Africa.

The Bay of Bengal, off the coast of India, is sometimes called Cyclone Alley because of the large number of tropical storms that occur each year between May and November.

The Indian Ocean is home to the Kerguelen Plateau, an underwater volcanic landmass that's three times the size of Japan.

In 2004, a major earthquake and its after-shocks sent a series of massive waves called tsunamis racing across the Indian Ocean. Thousands of miles of coastline were affected.

ARCTIC OCEAN

STATS

Surface area
5,390,000 sq mi (13,960,100 sq km)

Earth's water area
4 percent

Greatest depth
**Molloy Deep
-18,599 ft (-5,669 m)**

Surface temperatures
**Summer high: 41°F (5°C)
Winter low: 28°F (-2°C)**

Tides
**Less than 1 ft (0.3 m)
variation throughout the ocean**

GEO WHIZ

Satellite monitoring of Arctic sea ice, which began in the late 1970s, shows that the extent of the sea ice is shrinking by approximately 11 percent every 10 years. Many scientists believe this is caused by global warming.

The geographic North Pole lies roughly in the middle of the Arctic Ocean under 13,000 feet (3,962 m) of water.

Many of the features on the Arctic Ocean floor are named for early Arctic explorers and bordering landmasses.

About 2,700 billion tons (2,400 billion t) of ice drifts out of the Arctic Ocean and into other bodies of water every year.

Fish living in the Arctic Ocean have proteins in their blood that protect them from freezing in the frigid waters, which can drop to about -4°F (-20°C).

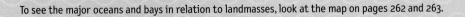

To see the major oceans and bays in relation to landmasses, look at the map on pages 262 and 263.

Coral Reefs

Just below the surface of the Caribbean Sea's crystal-clear water, miles of vivid corals shoot off in fantastic shapes that shelter tropical fish of every color. Coral reefs account for a quarter of all life in the ocean and are often called the rain forests of the sea. Like big apartment complexes, coral reefs provide a tough limestone skeleton for fish, shrimp, clams, and other organisms to live in—and plenty of food for them to eat, too.

And how does the coral get its color? It's all about the algae that clings to its limestone polyps. Algae and coral live together in a mutually helpful relationship. The coral provides a home to the algae and helps the algae convert sunlight to food that it uses. But as beautiful as coral reefs are, they are also highly sensitive. A jump of even two degrees in water temperature makes the reef rid itself of the algae, leaving the coral with a sickly bleached look. Pollution is another threat; it can poison the sensitive corals. Humans pose a threat, too: One clumsy kick from a swimmer can destroy decades of coral growth.

BY THE NUMBERS

50 million years ago coral reefs began growing on Earth.

1,500 species of fish live in the Great Barrier Reef in Australia.

80 percent of Caribbean coral reef has died in the last 35 years.

REEF FACTS

There's a
HEART-SHAPED
coral reef in Australia.

CORAL POLYPS are
related to
SEA ANEMONES.

MEET THE NAT GEO EXPLORER

ENRIC SALA

Dr. Enric Sala is a marine ecologist who studies the many species that live underwater and how they interact with each other. Through his research, he hopes to teach humans how to keep the Earth's oceans, coral reefs, and marine life healthy and protected.

What's a normal day like for you?
When I am at sea, I dive and collect data underwater three or four times every day.

What's the best place you've ever traveled to?
Millennium Atoll, a virgin coral reef in the middle of the Pacific Ocean that is full of sharks and beautiful corals. . .and no people!

Have you ever touched coral? What does it feel like?
I have touched coral, and it feels hard like a rock, with a little slimy thing on top of it. But to prevent damaging coral, you should leave it alone.

What would you suggest we do to help save coral?
Keep trying to help preserve the environment in general. Ask your parents what they are doing to save energy and recycle. Also, make sure that the seafood you eat is sustainable, and you will start a chain reaction.

Continents on the Move

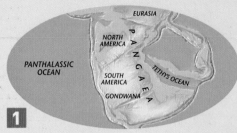

1

PANGAEA About 240 million years ago, Earth's landmasses were joined together in one super-continent that extended from pole to pole.

2

BREAKUP By 94 million years ago, Pangaea had broken apart into landmasses that would become today's continents. Dinosaurs roamed Earth during a period of warmer climates.

3

EXTINCTION About 65 million years ago, an asteroid smashed into Earth, creating the Gulf of Mexico. This impact may have resulted in the extinction of half the world's species, including the dinosaurs. This was one of several major mass extinctions.

4

ICE AGE By 18,000 years ago, the continents had drifted close to their present positions, but most far northern and far southern lands were buried beneath huge glaciers.

A LOOK INSIDE

The distance from Earth's surface to its center is 3,963 miles (6,378 km). There are four layers: a thin, rigid crust; the rocky mantle; the outer core, which is a layer of molten iron; and finally the inner core, which is solid iron.

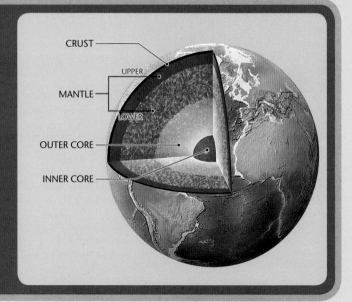

CRUST

UPPER

MANTLE

LOWER

OUTER CORE

INNER CORE

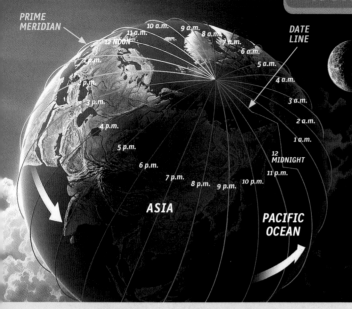

PRIME MERIDIAN

10 a.m. 9 a.m. 8 a.m.
11 a.m. 7 a.m.
12 NOON 6 a.m.
5 a.m.
1 p.m. 4 a.m.
2 p.m. 3 a.m.
3 p.m. 2 a.m.
1 a.m.
4 p.m.
5 p.m. 12 MIDNIGHT
6 p.m. 11 p.m.
7 p.m. 10 p.m.
8 p.m. 9 p.m.

DATE LINE

ASIA

PACIFIC OCEAN

TIME ZONES

Long ago, when people lived in relative isolation, they measured time by the position of the sun overhead. That meant that noon in one place was not the same as noon in a place 100 miles (160 km) to the west. Later, with the development of long-distance railroads, people needed to coordinate time. In 1884 a system of 24 standard time zones was adopted. Each time zone reflects the fact that Earth rotates west to east 15 degrees each hour.
Time is counted from the prime meridian, which runs through Greenwich, England.

Earth Shapers

Earth's features are constantly undergoing change—being built up, destroyed, or just rearranged. Below the Earth's surface are movable segments called plates. Plates are in constant, very slow motion. As the plates move, mountains are uplifted, volcanoes erupt, and new land is created.

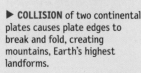

◀ FAULTING happens when two plates grind past each other, creating large cracks along the edges of the plates.

▲ VOLCANOES form when molten rock, called magma, rises to Earth's surface. Some volcanoes occur as one plate pushes beneath another plate. Other volcanoes result when a plate passes over a column of magma, called a hot spot, rising from the mantle.

▶ COLLISION of two continental plates causes plate edges to break and fold, creating mountains, Earth's highest landforms.

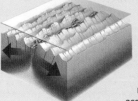

◀ SPREADING results when oceanic plates move apart. The ocean floor cracks, magma rises, and new crust is created. The Mid-Atlantic Ridge spreads about an inch—a few centimeters—a year, pushing Europe and North America farther apart.

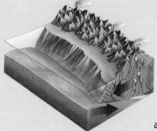

◀ SUBDUCTION occurs when an oceanic plate dives under a continental plate. This often results in volcanoes and earthquakes, as well as mountain building.

Countries Around the World
Where Crystals and Gems Are Mined

CANADA
Jade

POLAND
Amber

RUSSIA
Amber
Clear quartz

UNITED STATES
Clear quartz
Rose quartz

NORTH AMERICA

EUROPE

ASIA

AFGHANISTAN
Lapis lazuli

MYANMAR (BURMA)
Jade

MEXICO
Agate

AFRICA

SOUTH AMERICA

INDIA
Bloodstone

BRAZIL
Agate
Citrine
Clear quartz
Rose quartz

DEM. REP. OF THE CONGO
Malachite

SRI LANKA
Moonstone

AUSTRALIA

MADAGASCAR
Clear quartz

ANTARCTICA

See a great photo gallery of gems online.
science.nationalgeographic.com/
science/photos/gems.html

COOL CLICK

Bet you didn't **know**

A 14-pound (6-kg) **pearl** was found INSIDE a GIANT clam!

All the **MINED GOLD** in the **WORLD** can fill two OLYMPIC-SIZE **SWIMMING POOLS.**

The Queen of England has a CROWN studded with more than 3,000 PRECIOUS GEMS.

BIRTHSTNES

January

GARNET LOYALTY
Garnets were once thought to hold medicinal value and protect against poisons, wounds, and bad dreams. They come in red, black, and green, or are colorless.

February

AMETHYST SINCERITY
Amethysts were believed to help people stay awake and think clearly. They are found in geodes (rock formations) and range from light mauve to deep purple.

March

AQUAMARINE COURAGE
This gem was thought to heal illnesses of the stomach, liver, jaws, and throat. It ranges from deep blue to blue-green. The most valued and rare are the deep blue gems.

April

DIAMOND ENDURING LOVE
People associate these gems with romance, mystery, power, greed, and magic. The hardest natural substance on Earth, diamonds are a form of carbon.

May

EMERALD PURE LOVE
Emeralds were thought to prevent epilepsy, stop bleeding, cure fevers and diarrhea, and keep the wearer from panicking. These gems are light to deep green.

June

PEARL INNOCENCE
Pearls were thought to possess magical powers; as a result, there used to be laws about who could own and wear them (powerful, rich people). No two pearls are exactly alike.

July

RUBY CONTENTMENT
A ruby supposedly brought good health, cured bleeding, guarded against wickedness, and foretold misfortune. Rubies are a red form of the mineral corundum.

August

PERIDOT HAPPINESS
People felt that peridots could ward off anxiety, help one speak better, and improve relationships. Peridot is the only gem ever found in meteorites.

September

SAPPHIRE CLEAR THINKING
Once a source of protection for travelers, sapphires brought peace and wisdom. Some are pale; others are brilliant blue. They also come in orange, green, yellow, and pink.

October

OPAL HOPE
An opal was believed to bring beauty, success, and happiness, as well as to ward off heart and kidney failure and prevent fainting. Opals form over a long, long time.

November

TOPAZ FAITHFULNESS
Legends proclaimed that a topaz made one clear-sighted, increased strength, and warned of poison. Topazes come in a range of colors: gold, pink, or green, or colorless.

December

TURQUOISE SUCCESS
Some believed turquoise was a love charm. If a man gave a woman turquoise jewelry, he was pledging his love for her. It forms where mineral-rich water seeps into rocky gaps.

Biomes

A BIOME, OFTEN CALLED A MAJOR LIFE ZONE, is one of the natural world's major communities where plants and animals adapt to their specific surroundings. Biomes are classified depending on the predominant vegetation, climate, and geography of a region. They can be divided into six major types: forest, fresh water, marine, desert, grassland, and tundra. Each biome consists of many ecosystems.

Biomes are extremely important. Balanced ecological relationships between biomes help to maintain the environment and life on Earth as we know it. For example, an increase in one species of plant, such as an invasive one, can cause a ripple effect throughout the whole biome.

Since biomes can be fragile in this way, it is important to protect them from negative human activity, such as deforestation and pollution. We must work to conserve these biomes and the unique organisms that live within them.

FOREST

The forest biomes have been evolving for about 420 million years. Today, forests occupy about one-third of Earth's land area. There are three major types of forests: tropical, temperate, and boreal (taiga). Forests are home to a diversity of plants, some of which may hold medicinal qualities for humans, as well as thousands of unseen and undiscovered animal species. Forests can also absorb carbon dioxide, a greenhouse gas, and give off oxygen.

FRESH WATER

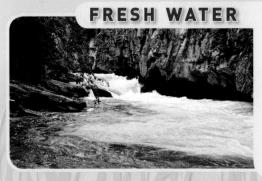

Most water on Earth is salty, but freshwater ecosystems include lakes, ponds, wetlands, rivers, and streams—all of which usually contain less than one percent salt concentration. The countless animal and plant species that live in a freshwater biome vary from continent to continent, but include algae, frogs, turtles, fishes, and the larvae of many insects. Throughout the world, people use food, medicine, and other resources from this biome.

MARINE

The marine biome covers almost three-fourths of Earth's surface, making it the largest habitat on our planet. The five oceans make up the majority of the marine biome. Coral reefs are considered to be the most biodiverse of any of the biome habitats. The marine biome is home to more than one million plant and animal species. Some of the largest animals on Earth, such as the blue whale, live in the marine biome.

DESERT

Covering about one-fifth of Earth's surface, deserts are places where precipitation is less than 10 inches (25 cm) per year. Although most deserts are hot, there are other kinds, as well. The four major kinds of deserts in the world include: hot, semi-arid, coastal, and cold. Far from being barren wastelands, deserts are biologically rich habitats with a vast array of animals and plants that have adapted to the harsh conditions there.

GRASSLAND

Biomes called grasslands are characterized by having grasses instead of large shrubs or trees. Grasslands generally have precipitation for only about half to three-fourths of the year. If it were more, they would become forests. Widespread around the world, grasslands can be divided into two types: tropical (savannas) and temperate. Grasslands are home to some of the largest land animals on Earth, such as elephants, hippopotamuses, rhinoceroses, and lions.

TUNDRA

The coldest of all biomes, tundras are characterized by an extremely cold climate, simple vegetation, little precipitation, poor nutrients, and short growing seasons. There are two types of tundra: arctic and alpine. A very fragile environment, tundras are home to few kinds of vegetation. Surprisingly, though, there are quite a few animal species that can survive the tundra's extremes, such as wolves, caribou, and even mosquitoes.

HOW DOES Your Garden GROW?

The plant kingdom is more than 300,000 organisms strong, growing all over the world: on top of mountains, in the sea, in frigid temperatures—everywhere. Without plants, life on Earth would not be able to survive. Plants provide food and oxygen for animals and humans.

Three characteristics make plants distinct:

1 Most have chlorophyll (a green pigment that makes photosynthesis work and turns sunlight into energy), while some are parasitic.

2 They cannot change their location on their own.

3 Their cell walls are made from a stiff material called cellulose.

Photosynthesis

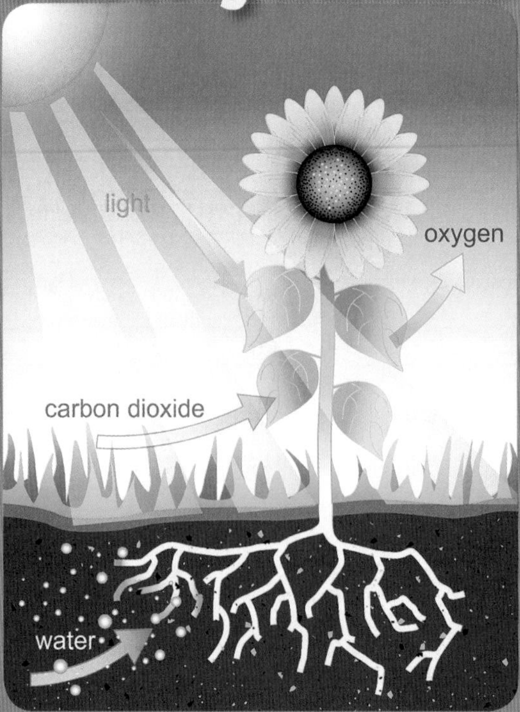

light

oxygen

carbon dioxide

water

Plants are lucky—they don't have to hunt or shop for food. Most use the sun to produce their own food. In a process called photosynthesis, the plant's chloroplast (the part of the plant where the chemical chlorophyll is located) captures the sun's energy and combines it with carbon dioxide from the air and nutrient-rich water from the ground to produce a sugar called glucose. Plants burn the glucose for energy to help them grow. As a waste product, plants emit oxygen, which humans and other animals need to breathe. When animals breathe, we exhale carbon dioxide, which the plants then use for more photosynthesis—it's all a big, finely tuned system. So the next time you pass a lonely houseplant, give it thanks for helping you live.

Try This!

CREATE A HUMMINGBIRD GARDEN!

MORE THAN 335 DIFFERENT SPECIES of colorful hummingbirds live around the world—probably near you. These tiny birds, with their sparkling iridescent feathers, are fun to watch as they dart from flower to flower. Use plants native to your area to create a garden that will attract hummingbirds to your yard. By growing native plants you'll have a garden that thrives naturally and is good for the environment. Here are some hummingbird favorites to plant in your garden.

A hummingbird's wings beat 40 to 80 times a second.

Hummingbirds are the only birds that can fly backward.

TO ATTRACT HUMMINGBIRDS

Hovering all day can be exhausting, so hummingbirds need to refuel often. They feed on the flowers' nectar, which is rich in energy. A hummingbird can drink half its weight in just one day. Hummingbirds will feed from any nectar-producing flower, no matter what its shape or color. Attract your feathered friends by filling your garden with these "flight fuel" flowers.

BEE BALM

TRUMPET CREEPER

PENSTEMON

BLUE SAGE

World Climate

Weather is the condition of the atmosphere—temperature, precipitation, humidity, wind—at a given place at a given time. Climate, however, is the average weather for a particular place over a long period of time. Different places on Earth have different climates, but climate is not a random occurrence. There is a pattern that is controlled by factors such as latitude, elevation, prevailing winds, the temperature of ocean currents, and location on land relative to water. Climate is generally constant, but evidence indicates that human activity is causing a change in the patterns of climate.

CLIMATE FACTS

Deforestation, fossil fuels, and landfills all release greenhouse gases, which contributes to climate change.

During one period of time about 125,000 years ago, there was no summer ice at the North Pole and the sea level was about 15 feet (5 m) higher than today.

As the Earth warms due to climate change, sea levels will rise. Melting ice from the glaciers and polar ice caps contributes to the rising levels.

Ever wonder what global warming looks like? Check out Klimapark in Norway. With tours of glaciers, snowdrifts, and melt-offs, and a trip through an ice tunnel, visitors to this climate change park witness the environmental impact of global warming firsthand.

GLOBAL CLIMATE ZONES

ARCTIC OCEAN
ATLANTIC OCEAN
PACIFIC OCEAN
PACIFIC OCEAN
INDIAN OCEAN

Climatologists, people who study climate, have created different systems for classifying climates. An often used system is called the Köppen system, which classifies climate zones according to precipitation, temperature, and vegetation. It has five major categories—Tropical, Dry, Temperate, Cold, and Polar—with a sixth category for locations where high elevations override other factors.

Climate

Tropical   Dry   Temperate   Cold   Polar

Bet you didn't know

Temperature Tips

There are two commonly used temperature scales, **Fahrenheit** (used in the U.S.) and **Celsius** (used in most countries of the world). Although they both measure temperature, the numbers are different. For example, **water freezes at 32°F or 0°C.**

To convert from Fahrenheit to Celsius, subtract 32, then multiply by 5, and divide by 9.

To convert from Celsius to Fahrenheit, multiply by 9, divide by 5, and then add 32.

Example: If water boils at 100°C, and we want to know what temperature that is in Fahrenheit, we'd use the second formula:
100°C x 9 = 900
900 ÷ 5 = 180
180 + 32 = 212°F

CLIMATE CHANGE

Earth's climate history has been a story of ups and downs, with warm periods followed by periods of bitter cold. The early part of the 20th century was marked by colder than average temperatures (see graph below), followed by a period of gradual and then steady increase. Scientists are concerned that the current warming trend is more than a natural cycle. One sign of change is the melting of glaciers in Greenland and Antarctica. If glaciers continue to melt, areas of Florida (shown above in red) and other coastal land will be underwater.

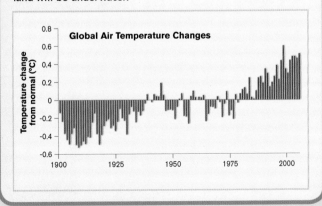

Global Air Temperature Changes

Freaky Weather

AN AURORA GLOWS OVER
REYKJAVIK, ICELAND.

Nature can be unbelievably powerful. A major earthquake can topple huge buildings and bring down entire mountainsides. Hurricanes, blizzards, and tornadoes can paralyze major cities. But as powerful as these natural disasters are, here are six other episodes of wacky weather that will really *blow* you away!

1

FLAMING TWISTERS

Wildfires are so powerful they can create their own weather. As these fires burn, they consume huge quantities of oxygen. The intense heat causes the air to rise. When fresh air swoops in and replaces it, strong winds are produced, sometimes causing swirling tornadoes of fire that can be 50 feet (15 m) wide and grow as tall as a 40-story building!

2

DODGEBALLS

About 1,000 years ago hundreds of people were mysteriously killed in the Himalaya Mountains. Research has revealed that they were caught in a hailstorm that dropped chunks of ice the size of baseballs on the victims' heads at more than a hundred miles an hour. Hail is formed when raindrops are carried into extremely cold areas of the atmosphere by powerful vertical winds. The longer the specks of ice bounce around in the wind, the bigger they become. When the clumps of ice grow too big for the winds to hold up, they fall to the ground as hail.

3

MYSTERY WAVES

Imagine you're on an ocean liner when a wall of water ten stories tall races toward you like an unstoppable freight train. It's a rogue wave, also called a freak wave, which can appear without any warning at any time in the open sea. These waves were once considered myths, but scientists now know they are very real—and very dangerous to even the largest ships.

IT'S RAINING FROGS!

Thousands of small frogs rained on a town in Serbia, sending residents scurrying for cover. Had the town gone crazy? Probably not. Scientists believe that waterspouts and tornadoes can suck up the surfaces of lakes, marshes, and other bodies of water, taking frogs and fish along for the ride. The tornadoes can then drop them miles away.

4

5

GREAT BALLS OF FIRE

During a thunderstorm, a glowing ball the size of your head suddenly appears. It hovers a few feet above the ground, drops down, dances across the yard, and then darts up into the air before it fades away. This freaky phenomenon is ball lightning. Sometimes it disappears with a small explosion. Some scientists think that when normal lightning strikes the ground, it vaporizes a mineral called silicon found in soil. This silicon forms a kind of bubble that burns in the oxygen around it.

SNOWBALL FACTORY

You head outside after a snowstorm and see dozens of log- or drum-shaped snowballs. These rare creations are called snow rollers, formed when wet snow falls on icy ground, so snow can't stick to it. Pushed by strong winds, the snow rolls into logs. Maybe this is nature's way of saying it's time for a snowball fight.

6

Lightning!

There are about 3,000 **LIGHTNING FLASHES** on Earth every minute.

Clouds suddenly appeared on the horizon, the sky turned dark, and it started to rain as Sabrina was hiking through the Grand Canyon with her parents.

As lightning flashed around them, Sabrina and her parents ran for cover. "When it stopped raining, we thought it was safe," says Sabrina. They started to hike back to their car along the trail. Then *zap!* A lightning bolt struck nearby. It happened so fast that the family didn't know what hit it. A jolt of electricity shot through their bodies. "It felt like a strong tingling over my whole body," says Sabrina. "It really hurt."

Sabrina and her family were lucky. The lightning didn't zap them directly, and they recovered within minutes. Some people aren't so lucky. Lightning kills thousands of people each year.

Lightning is a giant electric spark similar to the small spark you get when you walk across a carpet and touch a metal doorknob—but much stronger. One flash can contain a billion volts of electricity—enough to light a 100-watt incandescent bulb for three months. Lightning crackles through the air at a temperature five times hotter than the surface of the sun. The intense heat makes the surrounding air expand rapidly, creating a sound we know as thunder. Getting hit by lightning is rare, but everyone must be careful.

"For the first few years after I was struck, I was so scared every time there was a storm," says Sabrina. "Now I'm not scared. But I'm always cautious."

LIGHTNING SAFETY TIPS

INSIDE

Stay inside for 30 minutes after the last lightning or thunder.

Don't take baths or showers or wash dishes.

Avoid using landline phones (cell phones are okay), computers, TVs, and other electrical equipment.

OUTSIDE

Get into an enclosed structure or vehicle and shut the windows.

Stay away from bodies of water.

Avoid tall objects such as trees.

If you're in the open, crouch down (but do not lie flat) in the lowest place you can find.

Natural Disasters

Every world region has its share of natural disasters—the mix just varies from place to place. The Ring of Fire—grinding tectonic plate boundaries that follow the coasts of the Pacific Ocean—shakes with volcanic eruptions and earthquakes. Lives and livelihoods here and along other oceans can be swept away by tsunamis. North America's heartland endures blizzards in winter and tornadoes that can strike in spring, summer, or fall. Tropical cyclones batter many coastal areas in Asia and Australia with ripping winds, torrents of rain, and huge storm surges along their deadly paths.

HURRICANE

HURRICANES IN 2012

HELLO, MY NAME IS...

Hurricane names come from six official international lists. The names alternate between male and female. When a storm becomes a hurricane, a name from the list is used, in alphabetical order. Each list is reused every six years. A name "retires" if that hurricane caused a lot of damage or many deaths.

Alberto
Beryl
Chris
Debby
Ernesto
Florence
Gordon
Helene
Isaac
Joyce
Kirk
Leslie
Michael
Nadine
Oscar
Patty
Rafael
Sandy
Tony
Valerie
William

A monster storm with 150-mile-an-hour (240 kph) winds churns west across the Atlantic Ocean. Scientists at the National Hurricane Center in Miami have tracked it for days using satellite images. Now they're worried it may threaten the United States.

It's time for the "hurricane hunters" to go to work! All ships and airplanes have been warned away from this monster. But two four-engine airplanes head toward the storm. Their mission? To collect data inside the hurricane that will tell meteorologists where the storm is going, when it will get there, and how violent it will be.

The word "hurricane" comes from Huracan, the god of big winds and evil spirits once worshipped by the Maya people of Central America. These superstrong storms—which usually last for nine days—are the most destructive during their first 12 hours onshore, when high winds can topple homes and cause major flooding.

To help people prepare for a hurricane that's hustling to shore, the U.S. National Oceanic and Atmospheric Administration (NOAA) sends out the "hurricane hunters," who fly straight into the storm to determine characteristics such as temperature, air pressure, wind speed, and wind direction. It's a dangerous job, but by mission's end, the hunters' work will keep everyone in the hurricane's path safe.

Scale of Hurricane Intensity

CATEGORY	ONE	TWO	THREE	FOUR	FIVE
DAMAGE	Minimal	Moderate	Extensive	Extreme	Catastrophic
WINDS	74–95 mph (119–153 kph)	96–110 mph (154–177 kph)	111–130 mph (178–209 kph)	131–155 mph (210–249 kph)	Over 155 mph (249+ kph)
(DAMAGE refers to wind and water damage combined.)					

Earthquake

When a massive earthquake rocked Haiti in January 2010, the world realized just how destructive these forces of nature can be. The 7.0-magnitude quake lasted less than a minute, but the damage to the densely populated area was devastating. Homes and buildings collapsed, killing around 230,000 people and injuring 300,000. More than a million people were displaced near the country's capital of Port-au-Prince, sparking a worldwide relief effort for the ailing country.

Just one month later, a massive 8.8-magnitude quake all but destroyed certain parts of Chile. It was so strong that experts say it shifted the Earth's axis and shortened days by 1.26 microseconds!

Thousands of earthquakes occur each day. But unlike these recent quakes, most are too weak to feel. "Earthquakes don't kill people—falling buildings do," says Lucy Jones, a seismologist, who studies earthquakes at the U.S. Geological Survey in California. "You can't stop an earthquake. The best thing you can do is prepare."

Police on horseback patrol Concepción, Chile, following a 2010 earthquake.

Tornado

"One time a tornado we were filming was coming right at us," says filmmaker Sean Casey. "As it moved closer, the wind picked up, and we felt as if the wind were pulling us into the tornado." Casey wants to film the perfect tornado. So when he sees one, he plants himself nearby with his cameras. That's not the safest thing to do. "The trick is knowing when to get out of there," says Casey.

With swirling winds that can top 300 miles an hour (483 kph), twisters can rip up trees, turn houses into piles of twisted wood, and toss cars around like toys. They're nature's most violent storms.

People like Casey chase tornadoes to make large-format films. But to find the storms, Casey tags along with a group of meteorologists. These weather scientists chase storms to find out why tornadoes form in some thunderstorms but not in others. The data that these meteorologists collect could make it easier to predict tornadoes.

Casey's team of filmmakers and scientists have had close calls. "We were following a storm one day and the wind pushed our 13-ton (11.8-t) radar truck backward," remembers Casey.

Volcano

No Fly Zone

Throughout April 2010, thousands of commercial flights in and out of Europe were canceled while Eyjafjallajökull erupted. Aviation authorities made the rare decision to shut down the airspace in fear that the tiny particles of rock, glass, and sand in the volcanic ash cloud could potentially jam jet engines and cause planes to crash. What resulted was the largest air traffic shutdown since World War II.

AT FIRST, the eruption of Eyjafjallajökull—one of Iceland's 22 active volcanoes—brought a burst of excitement to the country. People came from far and wide to see ash and molten rock spewing up to 30,000 feet (9,000 m) in the sky. In the midst of only its fourth eruption since the Vikings settled Iceland in the ninth century, Eyjafjallajökull (pronounced ay-uh-fyat-luh-yoe-kuutl) was truly a sight to behold—from afar, of course.

But within weeks of its first burst of ash, Eyjafjallajökull proved just how powerful volcanoes really are. Its release of hot gases and lava melted ice, forcing hundreds of people to flee rising floodwaters. The volcanic ash also caused the cancellation of many flights and disrupted air traffic across northern Europe, stranding thousands of passengers around the world (see sidebar).

Although most volcanoes don't cause so much damage, there are thousands of others just waiting to erupt like Eyjafjallajökull. In fact, scientists consider about 1,900 volcanoes on Earth to be active. Some others are dormant, which means they show no signs of erupting now but may become active in the future. Volcanoes are found on both land and sea (many islands were once volcanoes that later sprouted from the ocean), as well as throughout the solar system. The largest known volcano is Olympus Mons on Mars, standing almost three times taller than Mount Everest!

While there's nothing we can do to stop a volcano from becoming active, scientists study volcanoes to get a better estimate of when an eruption may occur. That way, they can warn people in the area to stay far away from the volcano—potentially saving thousands of lives.

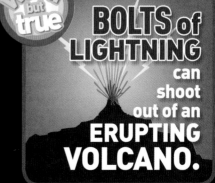

Weird but true

BOLTS of LIGHTNING can shoot out of an ERUPTING VOLCANO.

Avalanche!

A million tons (907,184 t) of snow rumble eight miles (13 km) downhill, kicking up a cloud of snow dust visible a hundred miles (161 km) away.

This is not a scene from a disaster movie—this describes reality one day in April 1981. The mountain was Mount Sanford in Alaska, and the event was one of history's biggest avalanches. Amazingly, no one was hurt, and luckily, avalanches this big are rare.

An avalanche is a moving mass of snow that may contain ice, soil, rocks, and uprooted trees. The height of a mountain, the steepness of its slope, and the type of snow lying on it all help determine the likelihood of an avalanche. Avalanches begin when an unstable mass of snow breaks away from a mountainside and moves downhill. The growing river of snow picks up speed as it rushes down the mountain. Avalanches have been known to reach speeds of 155 miles an hour (249 kph)—about the same as the record for downhill skiing.

To protect yourself and stay safe when you play in the mountains, follow our safety tips.

Safety TIPS

SAFETY FIRST
Before heading out, check for avalanche warnings.

EQUIPMENT
When hiking, carry safety equipment, including a long probe, a small shovel, and an emergency avalanche rescue beacon that signals your location.

NEVER GO IT ALONE
Don't hike in the mountain wilderness without a companion.

CAUGHT
If caught in the path of an avalanche, try to get to the side of it. If you can't, grab a tree as an anchor.

90 percent of AVALANCHE INCIDENTS are triggered by humans.

Bet you didn't know

7 *frrr*-ozen facts to keep you cool

1 The largest **frozen** smoothie on record was more than 195 gallons (738 L) — enough to fill **four bathtubs.**

2 Snowflakes get **smaller** as the temperature drops.

3 The **tallest snowman** ever built was **higher** than a **ten-story** building.

4 Small **icebergs** are called **growlers** and **bergy bits.**

5 Antarctica is a **desert,** even though it's covered mostly in **ice.**

6 There have been at least **four major ice ages** in Earth's history.

7 Nomads created **ice skates** made of **bone** at least **4,000** years ago.

SPEAK NATURALLY

Oral Reports Made Easy

Does the thought of public speaking start your stomach churning like a tornado? Would you rather get caught in an avalanche than give a speech?

Giving an oral report does not have to be a natural disaster. The basic format is very similar to a written essay. There are two main elements that make up a good oral report—the writing and the presentation. As you write your oral report, remember that your audience will be hearing the information as opposed to reading it. Follow the guidelines below, and there will be clear skies ahead.

TIP:
Remember to dress nicely on the day you give your report. Your appearance is a form of nonverbal communication and makes an impact on your audience.

Writing Your Material

Follow the steps in the "How to Write a Perfect Essay" section on p. 228, but prepare your report to be spoken rather than written.

Try to keep your sentences short and simple. Long, complex sentences are harder to follow. Limit yourself to just a few key points. You don't want to overwhelm your audience with too much information. To be most effective, hit your key points in the introduction, elaborate on them in the body, and then repeat them once again in your conclusion.

An oral report has three basic parts:

- **Introduction**—This is your chance to engage your audience and really capture their interest in the subject you are presenting. Use a funny personal experience or a dramatic story, or start with an intriguing question.

- **Body**—This is the longest part of your report. Here you elaborate on the facts and ideas you want to convey. Give information that supports your main idea and expand on it with specific examples or details. In other words, structure your oral report in the same way you would a written essay so that your thoughts are presented in a clear and organized manner.

- **Conclusion**—This is the time to summarize the information and emphasize your most important points to the audience one last time.

Preparing Your Delivery

1 Practice makes perfect.
Practice! Practice! Practice! Confidence, enthusiasm, and energy are key to delivering an effective oral report, and they can best be achieved through rehearsal. Ask family and friends to be your practice audience, and ask them for feedback when you're done. Were they able to follow your ideas? Did you seem knowledgeable and confident? Did you speak too slow or too fast, too soft or too loud? The more times you practice giving your report, the more you'll master the material. Then you won't have to rely so heavily on your notes or papers and can give your report in a relaxed and confident manner

2 Present with everything you've got.
Be as creative as you can. Incorporate videos, sound clips, slide presentations, charts, diagrams, and photos. Visual aids help stimulate your audience's senses and keep them intrigued and engaged. They can also help to reinforce your key points. And remember that when you're giving an oral report, you're a performer. Take charge of the spotlight and be as animated and entertaining as you can. Have fun with it.

COOL CLICK

Need a good subject? Go online. kidsblogs.national geographic.com/kidsnews

3 **Keep your nerves under control.**

Everyone gets a little nervous when speaking in front of a group. That's normal. But the more preparation you've done—meaning plenty of researching, organizing, and rehearsing—the more confident you'll be. Preparation is the key. And if you make a mistake or stumble over your words, just regroup and keep going. Nobody's perfect, and nobody expects you to be.

PRESENTATION CHECKLIST

 Get a good night's sleep before your presentation.

 Have a healthy meal or nutritious snack beforehand.

 When you think you're fully prepared, practice it one more time.

 Maintain eye contact with your audience throughout your report.

 Take a deep breath, relax, and have fun with it.

FUN TIP
If you're fighting nerves, try to picture your listeners in their Halloween costumes.

CONNECTING WORDS

Effective use of connecting words will make your oral report go smoothly. Connecting words help the listener understand as you transition from one idea to the next.

Here are some words you can use to make your oral report flow:

also	next
anyway	nonetheless
consequently	now that
finally	otherwise
furthermore	since
however	still
incidentally	then
instead	therefore
likewise	thus
meanwhile	until
moreover	whether
nevertheless	while

Awesome Adventure

Whitewater rafters splash through the Firth River
in Ivvavik National Park in Yukon Territory, Canada.

DARE TO EX

Do you have what it takes to be a great explorer? Read the stories of thre

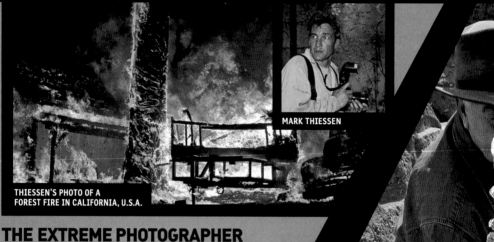

MARK THIESSEN

THIESSEN'S PHOTO OF A
FOREST FIRE IN CALIFORNIA, U.S.A.

THE EXTREME PHOTOGRAPHER

Mark Thiessen on photographing a raging wildfire sweeping across the desert in Idaho, U.S.A.:

"All of your senses just come alive when you're in the middle of photographing fire. You never know what's going to happen next. The wind is rushing and blowing sagebrush stumps right past our truck in a shower of sparks. It's night, and it can be very disorienting. To our left is a huge wall of flame that's coming in our direction. The flames start to twirl together and you get this 30-foot [9-m]-tall fire tornado. It's so fascinating, but also so dangerous. When I leave the fire, I'm exhilarated, exhausted, and I feel like I really lived."

Want to be a photographer?

STUDY: Anything— then take pictures!

WATCH: *Winged Migration*

READ: *National Geographic*

DO: Learn physical skills— climbing, hiking, skateboarding—to get you to great places to take photos.

ADVICE: "Shoot in the early morning or late afternoon

THE ARCHAEOLOGIST

Zahi Hawass on what it was like to discover Egypt's Valley of the Golden Mummies, an ancient cemetery containing thousands of mummies:

"I entered the first chamber of the tomb and saw 31 mummies, each one covered in gold. My hair went up to the ceiling and my heart began trembling as my eyes gazed at each mummy. I am able to live with the secrets of the pharaohs every day of my life. When you discover something, you are releasing magic into the world. History is dark, but through science we can bring it to life again."

Want to be an archaeologist?

STUDY: Science, geography, history

WATCH: The *Indiana Jones* movie series

READ: *The Curse of the Pharaohs: My Adventures With Mummies*, by Zahi Hawass

DO: Go to museums, and play pharaoh-inspired puzzles and games.

ADVICE: "It's not enough to just

XPLORE

...amous adventurers, and see how you can get started on the same path.

DERECK AND BEVERLY JOUBERT

B346ACY

THE JOUBERTS FILMING
A LEOPARD IN BOTSWANA

THE WILDLIFE FILMMAKERS

Dereck and Beverly Joubert are award-winning filmmakers from Botswana. Here, Beverly describes how they bonded with a young leopard while filming in Africa.

"[The leopard] had been watching us from her tree as Dereck worked on his laptop in our car. Suddenly, she left the tree, came up to the vehicle, and climbed onto [the passenger] seat. Then, amazingly, she raised a paw, put it on the keyboard of Dereck's computer, and looked him in the face. This was a very touching moment, but we knew this was inappropriate behavior for her, especially if acted out with tourists. So we gently encouraged her to leave the vehicle by turning on the heater, which produced a sound similar to the growl of disapproval a mother leopard might make."

ZAHI HAWASS
POINTS TO A
2,300-YEAR-
OLD MUMMY

Want to be a wildlife filmmaker?

STUDY: Biology and psychology to help you better understand animal behavior

WATCH: *Living With Big Cats*

READ: *Eye of the Leopard*, by Dereck and Beverly Joubert

DO: Grab your digital camcorder, head to the zoo, and film your favorite animals.

ADVICE: "You want to see (the

GOING TO
EXTREMES

Researchers hunt for life that seems out of this world.

Diving into a maze of underwater caves is all in a day's work for extremophile-hunting scientists and researchers. Extremophiles are microscopic life-forms that live in extreme environments that are too dry, too hot, too cold, too dark, or too toxic for the likes of us.

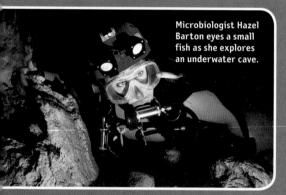

Microbiologist Hazel Barton eyes a small fish as she explores an underwater cave.

Scientists know that human beings are nature's wimps. We need a cushy environment to survive—lots of water, abundant sunshine, oxygen, and moderate temperatures. Most places on Earth—and in the rest of the solar system—just aren't like that.

SEARCHING THE DEEP

Finding extremophiles can be dangerous because of the remote places in which they live and grow. But some daring scientists are willing to take the risks because the rewards could be great.

The next important antibiotic could come from one of these organisms. Some have already helped scientists make new tests to identify people who are more likely to get certain diseases.

Heat-loving extremophiles were probably among the earliest forms of life on Earth. Scientists are even working with samples from caves to support the idea that microbes once lived under the surface of planets like Mars.

With so much to gain, scientists will keep chipping rock from cliffs, scraping scum from hot springs, and sampling the walls of deep ice caves to find extremophiles. Scientists are really going to extremes in the search for life.

Raging Danger!

On New Britain Island, part of Papua New Guinea, a white-water river vanishes into a limestone cave. Following the torrent underground, a team discovers breathtaking waterfalls and theater-size chambers. The island is home to a massive sinkhole, also called a doline. The team of 12 cavers from Britain, France, and the United States traveled to New Britain Island to descend into Ora, one of the island's largest sinkholes, and probe the cave at the bottom.

"In Ora you remain wet almost all the time," says explorer Herb Laeger. Following the riverbank underground, the team was forced to cross several times when the bank vanished. Complicated and dangerous, the crossings required one team member to swim the river and fix a line for the others.

During their two-month expedition, the team explored some 8 miles (13 km) of river caves, discovering waterfalls, lakes, and spectacular mineral formations. Exploring the damp, dark world by headlamp, expedition leader David Gill says that most of the time "you're watching where you're putting your feet."

Near the end of the expedition, the team spotted a previously unknown doline from the air, a river visible deep within it. "You cannot really get much better than this," says Gill. "It's an incredibly exotic, beautiful, untouched area."

DINOSAUR FOOTPRINTS

TRACKS TELL PREHISTORIC SECRETS

Footprints impressed on the Earth millions of years ago are changing the field of dinosaur paleontology.

"There is much to be learned from a corpse, even one that has been dead for millions of years," says Rich McCrea, a curator at the Peace Region Paleontology Research Centre in British Columbia, Canada. He is a member of a small but growing field of scientists who have dedicated themselves to the study of fossilized dinosaur tracks. "Tracks, even those millions of years old, represent the activity of animals that were living," he said.

LEARNING FROM TRACKS

Tracks are one of the closest ways a human can get to understanding dinosaurs as breathing, functioning animals. They show where and how dinosaurs walked, their posture, and gait. They show which dinosaurs roamed solo and which traveled in groups.

Coal mining sites have revealed thousands of footprints of dinosaurs. For example, McCrea spends much of his time studying tracks near the mining town of Grande Cache, Alberta, Canada. "There are only a couple of sites where there is a real diversity of tracks," says McCrea. In the few places with multiple tracks, he found traces of small, medium, and large meat-eating, two-footed theropod dinosaurs, and also of birds.

Paleontologist
Paul Sereno

TRACK HUNTING

When scientists hunt for dinosaur tracks, they look for areas where ancient layers of sedimentary rock are exposed, such as cliffs, sea coasts, quarries, open-pit mines, and along the banks of rivers and streams.

Usually, tracks are not found in the same location as bones. This is mostly because the conditions that are ideal for preserving tracks are not very good for the fossilization of bone. "It doesn't mean the bones weren't there, but after 70 million years the bones would dissolve whereas the tracks wouldn't," says Anthony Martin, an ichnologist (one who studies tracks). "We can look forward to the discovery of tracks of more groups of extinct animals."

MEET THE NAT GEO EXPLORERS

LUKE DOLLAR

A National Geographic Emerging Explorer, Dollar is a conservation scientist who has studied lemurs and a predator called the fossa in Madagascar.

How did you become an explorer?

In college, I traveled to Madagascar to study lemurs. I saw one being eaten by a carnivore that no one knew anything about—the fossa. That was the beginning.

How do you spend your time in the field?

We spend about half of it researching and the other half working with local communities. Like, in Madagascar, we're trying to convince the local park service to install more speed bumps to reduce the number of animals hit by speeding cars.

Describe one of your favorite adventures.

Going bungee jumping in the Nile River and white-water rafting down it later in the day when I was in Uganda. That was a good day.

MYSTERY
IN THE DESERT

Y ou're flying over the desert near Nasca, Peru, when you spy huge drawings in the sand below. A whale that's as long as a real blue whale, a hummingbird with a wingspan the size of a 747 jumbo jet's—these 2,000-year-old geoglyphs have been a mystery since they were discovered about 80 years ago.

Ancient Peruvian people, called the Nasca, created more than 1,500 of these drawings, from monkeys to spiders to a line that stretches for nine miles (14 km). But for the Nasca, these drawings weren't about art. They were about survival.

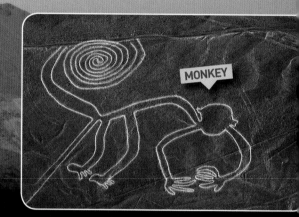

MONKEY

LINES IN THE SAND

Some archaeologists believe the Nasca created many of the geoglyphs during a drought that dried up rivers and wells. Since the Nasca likely believed that mountain and water gods controlled the rain, this would have been their way of asking the gods to send water. They drew huge creatures associated with these gods, such as hummingbirds and orcas. And they drew them so that even the gods could see them.

In the end, though, the water did not come, and the Nasca civilization ended around A.D. 650. They left no written communication, but researchers continue to read between the Nasca lines to learn more about these people. "For the Nasca, the landscape was alive," says archaeologist Johan Reinhard, a National Geographic explorer-in-residence. "It could get angry and jealous. It might send droughts to destroy the crops if someone didn't make the right offerings. They had to interact with the environment because it was a living thing."

BUILDING A NASCA LINE

How were the Nasca lines created, anyway? Scientists are pretty sure they've solved this mystery. Most of the figures are one continuous line. So working from small models, teams of 15 to 20 Nasca people would spread out from a single starting point with stakes, perhaps connected with string. They would line up the stakes, and each person would remove the dark desert rocks in his section to reveal the lighter sand underneath. They would repeat this process until a drawing was complete.

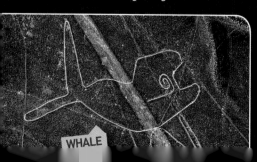

WHALE

NORTH AMERICA
ATLANTIC OCEAN
PACIFIC OCEAN
PERU
SOUTH AMERICA

Nasca lines

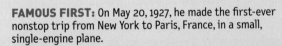

Fearless Fliers

Otto Lilienthal

FAMOUS FIRST: He successfully constructed and launched an early form of airplanes, also known as "gliders."

AWESOME AVIATION: Lilienthal built an artificial hill in Berlin, Germany, to launch some of the 18 different models of gliders he built. That way, the gliders could take off no matter which way the wind was blowing.

SCARES IN THE AIR: While on a flight in 1896, Lilienthal lost control of his glider and fell 56 feet (17 m). He died the next day. A few years later, the Wright Brothers picked up where he left off, adding a motor to a Lilienthal-inspired glider. In 1903, the Wright Brothers' "Flyer" became known as the world's first airplane to successfully take flight.

Charles Lindbergh

FAMOUS FIRST: On May 20, 1927, he made the first-ever nonstop trip from New York to Paris, France, in a small, single-engine plane.

AWESOME AVIATION: Lindbergh's cockpit didn't have a front window so he used a homemade periscope to look out the side for dangers. He also used charts, compasses, and the stars to guide his way.

SCARES IN THE AIR: For 2 hours during the 33½-hour flight, Lindbergh flew in total darkness and fell asleep with his eyes wide open!

Amelia Earhart

FAMOUS FIRST: On May 20, 1932, she became the first female pilot to make a solo flight across the Atlantic Ocean.

AWESOME AVIATION: For several hours during Earhart's cross-Atlantic trip, she flew at 12,000 feet (3,658 m), watching the sun set and the moon come up.

SCARES IN THE AIR: While crossing the ocean in 1932, a severe storm battered her plane, and then ice formed on the wings, sending Earhart into a dangerous spin. Later, flames shot out of the engine. A fuel leak dripped gas down the back of her neck—but she still managed to make land safely in Northern Ireland 15 hours after starting. In 1937, Earhart's plane disappeared mysteriously over the Pacific Ocean.

Bet you didn't know

The **FIRST** AIRPLANE JOURNEY across the United States took **49 DAYS.**

CRYSTAL

A ONCE HIDDEN CHAMBER REVEALS GIGANTIC, ICICLE-LIKE CRYSTALS.

I t looks like a mysterious alien hideaway, with crystal structures about the height of a three-story building jutting straight into the air and crisscrossing overhead. But Mexico's Cave of Crystals isn't science fiction. It's a real cave that miners discovered only ten years ago. And scientists had never seen anything like it.

SECRET WORLD

In 2000, miners looking for lead and silver beneath Mexico's Naica Mountain began pumping water out of a flooded chamber. They were shocked when they found a hidden gallery of giant icicle-like crystals beneath the watery depths almost a thousand feet (300 m) below the Earth's surface. Some of the crystals measured up to 37.4 feet (11.4 m) tall.

The Cave of Crystals is like no other cave in the world, but the massive glittering formations aren't the only things that make it unique. Most caves stay cool, around 60°F (15°C). But the Cave of Crystals rests atop what was once bubbling magma (hot, liquid rock). The leftover embers can make the mine hotter than the Sahara and wetter than a rain forest.

"It's like being in a sauna, only it's a thousand feet underground," says Juan Manuel García-Ruiz of the Spanish National Research Council in Granada, Spain. "As soon as I entered the cave I was dripping with sweat. My glasses fogged up from the humidity and I couldn't see."

The Cave of Crystals is made of a mineral called gypsum. Geologists call the cave's crystallized form of gypsum "selenite," after Selene, the Greek goddess of the moon. "They have the brightness and whiteness of moonlight," says crystal expert Juan Manuel García-Ruiz.

CAVE

How a Crystal Cave Grew

The superhot water that used to fill the cave contained molecules, or tiny particles, of chemicals. When those molecules bumped up against each other, they sometimes stuck together. Other molecules floating past glommed on as well, and a crystal would start to grow. Over half a million years, they grew gradually—the thickness of a human hair every 100 years—until they reached the size they are today.

DEATH-DEFYING SCIENTISTS

These harsh conditions are what allow the incredible crystals to grow into miniature Washington Monuments. Brave scientists put themselves in danger to study the cave, hoping to discover things such as the age of the crystals and whether tiny life-forms are living among them.

One Italian research team is developing cooling and breathing equipment to help scientists remain in the cave for long periods of time. "It's dangerous to stay too long," García-Ruiz says. "After ten minutes, I felt like I was boiling on the inside."

But to García-Ruiz and other scientists, the risk is worth the experience inside the mysterious cave. "You think you're looking at icicles, but when you touch them they're hot because it's 140°F (60°C) in there," he says. "When I first saw the cave, I was so happy that I laughed out loud like a crazy man!"

219

CHINA CONNECTION

DUDE: Marco Polo

EXPEDITION: One of the first Europeans to explore China

WHEN: Starting in 1271

Marco Polo's father and uncle ask him to travel with them from Italy to China—on horseback! The adventurous 17-year-old says yes! On his journey, Marco claims to hear "spirit voices" in the desert. But it's worth it when he reaches the huge, glittering palace of Kublai Khan, China's ruler. There he marvels at paper money, tattoos, and rhinoceroses. Marco turns his travels into a book, which later inspires another Italian with adventurous ambitions: Christopher Columbus.

WHAT'S IN IT FOR YOU: the discovery of America

**Lion wrestling.
Ice climbing.
Rat eating.**

These are just some of the extreme experiences five awesome adventurers faced while exploring Earth's uncharted, unforgiving unknown. Want to know who wore an American flag—as underwear? Explore on...if you dare!

WELCOME TO THE SUNSHINE STATE

DUDE: Ponce de León

EXPEDITION: Discovered Florida, now a U.S. state

WHEN: 1513

Wealth. Fame. The chance to be young again. That, according to legend, is what awaits the first person who dips his toes into the Fountain of Youth. But the problem is no one knows where the fabled fountain is located. Spanish explorer Ponce de León sails the Caribbean to Grand Turk Island. No fountain there. San Salvador Island, too, is fountain-free. Although Ponce never finds the fountain, he scores wealth and fame by being the first European to set foot in a land he calls Pascua Florida (Flowery Easter), or Florida to you and me.

WHAT'S IN IT FOR YOU: The discovery of the future home of Disney World

AFRICA

COOL DUDES
WHO CHANGED THE WORLD

AROUND THE WORLD IN... THREE YEARS

DUDE: Ferdinand Magellan

EXPEDITION: Led the first expedition to sail around the world

WHEN: Starting in 1519

Back then people thought the world was round, but no one had actually *proven* it by sailing all the way around the world—until Magellan. Terrible storms nearly sink the explorer's ships. Food runs so low that they eat rats. Three years later, just one of five ships returns to Spain. But it carries the first men to sail around the world.

WHAT'S IN IT FOR YOU: The knowledge that you won't ever fall off the edge of Earth

INTO AFRICA

DUDE: David Livingstone

EXPEDITION: First European to explore Central Africa extensively

WHEN: 1841 to 1873

For Scottish doctor-missionary David Livingstone, trudging through the deserts, rain forests, and mountains of unexplored Africa (and taking lots of notes) is a dream come true. He wrestles a lion and nearly loses an arm. He sees one of the world's largest waterfalls and names it Victoria, for England's queen. He searches for the source of the Nile River and drops from sight. Five years later newspaper reporter Henry Stanley tracks down Livingstone outside a grass hut and utters the famous line, "Dr. Livingstone, I presume?"

WHAT'S IN IT FOR YOU: The knowledge that you really *should* keep distance between yourself and a lion

IT'S LONELY AT THE TOP. COLD, TOO.

DUDE: Robert Peary

EXPEDITION: Led the expedition that was first to reach the geographic North Pole

WHEN: 1909

Robert Peary, his trusted partner Matthew Henson—a talented African-American explorer—and four other men are heading north. *Way* north. They scale 50-foot (15-m) cliffs of ice and endure subzero temperatures and dark fog. When they finally reach the North Pole, Peary unfurls an American flag sewn by his wife—which he's worn as a warm undergarment—and rightfully feels he's on top of the world.

WHAT'S IN IT FOR YOU: The knowledge that when exploring new territory, you should always pack a flag—it could come in handy!

NORTH POLE

TREE HIKING

Think the coolest wildlife lives on the ground? Think again— then climb a tree!

In forests all over the world, people are hiking in the treetops with help from canopy walkways, bridgelike trails made of metal or wood suspended high in the uppermost layer of the forest. Originally built for researchers studying wildlife in the treetops, tourists now pay to hike them to get a bird's-eye view of the forest. The money often helps pay for conservation efforts.

Some walkways can hang hundreds of feet in the air and stretch a quarter of a mile (400 m). The climb up can be made on steep stairs or on a gradually ascending walkway. You might see jaguars in Guyana, lemurs in Madagascar, or bald eagles in Montana.

Canopy creatures like to stay out of sight. So bring binoculars to scour the treetops. A bonus: Looking up will freak you out less than looking down!

Get Fit!

Hikers need strong legs. Try walking up and down a flight of stairs or a steep hill for five minutes without stopping. Repeat three to five times a day. For snacks on the trail, skip the candy bars and go for fresh fruit or high-energy munchies like nuts or granola.

PHILIPPINE EAGLE

MACAQUE

This hiker may see exotic animals like these in the forests of the Philippine island of Mindanao. He'll use walkways that are a hundred feet (30 m) in the air.

TOKAY GECKO

TARSIER

Bet you didn't know

A mountain climber carried the OLYMPIC TORCH to the top of Mount Everest.

Rising to an elevation of almost 11,072 feet (3.375 m), Fitz Roy Massif in southern Argentina's Patagonia region presents major challenges to adventurous climbers, who must contend with strong winds and bitter cold.

CAUGHT ON CAMERA

WHAT IS IT?
a gray whale, up close and personal

PLACE
off the coast of Mexico

I'm Annie Griffiths, and as a National Geographic photographer, I am lucky enough to go to some pretty wild places. A big part of the fun is how I get there. I have ridden elephants and camels, and traveled in helicopters, fishing boats, and hot-air balloons.

One of the most exciting adventures I have ever had was in Mexico, photographing gray whales. I was floating in a rubber raft and watching for whales. Suddenly, I felt a bump. The rubber raft actually began lifting out of the water!

A friendly whale had decided to play with us. She gently lifted our raft up out of the water, and slowly lowered us down again. She circled around us with her baby calf, so close that we could touch her nose and stroke her calf.

For more, read Annie's book *A Camera, Two Kids and a Camel: My Journey in Photographs.*

KidsDidIt!

EXPLORING PERU

Deep within a remote rain forest, a group of kids fish from a boat sitting on a lake. Suddenly, Peter Meehan feels a tug on his pole. He reels in the line and yanks the hook to the surface. Staring back at him is a piranha, bearing a mouthful of tiny, sharp teeth. "It's teeth were cruel-looking and very impressive!" recalls Peter.

Peter was one of 15 explorers on a National Geographic Kids Expedition Team who traveled to the country of Peru. The 10- to 14-year-olds and two teachers were winners of the annual National Geographic Kids Hands-On Explorer Challenge (HOEC), an essay and photo contest.

While visiting Peru's coast, highlands, and rain forest, the expedition team enjoyed surprises and discoveries around every corner. They took photos along the shore of the Pacific Ocean, presented gifts to a school high in the Andes mountains, and trekked through dense Amazonian jungle.

One of the most exciting highlights of the trip? Visiting Machu Picchu, considered one of the wonders of the world. Five hundred years ago, the Inca people built their magnificent city a mile and a half above sea level, but then abandoned it suddenly. The city was unknown to the outside world until 1911. It's now an archaeological site that the visitors had to reach by train, bus, and steep uphill hiking. "Our bus zig-zagged around 14 switch-backs up the mountain," says McKenna Tucker. "Then we climbed a path to a ledge overlooking all of Machu Picchu before heading down to explore."

And during their three-night stay in the rain forest lodge deep in the Tambopata National Reserve, the group slept in beds draped with mosquito netting, lured tarantulas from their holes, climbed a tall steel tower to the top of the forest canopy, and, yes, fished for piranhas in a lake.

"Every waking moment of this trip was an adventure," says Lijah Hanley. "We became a great team of explorers; we worked and played hard—together."

Members of a National Geographic Kids Expedition Team at Machu Picchu in Peru

Costumed Peruvian hosts greet the team.

Lijah's photo shows a piranha's impressive teeth.

A tarantula is lured from its hiding place.

HOW TO SURVIVE...

A LION ATTACK

1 CATFIGHT
Lions usually avoid confrontations with people. But if one lunges toward you, swing a tree branch, throw rocks, even gouge its eyes. Fighting back may make it slink away like the Cowardly Lion.

2 DON'T TAKE IT "LION DOWN"
Never crouch, kneel, or play dead. The lion might think you're ready to become a Kid McNugget.

3 ACT LIKE A PRO WRESTLER
Lions go after weaker prey, so show it that you rule. Scream, snarl, and bare your teeth (even if you have braces). Come on stronger than The Rock in a smackdown.

4 STRENGTH IN NUMBERS
Lions prefer to attack solitary prey, so make sure you safari with plenty of friends. Don't let the lion divide and conquer—keep your pals close by at all times.

5 SEE YA LATER
See an escape route? Don't wait for a permission slip, Einstein! Slowly back away—but never turn tail and run. You just might avoid a major "cat-astrophe."

QUICKSAND

BEWARE! QUICKSAND

1 NO MORE "SOUP-ERSTITIONS"
Quicksand isn't some bottomless pit waiting to suck you in. It's a soupy mixture of sand and water found near riverbanks, shorelines, and marshes. It's rarely more than a few feet (meters) deep, though it can be deeper.

2 GO WITH THE FLOAT
Not that you'd want to, but quicksand is actually easier to float on than water. So lean back, place your arms straight out from your sides, and let the sopping sand support your weight.

3 YOU FLAIL, YOU FAIL
Don't kick or struggle. That creates a vacuum, which only pulls you down. Ignore the gritty goop squishing into your underpants and remain calm.

4 LEG LIFTS
Conquer the quicksand with a slow stand. As you're lying back with your arms out, carefully inch one leg, then the other, to the surface.

5 ROLL OVER!
When both legs are afloat, pretend you're performing a dog trick. Keeping your face out of the muck, gently roll over the quicksand until you're on solid ground.

WILL MY TOY CAR SURVIVE A
CROC ATTACK?

My name is Brady Barr, and part of my job as a scientist is catching crocodiles. Crocs are big, fast, good at hiding, and always alert. They're not easy to catch, but I need to get hold of them to attach tracking tags and to gather data.

I talked with some creative kids who gave me a few great ideas to help me catch crocs. So on my next trip to Africa, I set off with my scientific equipment and toys (the kids' suggestion).

I'm helping wildlife biologists put tracking tags on a threatened population of Nile crocodiles. From our boat we spot a cluster of crocs. I set a remote-control car on the beach and steer it toward the basking crocs. I speed the car right up to one—chomp! The croc's teeth just miss the car, and it's not giving up! It chases the car and I work the joystick as if my life depends on it.

My little car is no match for a Nile crocodile—the croc's jaws close over my toy—and, temporarily, over my plans. The size and quick movements of the toy car must trigger a crocodile's predatory instinct. Conclusion: Use a faster car and improve my driving skills!

The kids' second idea: to disguise myself as a croc. I get into the water wearing a big rubber croc mask. My goal: Get close enough to wrestle a croc into our boat. When one giant male approaches, I raise the snout of my mask, which in "croc talk" lets him know I'm not looking for trouble. But he's angry—he arches his back and slaps the water with his chin. He thinks I'm a rival! At first I stand my ground, but as he comes closer, it gets too dangerous. I get out of the water ... fast! Conclusion: The disguise works.

Idea number three—I steer a remote-control boat, fitted with a small rubber croc head and a snare, toward the real crocs. Success! They act as if the boat's one of them and ignore it. Then, just as the boat's in position to snare one, the batteries die! Conclusion: The boat works, but next time I've got to remember more batteries!

A field test involves a lot of trial and error. What I learned this time will mean success the next time. Meanwhile, I reached my goal to be the first person to catch all 23 species of crocodilians!

18 EXTREME FEARS

PHOBIA	A FEAR OF
Anthophobia	Flowers
Coulrophobia	Clowns
Oneirophobia	Dreams
Panophobia	Everything
Osmophobia	Body odors
Arachnophobia	Spiders
Consecotaleophobia	Chopsticks
Chorophobia	Dancing
Philemaphobia	Kissing
Omphalophobia	Belly buttons
Botonophobia	Plants
Peladophobia	Bald people
Zoophobia	Animals
Dentophobia	Dentists
Herpetophobia	Reptiles and snakes
Lachanophobia	Vegetables
Scoleciphobia	Worms
Phasmophobia	Ghosts

A Near FATAL Attraction

Using Snake Venom to Save Lives

Snake venom is dangerous, complex, medically promising— and the ultimate adrenaline rush. What's not to love?

"It was the last night of a very long week," says herpetologist and molecular biologist Bryan Grieg Fry, describing the bite he suffered from one of the deadliest snakes on Earth. "Of course, it's always the last night. They never get you when you're fresh, and it was a new species, one that we hadn't caught before."

THE SNAKE WHISPERER

Fry is the director of the Australian Venom Research Unit at the University of Melbourne. In groundbreaking research on the toxins that squirt out of snake fangs, he has painted a startling new picture of the complexity of venom, and he has derived potential new drugs by studying its scary effects on human physiology, occasionally by experiencing those effects firsthand.

LOVE AT FIRST BITE

In the case of this deadly bite, he and his wife, Alexia, had flown to Weipa, Australia, to collect venom samples from a variety of sea snake (left) species, including Hardwick's sea snakes, elegant sea snakes, and rare Stokes sea snakes. Because the whole operation involved a lot of exposure to awfully dangerous animals—sea snakes are among the world's most poisonous reptiles, and their venom can cause horrible pain and a quick and ugly death—Fry had taken his standard precautions. He had contacted the head of the local emergency ward, explained what he'd be up to, and packed big syringes full of adrenaline and strong antihistamines. Then he got on with having a good time.

AMAZING SNAKES

Sea snakes have astonishing aquatic adaptations, such as valved nostrils to seal in air and lungs that can hold a breath for hours, but they do have to surface to breathe once in a while. When they do, a spotlight will catch a ripple of coils in its glare and Alexia and Fry will snatch them up.

Snake venoms are remarkable, Fry points out, for the sheer number of horrible effects that they can cause simultaneously. The venom of the seven-foot (2-m) -long Australian inland taipan (above, left and right), for example, carries more than 50 toxins, including some that abruptly lower blood pressure or destroy nerves.

It is precisely this complexity, however, that has led to Fry's most interesting discoveries. For decades it was assumed that snake venom had evolved separately in a range of snake species, based on the fact that many venomous snakes had close nonvenomous relatives. But modern research has allowed Fry to show that snake venom had a single point of biological origin, in the earliest of snakes, and that even the apparently nonvenomous snakes have active venom glands—they just lack a means for delivering it. Fry's research has raised the number of known venomous snakes from around 200 to 2,000-plus.

227

How to Write a Perfect Essay

Need to write an essay? Does the assignment feel as big as climbing Mount Everest? Fear not. You're up to the challenge! The following step-by-step tips will help you with this monumental task.

1 **BRAINSTORM.** Sometimes the subject matter of your essay is assigned to you, sometimes it's not. Either way, you have to decide what you want to say. Start by brainstorming some ideas, writing down any thoughts you have about the subject. Then read over everything you've come up with and consider which idea you think is the strongest. Ask yourself what you want to write about the most. Keep in mind the goal of your essay. (The four main types of essays are described on the next page.) Can you achieve the goal of the assignment with this topic? If so, you're good to go.

2 **WRITE A TOPIC SENTENCE.** This is the main idea of your essay, a statement of your thoughts on the subject. Again, consider the goal of your essay. Think of the topic sentence as an introduction that tells your reader what the rest of your essay will be about.

3 **OUTLINE YOUR IDEAS.** Once you have a good topic sentence, then you need to support that main idea with more detailed information, facts, thoughts, and examples. These supporting points answer one question about your topic sentence—"Why?" This is where research and perhaps more brainstorming come in. Then organize these points in the way you think makes the most sense, probably in order of importance. Now you have an outline for your essay.

4 **ON YOUR MARK, GET SET, WRITE!** Follow your outline, using each of your supporting points as the topic sentence of its own paragraph. Use descriptive words to get your ideas across to the reader. Go into detail, using specific information to tell your story or make your point. Stay on track, making sure that everything you include is somehow related to the main idea of your essay. Use transitions to make your writing flow (see p. 131 for "Write With Power").

5 **WRAP IT UP.** Finish your essay with a conclusion that summarizes your entire essay and restates your main idea.

6 **PROOFREAD AND REVISE.** Check for errors in spelling, capitalization, punctuation, and grammar. Look for ways to make your writing clear, understandable, and interesting. Use descriptive verbs, adjectives, or adverbs when possible. It also helps to have someone else read your work to point out things you might have missed. Then make the necessary corrections and changes in a second draft. Repeat this revision process once more to make your final draft as good as you can.

Types of Essays

NARRATIVE ESSAY

Purpose: A narrative essay tells a story about an event.

Example: "Caught on Camera" (p. 223)

Helpful Hints:
- Pick a topic that really interests you. Your excitement will come through in your writing.
- Tell your story with a clear beginning, middle, and end.
- Add fun or exciting details to highlight dramatic or unexpected moments.
- Use descriptive words to help give your reader a sense of what it was like to be there.

EXPOSITORY ESSAY

Purpose: An expository essay gives facts and information about a person, place, thing, or idea. Book reports, research papers, and biographies are types of expository writing.

Example: "Going to Extremes: Researchers Hunt for Life That Seems Out of This World" (p. 214)

Helpful Hints:
- Dig deep in your research to find interesting details.
- State your topic right away.
- Use transitional phrases to make your essay flow smoothly.

DESCRIPTIVE ESSAY

Purpose: A descriptive essay describes a person, place, or thing using sensory details to give the reader a better idea of what the subject is really like.

Example: "Treasures of the Tomb" (pp. 234-235)

Helpful Hints:
- Describe how the subject looks, sounds, tastes, smells, and feels.
- Use interesting comparisons.
- Be specific; find just the right adjectives and adverbs.

PERSUASIVE ESSAY

Purpose: A persuasive essay tries to convince the reader of your point of view using facts, statistics, details, and logic to make an argument.

Example: "Ocean Alert!" (p. 24)

Helpful Hints:
- State your opinion in the topic sentence.
- Use evidence to support your point of view.
- Consider the opposing views.
- Present a strong conclusion.

DON'T BE A COPYCAT

Plagiarism is presenting an idea or piece of writing as your own original work when it was actually created by someone else. It's a serious offense and will get you into trouble. Obvious examples of plagiarism include buying an essay from the Internet and handing it in as your own, or copying from a friend. Plagiarism can also occur by not citing your sources, so be careful.

In writing, you must give credit whenever you use information taken from another source. This is called citing your sources. Follow these basic guidelines to avoid plagiarism:

- **Take good notes** when researching. Keep a list of all research material you use, including details (title, author, page numbers, websites, etc.) about where you got specific pieces of information.

- **Use your own words.** Copying sentence structure but changing a few words is still plagiarism. Don't use more than three words in a row taken directly from another source.

- **Plagiarism** is not restricted to textbooks—don't copy material from the Internet, either.

- **Place quotation marks** around any phrase or sentence you take directly from another source, and cite it.

- **Double-check** your final text against your notes. Be sure that you've given credit where credit is due.

History
Happens

Egyptian pharaoh Tutankhamun's
solid gold funerary mask

GUARDIANS
OF THE TOMB

Back in 1974, some Chinese farmers were digging for water when they got a shock. Staring up from the soil was a face, eyes wide open, with features that looked almost human. But this was not a skeleton: It was one of thousands of life-size soldiers made of baked clay called terra cotta—and they had been buried for 2,200 years.

BURIED TREASURE

Row upon row of the soldiers—each face as different and as realistic as the next—were hidden in a pit the size of two football fields near Xi'an, which was China's capital city for nearly 2,000 years. Archaeologists eventually found four pits, some containing statues of horse-drawn chariots, cavalry (soldiers on horseback), and high-ranking officers.

BODY GUARDS

Who could have built this huge underground army? Experts assume it was China's first emperor, Qin Shihuangdi (chin she-hwong-dee). The brilliant but brutal ruler, who created the first unified China, was known for his big ideas and even bigger ego. It's believed that because Qin Shihuangdi had killed so many people during his reign, he may have wanted a large army to protect him from his victims' ghosts once he died. He probably had the clay soldiers created to guard his tomb, which was just one mile (1.6 km) away from where the pits were discovered.

FINAL REWARDS

As it turned out, the emperor's living enemies took revenge—not the dead ones. In 206 B.C., a few years after Qin Shihuangdi's death, invading armies destroyed the pits, burying the warriors and cracking every figure. The pits caved in more as time went on, and the soldiers were lost to the ages.

Experts have since pieced a thousand soldiers back together. But some 6,000 figures are still buried. As work continues, who knows what secrets these soldiers have yet to tell?

STATUES OF ARCHERS, LIKE THE ONE ABOVE, WERE BURIED HOLDING REAL CROSSBOWS.

ANCIENT CRAFTSMEN MADE THOUSANDS OF LIFE-SIZE TERRA COTTA WARRIORS, EACH WITH A UNIQUE FACE.

ASIA

CHINA

PACIFIC OCEAN

Terra cotta warriors

CHINA

HORSE-DRAWN CHARIOT

UNDER RECONSTRUCTION

Experts have painstakingly rebuilt and restored a thousand terra cotta warriors found in underground pits near the emperor's tomb. The complex is so vast that excavations may continue for generations.

A warrior's head poking out of the dirt still has traces of red paint. Originally all of the warriors were painted bright colors.

Workers brush dirt away from the collapsed roof that sheltered the terra cotta warriors.

A toppled terra cotta warrior lies in its 2,200-year-old underground tomb.

TREASURES OF THE TOMB

Discovering King Tut's INCREDIBLE RICHES

It's pitch-black. His hands trembling, British archaeologist Howard Carter makes a small hole in the tomb's second door. He inserts a candle. Next to him, British millionaire Lord Carnarvon blurts out, "Can you see anything?" After a moment of stunned silence, Carter replies, "Yes, wonderful things."

What Carter sees looks like the inside of a giant treasure chest. Gold gleams everywhere! There are glittering statues, a throne, and fabulous golden beds with posts shaped like the heads of wild animals. Precious items are heaped all over the room.

It's 1922. It has taken years of digging in the Valley of the Kings—a graveyard for ancient Egypt's richest kings—and $500,000 (in today's money) of Lord Carnarvon's cash, but Carter hit the jackpot. He discovered the tomb of Tutankhamun (Tut, for short), who became pharaoh at age nine and died ten years later around 1323 B.C.

HIDDEN TREASURES

Carter, Lord Carnarvon, and two others enter the cluttered first room, which they call the antechamber. Under a bed with posts in the shape of hippopotamus heads, Lord Carnarvon finds the entrance to another room. Soon known as the annex, this tiny chamber holds more than 2,000 everyday objects. They include boomerangs, shields, a box

The Truth About Tut

For centuries, experts suspected King Tut died in a dramatic fashion, either by a blow to the head or by poisoning. But now, studies reveal that he may have been plagued by poor health. Taking DNA from bones found in Tut's tomb, scientists conducted genetic tests. They also took CT scans. The results showed that Tut likely had malaria, a broken leg, and a bone disorder that caused a club foot—all of which may have led to his death at just 19 years old. And that staff seen in so many images of Tut? It was probably a cane to help the frail pharaoh walk.

Ceremonial instruments of royal authority

Collar on Tut's mummy

Buckle showing King Tut and his queen

Fan

Tut's gold sandals

Hippo's head bedpost

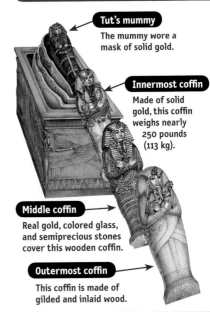

Tut's mummy
The mummy wore a mask of solid gold.

Innermost coffin
Made of solid gold, this coffin weighs nearly 250 pounds (113 kg).

Middle coffin
Real gold, colored glass, and semiprecious stones cover this wooden coffin.

Outermost coffin
This coffin is made of gilded and inlaid wood.

containing eye makeup, and 116 baskets of food. When Carter clears the annex out later, his workers need to be suspended by ropes to keep from stepping on things.

ANCIENT ROBBERS

The disorder in the annex indicates ancient grave robbers had looted the tomb. They left behind footprints and gold rings wrapped in cloth. Luckily, they'd been caught and the tomb resealed. That was more than 3,000 years ago.

The explorers are fascinated by two tall statues in the antechamber showing Tut dressed in gold. The figures seem to be guarding another room. Sweltering in the heat, the group crawls through a hole created by the ancient robbers.

AMAZING DISCOVERY

Before them stands a huge wooden box, or shrine, that glitters with a layer of gold. This room must be Tut's burial chamber! At the very center of the shrine is a carved sarcophagus, or coffin. Inside it are three nested coffins, each one more richly decorated than the one before. Inside the last, made of solid gold, lies the mummy of Tutankhamun. A 22-pound (10-kg) gold mask (above left) covers its head and shoulders. A collar made from 171 separate gold pieces rests on the mummy's chest, and gold sandals are on its feet.

On one side of the burial chamber is a doorway revealing the fourth room of the tomb— the treasury. Towering over the other objects is a gold-covered shrine guarded by goddesses. It holds Tut's liver, lungs, stomach, and intestines. Each vital organ is preserved, wrapped in linen, and placed in its very own small coffin.

Today, millions of people visit Cairo's Egyptian Museum each year to see Tut's treasures. The ancient Egyptians believed that "to speak the name of the dead is to make them live again." If that is true, Tutankhamun certainly lives on.

Tut's Extreme Makeover

Experts recreated the young king's face using skull measurements from digital images of the mummy. What can't the technology tell us? The color of Tut's eyes and skin, and the shape of his nose

Bet you didn't know

8 incredible facts about the ancient world

1 Australian Aborigines—the world's **oldest living culture**—have existed for at least **50,000** years!

2 The ancient **Aztecs** used cacao (cocoa) beans as **money.**

3 A red **flag** was a **signal** for **battle** in **ancient Rome.**

4 Ancient Egyptians took up to **70 days** to make a **mummy.**

5 **Dice** made of **BONE** were found in the **tombs** of ancient **Egypt.**

6 The Roman emperor **CALIGULA** wanted to make his horse a **senator,** according to **ancient sources.**

7 The ancient **Maya chewed gum** made from **tree sap.**

8 **Earth** is the only planet not named after a **Greek or Roman god.**

ancient Aboriginal art

THE ROMAN EMPIRE

North Sea

ATLANTIC OCEAN

E U R O P E

Rhine

Danube

Black Sea

Caspian Sea

Rome

Mediterranean Sea

Tigris

Euphrates

A S I A

A F R I C A

Arabia

Nile

Red Sea

0   500 miles
0   500 kilometers

MAP KEY
Roman Empire in A.D. 117

THE ANCIENT ROMANS FIRST CONQUERED the whole of Italy and then a vast empire. At its greatest extent, in A.D. 117, the Roman Empire covered some 2.3 million square miles (6 million sq km)—that's roughly two-thirds the size of the United States—and had an estimated population of 120 million. These people were ruled by emperors, the most famous of which was Julius Caesar.

The Roman Empire had an efficient government and a highly organized military. Its people made significant advances in technology and architecture. The empire helped lay the foundations for modern Western civilization.

Daily Life in Tudor England

The Tudor period, from 1485 to 1603 (118 years), saw the reign of five powerful monarchs.

Some of these colorful monarchs were kind; others were tyrannical. From the first Tudor monarch, Henry VII, to the last queen of the period, Elizabeth I, Tudor times were both romantic and turbulent.

The Tudor period was a time of frilly fashions, Shakespeare, and heroic explorers. But it wasn't all great feasts and beautiful music. For most, living in Tudor England was hard—to say the least.

There were four main social classes, or groups of people organized by power and status. Nobility, including dukes, barons, and the royal family, made up the smallest and richest class. Just below them was the gentry—wealthy landowners who lived in mansions with tons of servants—and knights. The next class consisted of professionals, such as merchants and lawyers. The largest and lowest class included farmhands, servants, and people living in poverty.

Cities were smaller than they are now, more like today's big towns, and most people lived in the countryside. There were no sewers, so sewage and polluted water ran right down the streets. Rats and other pests were everywhere. The lack of sanitation led to many outbreaks of plague and smallpox, and the lack of medical knowledge meant that many people faced illness and death.

Be very happy you didn't live in Tudor England, where having a bath was a rarity!

Bet you didn't know

Ancient EGYPTIANS mummified their pet DOGS, CATS, and MONKEYS.

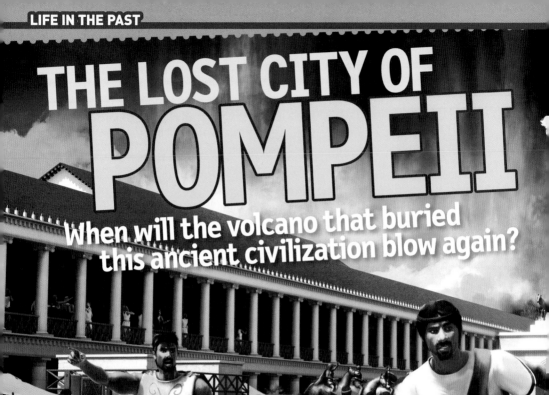

THE LOST CITY OF POMPEII

When will the volcano that buried this ancient civilization blow again?

A deafening boom roars through Pompeii's crowded marketplace. The ground shakes violently, throwing the midday shoppers off balance and toppling stands of fish and meat. People start screaming and pointing toward Mount Vesuvius, a massive volcano that rises above the bustling city, located in what is now southern Italy.

Vesuvius has been silent for nearly 2,000 years, but it roars back to life, shooting ash and smoke into the air. Almost overnight, the city and most of its residents have vanished under a blanket of ash and lava.

Now, almost 2,000 years later, scientists agree that Vesuvius is overdue for another major eruption—but no one knows when it will happen. Three million people live in the volcano's shadow, in the modern-day city of Naples, Italy. Correctly predicting when the eruption will take place will mean the difference between life and death for many.

THE SKY IS FALLING

Thanks to excavations that started in 1748 and continue to this day, scientists have been able to re-create almost exactly what happened in Pompeii on that terrible day.

"The thick ash turned everything black," says Pompeii expert Andrew Wallace-Hadrill.

"People couldn't see the sun. All the landmarks disappeared. They didn't have the foggiest idea which way they were going."

Some people ran for their lives, clutching their valuable coins and jewelry. Other people took shelter in their homes. But the debris kept falling. Piles grew as deep as nine feet (2.7 m) in some places, blocking doorways and caving in roofs.

Around midnight, the first of four searing-hot clouds, or surges, of ash, pumice, rock, and toxic gas rushed down the mountainside. Traveling toward Pompeii at up to 180 miles (290 km) an hour, it scorched everything in its path. Around 7 a.m., 18 hours after the

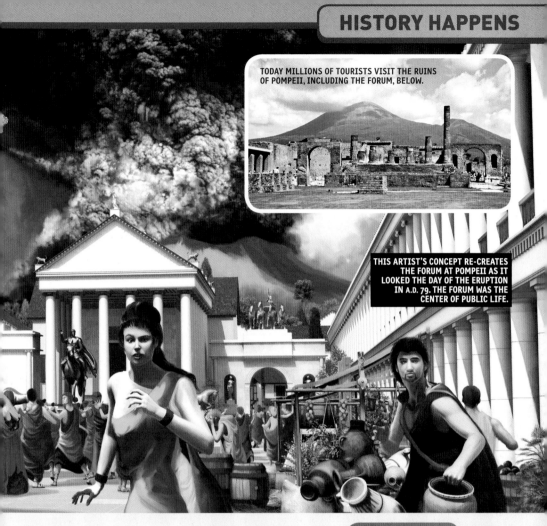

TODAY MILLIONS OF TOURISTS VISIT THE RUINS OF POMPEII, INCLUDING THE FORUM, BELOW.

THIS ARTIST'S CONCEPT RE-CREATES THE FORUM AT POMPEII AS IT LOOKED THE DAY OF THE ERUPTION IN A.D. 79. THE FORUM WAS THE CENTER OF PUBLIC LIFE.

eruption, the last fiery surge buried the city.

LOST AND FOUND

Visiting the ruins of Pompeii today is like going back in time. The layers of ash actually helped preserve buildings, artwork, and even the forms of bodies. "It gives you the feeling you can reach out and touch the ancient world," Wallace-Hadrill says.

There are kitchens with pots on the stove and bakeries with loaves of bread—now turned to charcoal—still in the ovens. Narrow corridors lead to magnificent mansions with elaborate gardens and fountains. Mosaics, or designs made out of tiles, decorate the walls and floors.

WARNING SIGNS

Pompeii's destruction may be ancient history, but there's little doubt that disaster will strike again. Luckily people living near Vesuvius today will likely receive evacuation warnings before the volcano blows.

Scientists are closely monitoring Vesuvius for shifts in the ground, earthquakes, and rising levels of certain gases, which could be signs of an upcoming eruption. The Italian government is also working on a plan to help people flee the area in an emergency.

CREEPY CASTS

Volcanic ash settled around many of the victims at the moment of death. When the bodies decayed, holes remained inside the solid ash. Scientists poured plaster into the holes to preserve the shapes of the victims.

239

7 Cool Things About the TOWER OF LONDON

As a palace, the Tower of London was a great place to live. As a prison, it wasn't so nice—especially since so many prisoners lost their heads! The place has been a lot of things in its nearly 1,000-year history. Today tourists can explore the Tower, in England, in the United Kingdom. Here are seven reasons why the Tower was—and still is— a cool place to be (as long as you weren't a prisoner, that is).

1

Ravens are like local superheroes. Well, sort of. Legend says if the ravens that live on the Tower grounds ever leave, the Tower will crumble and a disaster will befall England. No one knows when the ravens first showed up, but Charles II took the legend so seriously that in the 1670s he decreed that six ravens be kept there all the time. Today there are still always six— plus a couple of spares, just in case.

2

If you lived at the Tower today, your mom or dad might be in charge. The 35 Yeoman Warders and their families are among the few still allowed to live at the Tower. Established in 1509 as bodyguards for the king, today they give tours and manage the day-to-day details of the Tower. They're called "beefeaters," possibly because their job once allowed them to eat beef from the king's table.

3

You need a secret password at night. Called the "Word," the password changes every 24 hours and is a must-have to enter the Tower after hours. It's written on a piece of paper and delivered to the Yeoman on duty for the night.

4

You might see a ghost. Queen Anne Boleyn, who was executed on orders from her husband, King Henry VIII, is said to wander the grounds without her head. One building is believed to be so haunted that dogs refuse to enter.

5 You'd have lots of bling. England's **crown jewels** are still guarded in the Tower's **Jewel House,** a dazzling display of crowns, **robes,** jewelry, and scepters that dates back hundreds of years. More than **23,500 diamonds,** sapphires, rubies, and other gems adorn the **royal collection.**

6 You'd never have to worry about a prison break. The Tower was so secure only a few **escape attempts** succeeded. In 1716, one man sneaked out dressed in **women's clothing.** In 1100, a prisoner threw such a wild **party** for the guards they didn't notice him climbing over the wall to meet a waiting **boat!**

7 You could find buried gold. In 1662, a **gold-smith** named John Barkstead supposedly hid more than **$40,000** worth of stolen **gold** somewhere on Tower grounds. Many have searched for the **loot,** but it has never been found.

WAR!

Since the beginning of time, different countries, territories, and cultures have fueded with each other over land, power, and politics. Major military conflicts include the following wars:

1095–1291 THE CRUSADES
Starting late in the 11th century, these wars over religion in the Middle East were fought for nearly 200 years.

1337–1453 HUNDRED YEARS' WAR
France and England battled over rights to land for more than a century before the French eventually drove the English out in 1453.

1754–1763 FRENCH AND INDIAN WAR (part of Europe's Seven Years' War)
A nine-year war between the British and French for control of North America.

1775–1783 AMERICAN REVOLUTION
Thirteen British colonies in America united to reject the rule of the British government and form the United States of America.

1861–65 AMERICAN CIVIL WAR
Occurred when the northern states (the Union) went to war with the southern states, which had seceded, or withdrew, to form the Confederate States of America. Slavery was one of the key issues in the Civil War.

1910–1920 MEXICAN REVOLUTION
The people of Mexico revolted against the rule of dictator President Porfirio Diaz, leading to his eventual defeat and to a democratic government.

1914–18 WORLD WAR I
The assassination of Austria's Archduke Ferdinand by a Serbian nationalist sparked this wide-spreading war. The U.S. entered after Germany sunk the British ship *Lusitania*, killing more than 120 Americans.

1918–1920 RUSSIAN CIVIL WAR
A conflict pitting the Communist Red Army against the foreign-backed White Army. The Red Army won after four hostile years, leading to the establishment of the Union of Soviet Socialist Republics (U.S.S.R.) in 1922.

1936–39 SPANISH CIVIL WAR
Aid from Italy and Germany helped the Nationalists gain victory over the Communist-supported Republicans. The war resulted in the loss of more than 300,000 lives and increased tension in Europe leading up to World War II.

1939–1945 WORLD WAR II
This massive conflict in Europe, Asia, and North Africa involved many countries that aligned with the two sides: the Allies and the Axis. After the bombing of Pearl Harbor in Hawaii in 1941, the U.S. entered the war on the side of the Allies. More than 50 million people died during the war.

1946–49 CHINESE CIVIL WAR
Also known as the "War of Liberation," this pitted the Communist and Nationalist parties in China against each other. The Communists won.

1950–53 KOREAN WAR
Kicked off when the Communist forces of North Korea, with backing from the Soviet Union, invaded their democratic neighbor to the south. A coalition of 16 countries from the United Nations stepped in to support South Korea.

Peace!

Though there have been many times of war in our world, there have been even more times of peace. And the task of keeping once warring countries conflict-free is shared by everyone from individuals to countries to international organizations like the United Nations, which work to aid war-torn areas and make them a safe place to live. Here's a look at some major peacekeeping and humanitarian moments in history.

1950s–1975 VIETNAM WAR
Fought between the Communist North, supported by its allies including China, and the government of South Vietnam, supported by the United States and other anticommunist nations.

1967 SIX-DAY WAR
A battle for land between Israel and the neighboring states of Egypt, Jordan, and Syria. The outcome resulted in Israel's gaining control of coveted territory, including the Gaza Strip and the West Bank.

1990–91 PERSIAN GULF WAR
When Iraq invaded the country of Kuwait over oil conflicts, a coalition of 32 nations stepped in to destroy Iraq's forces.

**1991–PRESENT
SOMALI CIVIL WAR**
Began when Somalia's last president, a dictator named Mohamed Siad Barre, was overthrown. The war has led to years of fighting and anarchy.

**2001–PRESENT
WAR IN AFGHANISTAN**
After attacks in the United States by the terrorist group al-Qaeda, a coalition of more than 40 countries invaded Afghanistan to find Osama bin Laden and other al-Qaeda members.

2003–2010 WAR IN IRAQ
A coalition led by the U.S., and including Britain, Australia, and Spain, invaded Iraq over suspicions that Iraq had weapons of mass destruction.

c. 1274 B.C.: The **HITTITE-EGYPT TREATY** is signed between the Hittite and Egyptian empires after the Battle of Kadesh, establishing one of the world's earliest peace agreements.

1648: Signed in Europe, the **PEACE OF WESTPHALIA,** a series of peace treaties, ends the Thirty Years' War in the Holy Roman Empire and the Eighty Years' War between Spain and the Dutch Republic.

1901: The first **NOBEL PEACE PRIZE** is awarded to Frederic Passy, a French economist, and Swiss businessman Jean Henri Dunant. Future laureates will include Mother Teresa and the Dalai Lama.

1920: The **LEAGUE OF NATIONS,** an international organization to "promote international cooperation and to achieve peace and security," is formed following World War I. It eventually dissolves in 1946.

1945: The **UNITED NATIONS (UN)** is formed shortly after the end of World War II. Its mission is to enhance peace and security around the world.

1948: The first **UN PEACEKEEPING MISSION** is established with the deployment of troops to the Middle East to monitor the cease-fire between Israel and its Arab neighbors.

2008: Palau is the 156th country to become a party to the **MINE BAN TREATY.** The treaty calls for nations to stop producing land mines and destroy all their stockpiles within a four-year period.

The Constitution & Bill of Rights

The United States Constitution was written in 1787 by a group of political leaders from the 13 states that made up the U.S. at the time. Thirty-nine men, including Benjamin Franklin and James Madison, signed the document to create a national government. While some feared the creation of a strong federal government, all 13 states eventually ratified, or approved, the Constitution, making it the law of the land. The Constitution has three major parts: the preamble, the articles, and the amendments.

The preamble outlines the basic purposes of the government:

We the People of the United States, in order to form a more perfect Union, establish justice, insure domestic tranquility, provide for the common defense, promote the general welfare, and secure the blessings of liberty to ourselves and our posterity, do ordain and establish this Constitution for the United States of America.

Seven articles outline the powers of Congress, the President, and the court system:

Article I outlines the legislative branch—the Senate and the House of Representatives—and its powers and responsibilities.

Article II outlines the executive branch—the Presidency—and its powers and responsibilities.

Article III outlines the judicial branch—the court system—and its powers and responsibilities.

Article IV describes the individual states' rights and powers.

Article V outlines the amendment process.

Article VI establishes the Constitution as the law of the land.

Article VII gives the requirements for the Constitution to be approved.

The amendments, or additions to the Constitution, were put in later as needed. In 1791, the first ten amendments, known as the Bill of Rights, were added. Since then another 17 amendments have been added. This is the Bill of Rights:

1st Amendment: guarantees freedom of religion, speech, the press, and the right to assemble and petition

2nd Amendment: discusses the militia and the right of people to bear arms

3rd Amendment: prohibits the military or troops from using private homes without consent

4th Amendment: protects people and their homes from search, arrest, or seizure without probable cause or a warrant

5th Amendment: grants people the right to have a trial and prevents punishment before prosecution; protects private property from being taken without compensation

6th Amendment: guarantees the right to a speedy and public trial

7th Amendment: guarantees a trial by jury in certain cases

8th Amendment: forbids "cruel and unusual punishments"

9th Amendment: states that the Constitution is not all-encompassing and does not deny people other rights, as well

10th Amendment: grants the powers not covered by the Constitution to the states and the people

HIDDEN TREASURE

THE TREASURE: DECLARATION OF INDEPENDENCE

FOUND: IN A FOUR-DOLLAR PICTURE FRAME

NOW WORTH: $8.14 MILLION

The painting was ugly and torn, but its frame seemed worth paying four dollars for. When the buyer took home his flea market find, he found a copy of the Declaration of Independence behind the painting! Convinced it must be a fake, the buyer took the document to experts at Sotheby's auction house. Not only was it real, it also had real value: It sold for $8.14 million!

The **UNITED STATES GOVERNMENT** is divided into three branches: **executive, legislative** (see p. 246), and **judicial** (see p. 246). The system of checks and balances is a way to control power and to make sure one branch can't take the reins of government. For example, most of the President's actions require the approval of Congress. Likewise, the laws passed in Congress must be signed by the President before they can take effect. This system prevents one area of government from becoming so powerful as to overly influence the business of the nation.

White House

Executive Branch

The Constitution lists the central powers of the President: to serve as Commander in Chief of the armed forces; make treaties with other nations; grant pardons; inform Congress on the state of the union; and appoint ambassadors, officials, and judges. The executive branch includes the President and the governmental departments. Originally there were three departments—State, War, and Treasury. Today there are 15 departments (see chart below).

The White House used to be called the President's Palace, President's House, and the Executive Mansion. Theodore Roosevelt officially named it the White House in 1901.

Government of the United States

THE CONSTITUTION

LEGISLATIVE BRANCH	EXECUTIVE BRANCH	JUDICIAL BRANCH
CONGRESS	**President**	**U.S. Supreme Court**
Senate	**Vice President**	**U.S. courts of appeals**
House of Representatives		**U.S. district courts**

Department of Agriculture	Department of Commerce	Department of Defense	Department of Education	Department of Energy
Department of State	Department of the Treasury	Department of Justice	Department of Labor	Department of the Interior
Department of Veterans Affairs	Department of Transportation	Department of Housing and Urban Development	Department of Health and Human Services	Department of Homeland Security

Legislative Branch

This branch is made up of Congress—the Senate and the House of Representatives. The Constitution grants Congress the power to make laws. Congress is made up of elected representatives from each state. Each state has two representatives in the Senate, while the number of representatives in the House is determined by the size of the state's population. Washington, D.C., and the territories elect nonvoting representatives to the House of Representatives. The Founding Fathers set up this system as a compromise between big states—which wanted representation based on population—and small states—which wanted all states to have equal representation rights.

The U.S. Capitol in Washington, D.C.

Judicial Branch

The judicial branch is composed of the federal court system—the U.S. Supreme Court, the courts of appeals, and the district courts. The Supreme Court is the most powerful court. Its motto is "Equal Justice Under Law." This influential court is responsible for interpreting the Constitution and applying it to the cases that it hears. The decisions of the Supreme Court are absolute—they are the final word on any legal question.

The U.S. Supreme Court Building in Washington, D.C.

There are nine justices on the Supreme Court. They are appointed by the President of the United States and confirmed by the Senate.

Bet you didn't know

It's Against the Law to:

DYE OR COLOR the feathers and fur of baby chicks, ducklings, and rabbits in Kentucky.	LET A DONKEY SLEEP in a bathtub in Brooklyn, New York.
RIDE A SLED that's pulled by a car in Portland, Oregon.	THROW BANANA PEELS on the sidewalks of Mobile, Alabama.
DISTURB A BULLFROG in Hayden, Arizona.	HOOT LOUDLY after 11 p.m. on weekdays in Athens, Georgia.
RIDE A BIKE with your hands off the handlebars in Sun Prairie, Wisconsin.	RIDE A HORSE faster than ten miles an hour (16 kph) in the streets of Indianapolis, Indiana.
STEP OUT OF A PLANE while it's in the air in Maine.	GO TO COLLEGE in Winston-Salem, North Carolina, if you're under the age of seven.

U.S. Political Parties

Some of the Founding Fathers hoped that members of the new United States government would work together in harmony without dividing into opposing groups called parties. Yet, soon after George Washington became President, political parties began to form. Leaders partnered with others who shared their geographic background, foreign policy beliefs, or ideas for governing.

A LONG HISTORY

Today's leaders are primarily members of the Democratic and Republican parties. Each group can trace its origins to the 19th century.

Republican elephant mascot

The Democratic Party evolved from the early groups that opposed a strong federal government. Leaders such as Thomas Jefferson shaped these lawmakers into a collection of politicians known variously as the Democratic-Republicans, the National Republicans, and, eventually, the Democrats.

The modern Republican Party was formed during the 1850s to combat the spread of slavery. Its first successful presidential candidate was Abraham Lincoln. It is sometimes referred to as the Grand Old Party (GOP).

THE TWO-PARTY SYSTEM

Today, as then, the party with the largest number of elected members in the U.S. House of Representatives and the U.S. Senate holds a majority of influence over those chambers. Occasionally the same party will control both chambers of Congress and the Presidency. With that much political power, it can significantly influence the nature of government. Usually each party will control only one or two of these three areas. In that case, political parties have to compromise and cooperate with one another in order to enact new laws.

Democratic donkey mascot

SHIFTING THE VOTE

Often the presidential ballot will include candidates from third parties, those groups that exist beyond the two major parties. Occasionally a candidate has run for office as an independent— that is, without the support of a political party. No independent or third-party candidate has ever made it to the White House. Even so, these candidates may influence an election by dividing the support of voters or by directing attention to a particular issue or cause. In recent decades, third-party and independent candidates have frequently drawn support away from Republican and Democratic candidates in ways that helped secure a victory for the opposing major party.

SUCCESSION

If the President of the United States becomes incapacitated, dies, resigns, or is removed from office, there is an order of succession to determine who takes over as President. This order, specified by the Presidential Succession Act of 1947 and later amendments, is as follows:

1. Vice President
2. Speaker of the House of Representatives
3. President pro tempore of the Senate (highest-ranking senator)
4. Secretary of State
5. Secretary of the Treasury
6. Secretary of Defense
7. Attorney General
8. Secretary of the Interior
9. Secretary of Agriculture
10. Secretary of Commerce
11. Secretary of Labor
12. Secretary of Health and Human Services
13. Secretary of Housing and Urban Development
14. Secretary of Transportation
15. Secretary of Energy
16. Secretary of Education
17. Secretary of Veterans Affairs
18. Secretary of Homeland Security

UNITED STATES PRESIDENTS

The President of the United States is the chief of the executive branch, the Commander in Chief of the U.S. armed forces, and head of the federal government. Elected every four years, the President is the highest policy-maker in the nation. The 22nd Amendment (1951) says that no person may be elected to the office of President more than twice. There have been 44 Presidencies and 43 Presidents.

JAMES MONROE
5th President of the United States ★ 1817–1825
BORN April 28, 1758, in Westmoreland County, VA
POLITICAL PARTY Democratic-Republican
NO. OF TERMS two
VICE PRESIDENT Daniel D. Tompkins
DIED July 4, 1831, in New York, NY

GEORGE WASHINGTON
1st President of the United States ★ 1789–1797
BORN Feb. 22, 1732, in Pope's Creek, Westmoreland County, VA
POLITICAL PARTY Federalist
NO. OF TERMS two
VICE PRESIDENT John Adams
DIED Dec. 14, 1799, at Mount Vernon, VA

JOHN QUINCY ADAMS
6th President of the United States ★ 1825–1829
BORN July 11, 1767, in Braintree (now Quincy), MA
POLITICAL PARTY Democratic-Republican
NO. OF TERMS one
VICE PRESIDENT John Caldwell Calhoun
DIED Feb. 23, 1848, at the U.S. Capitol, Washington, D.C.

JOHN ADAMS
2nd President of the United States ★ 1797–1801
BORN Oct. 30, 1735, in Braintree (now Quincy), MA
POLITICAL PARTY Federalist
NO. OF TERMS one
VICE PRESIDENT Thomas Jefferson
DIED July 4, 1826, in Quincy, MA

ANDREW JACKSON
7th President of the United States ★ 1829–1837
BORN March 15, 1767, in the Waxhaw region, NC and SC
POLITICAL PARTY Democrat
NO. OF TERMS two
VICE PRESIDENTS 1st term: John Caldwell Calhoun
2nd term: Martin Van Buren
DIED June 8, 1845, in Nashville, TN

THOMAS JEFFERSON
3rd President of the United States ★ 1801–1809
BORN April 13, 1743, at Shadwell, Goochland (now Albemarle) County, VA
POLITICAL PARTY Democratic-Republican
NO. OF TERMS two
VICE PRESIDENTS 1st term: Aaron Burr
2nd term: George Clinton
DIED July 4, 1826, at Monticello, Charlottesville, VA

MARTIN VAN BUREN
8th President of the United States ★ 1837–1841
BORN Dec. 5, 1782, in Kinderhook, NY
POLITICAL PARTY Democrat
NO. OF TERMS one
VICE PRESIDENT Richard M. Johnson
DIED July 24, 1862, in Kinderhook, NY

JAMES MADISON
4th President of the United States ★ 1809–1817
BORN March 16, 1751, at Belle Grove, Port Conway, VA
POLITICAL PARTY Democratic-Republican
NO. OF TERMS two
VICE PRESIDENTS 1st term: George Clinton
2nd term: Elbridge Gerry
DIED June 28, 1836, at Montpelier, Orange County, VA

WILLIAM HENRY HARRISON
9th President of the United States ★ 1841
BORN Feb. 9, 1773, in Charles City County, VA
POLITICAL PARTY Whig
NO. OF TERMS one (cut short by death)
VICE PRESIDENT John Tyler
DIED April 4, 1841, in the White House, Washington, D.C.

JOHN TYLER

10th President of the United States ★ *1841–1845*
BORN March 29, 1790, in Charles City
County, VA
POLITICAL PARTY Whig
NO. OF TERMS one (partial)
VICE PRESIDENT none
DIED Jan. 18, 1862, in Richmond, VA

JAMES BUCHANAN

15th President of the United States ★ *1857–1861*
BORN April 23, 1791, in Cove Gap, PA
POLITICAL PARTY Democrat
NO. OF TERMS one
VICE PRESIDENT John Cabell Breckinridge
DIED June 1, 1868, in Lancaster, PA

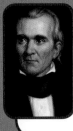

JAMES K. POLK

11th President of the United States ★ *1845–1849*
BORN Nov. 2, 1795, near Pineville,
Mecklenburg County, NC
POLITICAL PARTY Democrat
NO. OF TERMS one
VICE PRESIDENT George Mifflin Dallas
DIED June 15, 1849, at Nashville, TN

ABRAHAM LINCOLN

16th President of the United States ★ *1861–1865*
BORN Feb. 12, 1809,
near Hodgenville, KY
POLITICAL PARTY Republican (formerly Whig)
NO. OF TERMS two (assassinated)
VICE PRESIDENTS 1st term: Hannibal Hamlin
2nd term:
Andrew Johnson
DIED April 15, 1865, in Washington, D.C.

ZACHARY TAYLOR

12th President of the United States ★ *1849–1850*
BORN Nov. 24, 1784,
in Orange County, VA
POLITICAL PARTY Whig
NO. OF TERMS one (cut short by death)
VICE PRESIDENT Millard Fillmore
DIED July 9, 1850, in the White House,
Washington, D.C.

ANDREW JOHNSON

17th President of the United States ★ *1865–1869*
BORN Dec. 29, 1808, in Raleigh, NC
POLITICAL PARTY Democrat
NO. OF TERMS one (partial)
VICE PRESIDENT none
DIED July 31, 1875, in Carter's
Station, TN

MILLARD FILLMORE

13th President of the United States ★ *1850–1853*
BORN Jan. 7, 1800,
in Cayuga County, NY
POLITICAL PARTY Whig
NO. OF TERMS one (partial)
VICE PRESIDENT none
DIED March 8, 1874, in Buffalo, NY

Presidential Fitness Test

OUR COUNTRY'S PRESIDENTS have been
a sporty crew! Here's how some of them
have elected to stay fit:

★ **Barack Obama** shoots hoops on the
White House basketball courts.

★ **Richard Nixon** installed a one-lane
bowling alley underneath the driveway.

★ **Bill Clinton** ran laps around a quarter-
mile jogging track built just for him.

★ Golf-obsessed **Dwight D. Eisenhower**
hit the links.

★ **John Quincy Adams** was said to skinny-
dip in the Potomac River.

★ **FAILING MARKS: William Howard Taft**,
at more than 300 pounds, was the
heaviest President in history.

FRANKLIN PIERCE

14th President of the United States ★ *1853–1857*
BORN Nov. 23, 1804, in Hillsborough
(now Hillsboro), NH
POLITICAL PARTY Democrat
NO. OF TERMS one
VICE PRESIDENT William Rufus De Vane King
DIED Oct. 8, 1869, in Concord, NH

ULYSSES S. GRANT

18th President of the United States ★ 1869–1877

BORN April 27, 1822,
in Point Pleasant, OH

POLITICAL PARTY Republican

NO. OF TERMS two

VICE PRESIDENTS 1st term: Schuyler Colfax
2nd term: Henry Wilson

DIED July 23, 1885, in Mount McGregor, NY

RUTHERFORD B. HAYES

19th President of the United States ★ 1877–1881

BORN Oct. 4, 1822,
in Delaware, OH

POLITICAL PARTY Republican

NO. OF TERMS one

VICE PRESIDENT William Almon Wheeler

DIED Jan. 17, 1893, in Fremont, OH

JAMES A. GARFIELD

20th President of the United States ★ 1881

BORN Nov. 19, 1831, near Orange, OH

POLITICAL PARTY Republican

NO. OF TERMS one (assassinated)

VICE PRESIDENT Chester A. Arthur

DIED Sept. 19, 1881, in Elberon, NJ

CHESTER A. ARTHUR

21st President of the United States ★ 1881–1885

BORN Oct. 5, 1829, in Fairfield, VT

POLITICAL PARTY Republican

NO. OF TERMS one (partial)

VICE PRESIDENT none

DIED Nov. 18, 1886, in New York, NY

GROVER CLEVELAND

*22nd and 24th President of the United States
1885–1889 ★ 1893–1897*

BORN March 18, 1837, in Caldwell, NJ

POLITICAL PARTY Democrat

NO. OF TERMS two (nonconsecutive)

VICE PRESIDENTS 1st administration:
Thomas Andrews Hendricks
2nd administration:
Adlai Ewing Stevenson

DIED June 24, 1908, in Princeton, NJ

BENJAMIN HARRISON

23rd President of the United States ★ 1889–1893

BORN Aug. 20, 1833,
in North Bend, OH

POLITICAL PARTY Republican

NO. OF TERMS one

VICE PRESIDENT Levi Parsons Morton

DIED March 13, 1901, in Indianapolis, IN

WILLIAM MCKINLEY

25th President of the United States ★ 1897–1901

BORN Jan. 29, 1843, in Niles, OH

POLITICAL PARTY Republican

NO. OF TERMS two (assassinated)

VICE PRESIDENTS 1st term:
Garret Augustus Hobart
2nd term:
Theodore Roosevelt

DIED Sept. 14, 1901, in Buffalo, NY

THEODORE ROOSEVELT

26th President of the United States ★ 1901–1909

BORN Oct. 27, 1858, in New York, NY

POLITICAL PARTY Republican

NO. OF TERMS one, plus balance of
McKinley's term

VICE PRESIDENTS 1st term: none
2nd term: Charles
Warren Fairbanks

DIED Jan. 6, 1919, in Oyster Bay, NY

WILLIAM HOWARD TAFT

27th President of the United States ★ 1909–1913

BORN Sept. 15, 1857, in Cincinnati, OH

POLITICAL PARTY Republican

NO. OF TERMS one

VICE PRESIDENT James Schoolcraft
Sherman

DIED March 8, 1930, in Washington, D.C.

WOODROW WILSON

28th President of the United States ★ 1913–1921

BORN Dec. 29, 1856,
in Staunton, VA

POLITICAL PARTY Democrat

NO. OF TERMS two

VICE PRESIDENT Thomas Riley Marshall

DIED Feb. 3, 1924, in Washington, D.C.

WARREN G. HARDING

29th President of the United States ★ *1921–1923*
BORN Nov. 2, 1865, in Caledonia
(now Blooming Grove), OH
POLITICAL PARTY Republican
NO. OF TERMS one (died while in office)
VICE PRESIDENT Calvin Coolidge
DIED Aug. 2, 1923, in San Francisco, CA

CALVIN COOLIDGE

30th President of the United States ★ *1923–1929*
BORN July 4, 1872, in Plymouth, VT
POLITICAL PARTY Republican
NO. OF TERMS one, plus balance of
Harding's term
VICE PRESIDENTS 1st term: none
2nd term:
Charles Gates Dawes
DIED Jan. 5, 1933, in Northampton, MA

HERBERT HOOVER

31st President of the United States ★ *1929–1933*
BORN Aug. 10, 1874,
in West Branch, IA
POLITICAL PARTY Republican
NO. OF TERMS one
VICE PRESIDENT Charles Curtis
DIED Oct. 20, 1964, in New York, NY

FRANKLIN D. ROOSEVELT

32nd President of the United States ★ *1933–1945*
BORN Jan. 30, 1882, in Hyde Park, NY
POLITICAL PARTY Democrat
NO. OF TERMS four (died while in office)
VICE PRESIDENTS 1st & 2nd terms: John
Nance Garner; 3rd term:
Henry Agard Wallace; 4th
term: Harry S. Truman
DIED April 12, 1945,
in Warm Springs, GA

HARRY S. TRUMAN

33rd President of the United States ★ *1945–1953*
BORN May 8, 1884, in Lamar, MO
POLITICAL PARTY Democrat
NO. OF TERMS one, plus balance of
Franklin D. Roosevelt's term
VICE PRESIDENTS 1st term: none
2nd term:
Alben William Barkley
DIED Dec. 26, 1972, in Independence, MO

DWIGHT D. EISENHOWER

34th President of the United States ★ *1953–1961*
BORN Oct. 14, 1890, in Denison, TX
POLITICAL PARTY Republican
NO. OF TERMS two
VICE PRESIDENT Richard M. Nixon
DIED March 28, 1969,
in Washington, D.C.

JOHN F. KENNEDY

35th President of the United States ★ *1961–1963*
BORN May 29, 1917, in Brookline, MA
POLITICAL PARTY Democrat
NO. OF TERMS one (assassinated)
VICE PRESIDENT Lyndon B. Johnson
DIED Nov. 22, 1963,
in Dallas, TX

LYNDON B. JOHNSON

36th President of the United States ★ *1963–1969*
BORN Aug. 27, 1908,
near Stonewall, TX
POLITICAL PARTY Democrat
NO. OF TERMS one, plus balance of
Kennedy's term
VICE PRESIDENTS 1st term: none
2nd term: Hubert
Horatio Humphrey
DIED Jan. 22, 1973, near San Antonio, TX

PRESIDENTIAL PETS

George W. Bush's **DOG** Spot was the daughter of another presidential pooch, George Herbert Walker Bush's dog Millie.

Thomas Jefferson had two pet **GRIZZLY BEARS** that lived in a cage on the South Lawn.

Benjamin Harrison's **PET GOAT** Old Whiskers once escaped down Pennsylvania Avenue and had to be wrangled back into the White House.

John F. Kennedy and his family had dogs, rabbits, guinea pigs, and the **FIRST PONY**, Macaroni.

John Quincy Adams briefly kept an **ALLIGATOR** in the East Room during his presidency.

RICHARD NIXON

37th President of the United States ★ 1969–1974
BORN Jan. 9, 1913, in Yorba Linda, CA
POLITICAL PARTY Republican
NO. OF TERMS two (resigned)
VICE PRESIDENTS 1st term & 2nd term
(partial): Spiro Theodore
Agnew; 2nd term
(balance): Gerald R. Ford
DIED April 22, 1994, in New York, NY

GERALD R. FORD

38th President of the United States ★ 1974–1977
BORN July 14, 1913, in Omaha, NE
POLITICAL PARTY Republican
NO. OF TERMS one (partial)
VICE PRESIDENT Nelson Aldrich
Rockefeller
DIED Dec. 26, 2006, in Rancho Mirage, CA

JIMMY CARTER

39th President of the United States ★ 1977–1981
BORN Oct. 1, 1924,
in Plains, GA
POLITICAL PARTY Democrat
NO. OF TERMS one
VICE PRESIDENT Walter Frederick
(Fritz) Mondale

RONALD REAGAN

40th President of the United States ★ 1981–1989
BORN Feb. 6, 1911, in Tampico, IL
POLITICAL PARTY Republican
NO. OF TERMS two
VICE PRESIDENT George H. W. Bush
DIED June 5, 2004, in Los Angeles, CA

GEORGE H. W. BUSH

41st President of the United States ★ 1989–1993
BORN June 12, 1924, in Milton, MA
POLITICAL PARTY Republican
NO. OF TERMS one
VICE PRESIDENT James Danforth (Dan)
Quayle III

BILL CLINTON

42nd President of the United States ★ 1993–2001
BORN Aug. 19, 1946,
in Hope, AR
POLITICAL PARTY Democrat
NO. OF TERMS two
VICE PRESIDENT Albert Gore, Jr.

GEORGE W. BUSH

43rd President of the United States ★ 2001–2009
BORN July 6, 1946,
in New Haven, CT
POLITICAL PARTY Republican
NO. OF TERMS two
VICE PRESIDENT Richard Bruce Cheney

BARACK OBAMA

*44th President of the United States ★
2009–present*
BORN August 4, 1961,
in Honolulu, HI
POLITICAL PARTY Democrat
VICE PRESIDENT Joseph Biden

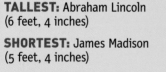

Standout Presidents

OLDEST: Ronald Reagan,
who was elected at the age of 69

TALLEST: Abraham Lincoln
(6 feet, 4 inches)

SHORTEST: James Madison
(5 feet, 4 inches)

BIGGEST FEET: Warren G. Harding,
size 14

MOST TRAVELED: Bill Clinton,
who took 133 trips abroad as President

MOST CHILDREN: John Tyler,
with 15 offspring

FAST FACT

Barack Obama
is only the sixth president
to have brown eyes.

The Indian Experience

American Indians are indigenous to North and South America—they are the people who were here before Columbus and other European explorers came to these lands. They lived in nations, tribes, and bands across both continents. For decades following the arrival of Europeans in 1492, American Indians clashed with the newcomers who had ruptured the Indians' way of living.

Tribal Land

During the 19th century, both United States legislation and military action restricted the movement of American Indians, forcing them to live on reservations and attempting to dismantle tribal structures. For centuries Indians were often displaced or killed, or became assimilated into the general U.S. population. In 1924 the Indian Citizenship Act granted citizenship to all American Indians. Unfortunately, this was not enough to end the social discrimination and mistreatment that many Indians have faced. Today, American Indians living in the U.S. still face many challenges.

Healing the Past

Many members of the 560-plus recognized tribes in the United States live primarily on reservations. Some tribes have more than one reservation, while others have none. Together these reservations make up less than 3 percent of the nation's land area. The tribal governments on reservations have the right to form their own governments and enforce laws, similar to individual states. Many feel that this sovereignty is still not enough to right the wrongs of the past: They hope for a change in the U.S. government's relationship with American Indians.

A young Cherokee man dressed in traditional costume

5 BIGGEST INDIAN NATIONS

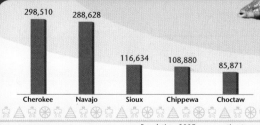

Cherokee	Navajo	Sioux	Chippewa	Choctaw
298,510	288,628	116,634	108,880	85,871

Population, 2007 census estimates

Most American Indians in the U.S. live in the West, with California, Oklahoma, and Arizona having the largest populations

The largest group of American Indians living in the United States is the Cherokee nation. This nation is concentrated mainly in the

CIVIL RIGHTS

Fighting for Your Rights:

Although the Constitution protects the civil rights of American citizens, it has not always been able to protect all Americans from persecution or discrimination. During the first half of the 20th century, many Americans, particularly African Americans, were the subject of widespread discrimination and racism. By the mid-1950s, many people were eager to end the bonds of racism and restore freedom to all men and women.

The civil rights movement of the 1950s and 1960s sought to end the racial discrimination against African Americans, especially in the southern states. The movement wanted to restore the fundamentals of economic and social equality to those who had been oppressed.

The Little Rock Nine

The Little Rock Nine study during the weeks when they were blocked from school.

September 4, 1957, marked the first day of school at Little Rock Central High in Little Rock, Arkansas. But this was no ordinary back-to-school scene: Armed soldiers surrounded the entrance, awaiting the arrival of Central's first-ever African-American students. The welcome was not warm, however, as the students—now known as the Little Rock Nine—were refused entry into the school by the soldiers and a group of protesters, angry about the potential integration. This did not deter the students, and they gained the support of President Dwight D. Eisenhower to eventually earn their right to go to an integrated school. Today, the Little Rock Nine are still considered civil rights icons for challenging a racist system—and winning!

Key Events in the Civil Rights Movement

1954	The Supreme Court case *Brown* v. *Board of Education* declares school segregation illegal.
1955	Rosa Parks refuses to give up her bus seat to a white passenger and spurs a bus boycott.
1957	The Little Rock Nine help integrate schools.
1960	Four black college students begin sit-ins at a restaurant in Greensboro, North Carolina.
1961	Freedom Rides begin to southern states to protest segregation in transportation.
1963	Martin Luther King, Jr., leads the famous March on Washington.
1964	The Civil Rights Act, signed by President Lyndon Johnson, prohibits discrimination based on race, color, religion, sex, and national origin.
1967	Thurgood Marshall becomes the first African American to be named to the Supreme Court.
1968	President Lyndon B. Johnson signs the Civil Rights Act of 1968, which prohibits discrimination in the sale, rental, and financing of housing.

Never Back Down: Prominent figures who emerged from the civil rights movement included Martin Luther King, Jr., Rosa Parks, John F. Kennedy, and Malcolm X. Here's more about these powerful leaders.

ROSA PARKS 1913 (Alabama, U.S.) – 2005 (Michigan, U.S.)

After refusing to give up her bus seat to a white passenger, activist Parks sparked a 381-day boycott of the city bus line in Montgomery, Alabama. This eventually led to the 1956 Supreme Court ruling declaring segregation illegal on public buses, giving Parks the unofficial title of "The Mother of the Modern-Day Civil Rights Movement."

Did you know? At the time of her arrest, Parks was 42 and on her way home from work as a seamstress. Aside from being arrested, she was fined $14 for refusing to give up her seat.

JOHN F. KENNEDY 1917 (Massachusetts, U.S.) – 1963 (Texas, U.S.)

As President, Kennedy used executive orders and pleas to the public to show his support of civil rights. This included sending 400 U.S. Marshals to Alabama in 1961 to protect the "Freedom Riders," a group of men and women who boarded buses, trains, and planes to the deep South to test the 1960 U.S. Supreme Court ruling outlawing racial segregation. Kennedy was assassinated during a presidential motorcade in Dallas, Texas, on November 22, 1963.

Did you know? Kennedy was the first U.S. President born in the 20th century.

MALCOLM X 1925 (Nebraska, U.S.) – 1965 (New York, U.S.)

A preacher and talented public speaker, Malcolm X believed that people would be set free of racism by working together, and encouraged his African-American followers to be proud of their race. He also advocated peace and unity among all people, regardless of the color of their skin. While giving a speech in Harlem, New York, Malcolm X was shot and killed by three members of the Nation of Islam, the religious organization he once belonged to.

Did you know? Malcolm X was born with the last name "Little," but changed it to "X" once he joined the Nation of Islam.

MARTIN LUTHER KING, JR. 1929 (Georgia, U.S.) – 1968 (Tennessee, U.S.)

Civil rights leader Dr. Martin Luther King, Jr., born in Atlanta, Georgia, in 1929, never backed down in his stand against racism. He dedicated his life to achieving equality and justice for Americans of all colors. From a family of preachers, King experienced racial prejudice early in life. As an adult fighting for civil rights, his speeches, marches, and mere presence motivated people to fight for justice for all. His March on Washington in 1963 was one of the largest activist gatherings in our nation's history. King was assassinated by James Earl Ray on April 4, 1968.

Did you know? King received the Nobel Prize for Peace in 1964.

Brilliant Biographies

A biography is the story of a person's life. It can be a brief summary or a long book. Biographers—those who write biographies—use many different sources to learn about their subjects. You can write your own biography of a famous person who you find inspiring.

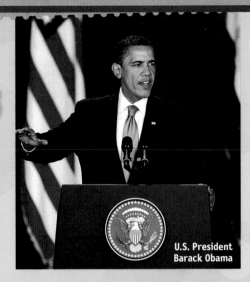

U.S. President
Barack Obama

How to Get Started

Choose a subject you find interesting. If you think Cleopatra is cool, you have a good chance of getting your reader interested, too. If you're bored by ancient Egypt, your reader will be snoring after your first paragraph.

Your subject can be almost anyone: an author, an inventor, a celebrity, a politician, or a member of your family. To find someone to write about, ask yourself these simple questions:

1. Who do I want to know more about?
2. What did this person do that was special?
3. How did this person change the world?

Do Your Research

- Find out as much about your subject as possible. Read books, news articles, and encyclopedia entries. Watch video clips and movies, and search the Internet. Conduct interviews, if possible.

- Take notes, writing down important facts and interesting stories about your subject.

Writing the Biography

- Come up with a title. Include the person's name.

- Write an introduction. Consider asking a probing question about your subject.

- Include information about the person's child-hood. When was this person born? Where did he or she grow up? Whom did he or she admire?

- Highlight the person's talents, accomplishments, and personal attributes.

- Describe the specific events that helped to shape this person's life. Did this person ever have a problem and overcome it?

- Write a conclusion. Include your thoughts about why it is important to learn about this person.

- Once you have finished your first draft, revise and then proofread.

Here's a SAMPLE BIOGRAPHY for President Barack Obama.
Of course, there is so much more for you to research, uncover, and reveal!

Barack Obama—Number 44

Barack Obama is the 44th President of the United States and the first African American to hold the office.

Obama was born on August 4, 1961, in Honolulu, Hawaii. As a child he lived in Indonesia. In elementary school he once wrote an essay titled "I Want to Become President." Some dreams start early! Later, Obama graduated from Columbia University and earned a degree in law from Harvard Law School.

Obama was a Democratic Illinois state senator from 1997 to 2004. He gave the keynote address at the 2004 Democratic National Convention, an honor that helped him on the path to his successful presidential candidacy.

He is married to Michelle Robinson Obama and has two daughters, Malia and Sasha. Obama is a good example for them—and kids everywhere. If you work hard, your dreams can come true.

REVEAL YOUR SOURCES

A bibliography is a list of all the sources you used to get information for your essay, such as books, magazine articles, interviews, and websites. It is included at the end of your essay or report.

The bibliography should list sources in alphabetical order by author's last name. If a source doesn't have an author, then it should be alphabetized by title.

BOOK
Author (last name, first name). *Title*. City of publisher: publisher, date of publication.

Ex: Allen, Thomas B. *George Washington, Spymaster*. Washington, D.C.: National Geographic, 2004.

ENCYCLOPEDIA
Author (last name, first name) (if given). "Article title." *Name of Encyclopedia*. Edition. Volume. City of publisher: publisher, date of publication.

Ex: "Gerbil." *The Encyclopedia Britannica*. 15th ed. Vol. 5. Chicago: Encyclopedia Britannica, 2007.

MAGAZINE/NEWSPAPER ARTICLE
Author (last name, first name). "Article title." *Name of magazine*. Date: page numbers.

Ex: Elder, Scott. "Great Migrations." NATIONAL GEOGRAPHIC KIDS. Nov. 2010: pp. 20–25.

DVD/FILM
Title of film. Director's name. Year of original film's release. Format. Name of distributor, year, video/DVD/etc. produced.

Ex: *Lewis & Clark: Great Journey West*. Dir. Bruce Neibaur. 2002. Large-format film. National Geographic, 2002.

INTERVIEW
Person interviewed (last name, first name). Type of interview (personal, telephone, email, etc.). Date of interview.

Ex: Hiebert, Fredrik. Personal interview. April 28, 2011.

WEBSITE
Author (last name, first name) (if given). *Title of the site*. Editor. Date and/or version number. Name of sponsoring institution. Date of access. <URL>.

Ex: Hora, Reenita Malhotra. *Diwali, India's Festival of Light*. 2008. National Geographic. May 12, 2011. <http://kids.national geographic.com/kids/stories/peopleplaces/diwali>.

COOL CLICK

Want to find out more about sources and books? The Library of Congress has a great website. loc.gov/families

TIP:
If you keep track of all your sources as you use them, compiling the information to create your bibliography can be done in a snap.

Geography
Rocks

Tanzania's Mount Kilimanjaro looms behind
a group of African elephants.

THE POLITICAL WORLD

Earth's land area is made up of seven continents, but people have divided much of the land into smaller political units called countries. Australia is a continent made up of a single country, and Antarctica is set aside for scientific research. But the other five continents include almost 200 independent countries. The political map shown here depicts boundaries—imaginary lines created by treaties—that separate countries. Some boundaries, such as the one between the United States and Canada, are very stable and have been recognized for many years.

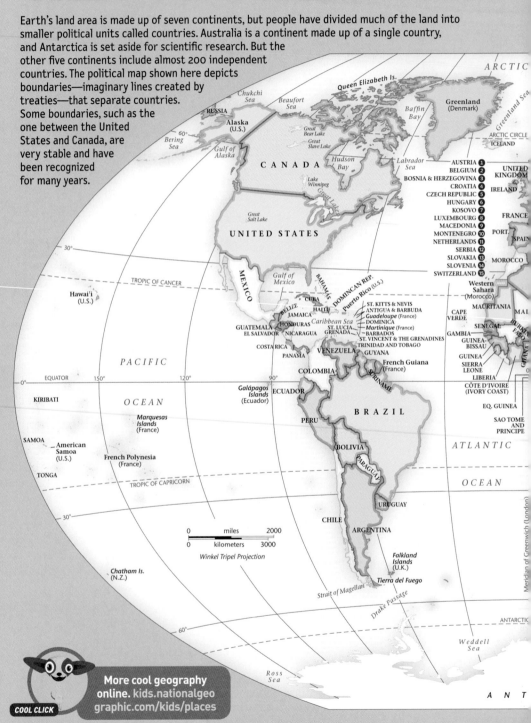

More cool geography online. kids.nationalgeographic.com/kids/places

Other boundaries, such as the one between Ethiopia and Eritrea in northeast Africa, are relatively new and still disputed. Countries come in all shapes and sizes. Russia and Canada are giants; others, such as Luxembourg, are small. Some countries are long and skinny—look at Chile in South America! Still other countries—such as Indonesia and Japan in Asia—are made up of groups of islands. The political map is a clue to the diversity that makes Earth so fascinating.

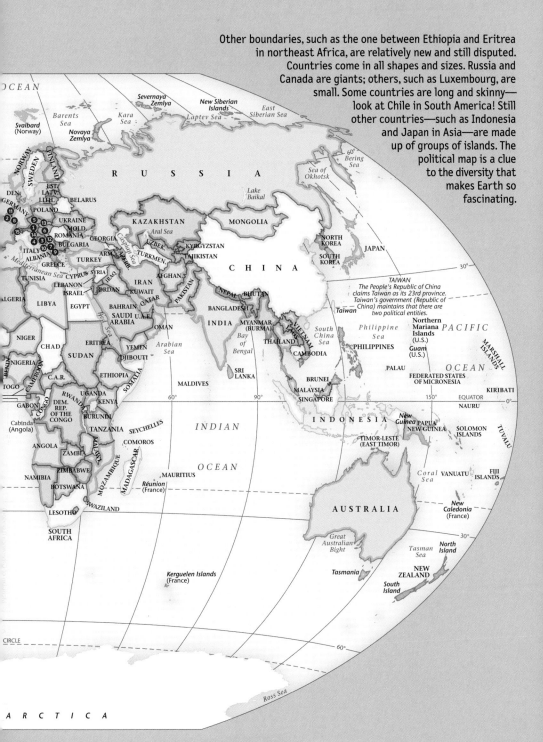

TAIWAN
The People's Republic of China claims Taiwan as its 23rd province. Taiwan's government (Republic of China) maintains that there are two political entities.

THE PHYSICAL WORLD

Earth is dominated by large landmasses called continents—seven in all—and by an interconnected global ocean that is divided into four parts by the continents. More than 70 percent of Earth's surface is covered by oceans, and the remaining 30 percent is made up of land areas.

Different landforms give variety to the surface of the continents. The Rockies and Andes mark the western edge of the Americas, and the Himalaya tower above southern Asia. The Plateau of Tibet forms the rugged core of Asia, while

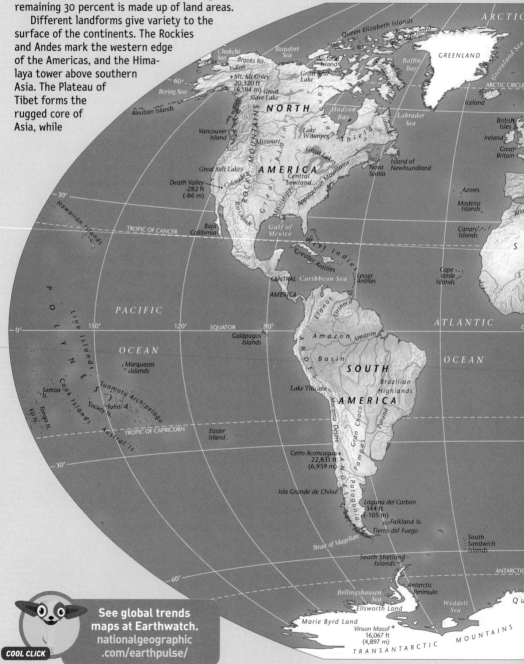

See global trends maps at Earthwatch.
nationalgeographic.com/earthpulse/

COOL CLICK

the Northern European Plain extends from the North Sea to the Ural Mountains. Much of Africa is a plateau, and dry plains cover large areas of Australia. Mountains rise more than 16,000 ft (4,877 m) above Antarctica's massive ice sheets. Mountains and trenches make the ocean floors as varied as any continent. A mountain chain called the Mid-Atlantic Ridge runs the length of the Atlantic Ocean. In the western Pacific, trenches drop deep into the ocean floor.

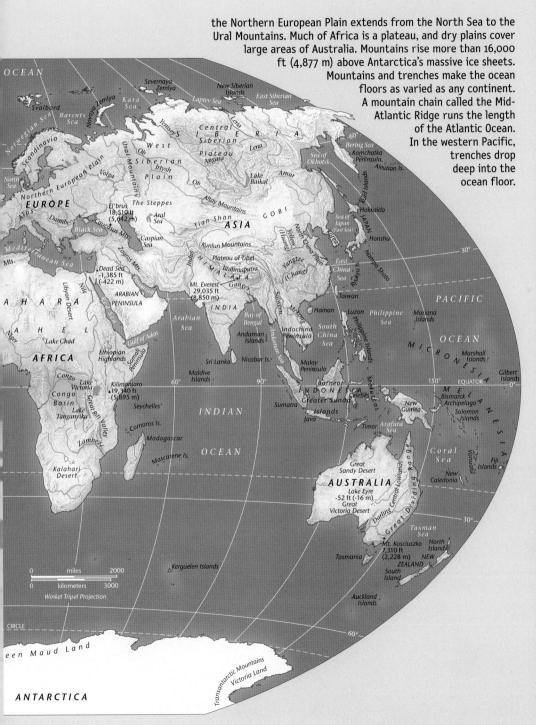

KINDS OF MAPS

Maps are special tools that geographers use to tell a story about Earth. Maps can be used to show just about anything related to places. Some maps show physical features, such as mountains or vegetation. Maps can also show climates or natural hazards and other things we cannot easily see. Other maps illustrate different features on Earth—political boundaries, urban centers, and economic systems.

AN IMPERFECT TOOL

Maps are not perfect. A globe is a scale model of Earth with accurate relative sizes and locations. Because maps are flat, they involve distortions of size, shape, and direction. Also, cartographers—people who create maps—make choices about what information to include. Because of this, it is important to study many different types of maps to learn the complete story of Earth. Three commonly found kinds of maps are shown on this page.

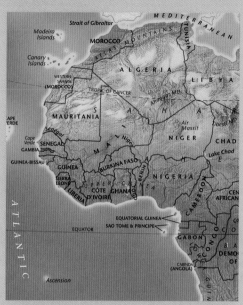

PHYSICAL MAPS. Earth's natural features—landforms, water bodies, and vegetation—are shown on physical maps. The map above uses color and shading to illustrate mountains, lakes, rivers, and deserts of western Africa. Country names and borders are added for reference, but they are not natural features.

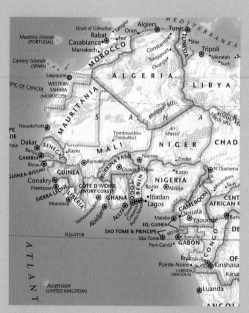

POLITICAL MAPS. These maps represent characteristics of the landscape created by humans, such as boundaries, cities, and place-names. Natural features are added only for reference. On the map above, capital cities are represented with a star inside a circle, while other cities are shown with black dots.

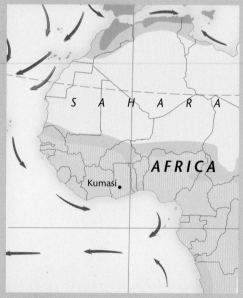

THEMATIC MAPS. Patterns related to a particular topic, or theme, such as population distribution, appear on these maps. The map above displays the region's climate zones, which range from tropical wet (bright green) to tropical wet and dry (light green) to semiarid (dark yellow) to arid or desert (light yellow).

KINDS OF ENVIRONMENTS

The world is full of a wondrous selection of natural geographic features. If you take a look around, you'll be amazed by the beauty of our world. From roaring rivers to parched deserts, from underwater canyons to jagged mountains, Earth is covered with beautiful and diverse environments.

Here are examples of the most common types of geographic features found around the world.

RIVER

As a river moves through flatlands, it twists and turns. Above, the Rio Los Amigos winds through a rain forest in Peru.

CANYON

Steep-sided valleys called canyons are created mainly by running water. Buckskin Gulch (above) is the deepest slot canyon in the American Southwest.

DESERT

Deserts are land features created by climate, specifically by a lack of water. Above, a camel caravan crosses the Sahara in North Africa.

OASIS

Occasionally water rises from deep below a desert, creating a refuge that supports trees and sometimes crops, as in this oasis in Africa.

MOUNTAIN

Mountains are Earth's tallest landforms, and Mount Everest (above) rises highest of all, at 29,035 feet (8,850 m) above sea level.

GLACIER

Glaciers—"rivers" of ice—such as Alaska's Hubbard Glacier (above) move slowly from mountains to the sea. Global warming is shrinking them.

VALLEY

Valleys, cut by running water or moving ice, may be broad and flat or narrow and steep, such as the Indus River Valley in Ladakh, India (above).

WATERFALL

Waterfalls form when a river reaches an abrupt change in elevation. Above, Kaitur Falls, in Guyana, descends 800 feet (244 m).

AFRICA

T he massive continent of Africa, where humankind began millions of years ago, is second only to Asia in size. The 53 independent countries of Africa are home to a wide variety of cultures and traditions. In many areas traditional tribal life is still very common, such as among the Maasai people of Kenya and Tanzania.

Maasai women in native costume

From Arabic and Nubian, to Zulu and Sandawe, some 1,600 languages are spoken in Africa—more than on any other continent.

Although rich in natural resources, from oil to coal to gemstones and precious metals, Africa is the poorest continent, long plagued by out-side interference, corruption, and disease.

Africa spans nearly as far from west to east as it does from north to south. The Sahara—the world's largest desert— covers Africa's northern third, while bands of grassland, tropical rain forest, and more desert lie to the south. The rain forests of Africa are home to half of the continent's animal species. Wild creatures, such as lions, roam sub-Saharan Africa, and water-loving hippos live near the great lakes of this large continent.

The first great civilization in Africa arose 6,000 years ago on the banks of the lower Nile. Today, though the continent is still largely rural, Africans increasingly migrate to booming cities such as Cairo, Egypt; Lagos, Nigeria; and Johannesburg, South Africa.

MORE THAN 12,000 SQUARE MILES (31,080 SQ KM)	SURFACE AREA OF THE CENTRAL AFRICAN FRESHWATER LAKE, LAKE TANGANYIKA
3,475,000 SQUARE MILES (9,000,209 SQ KM)	AREA OF THE SAHARA, LARGEST HOT DESERT ON EARTH
11	NUMBER OF OFFICIAL LANGUAGES IN THE COUNTRY OF SOUTH AFRICA

COOL CLICK

Go online to learn more about all of the continents.
travel.national geographic.com/places/ continents/

GIRAFFES' TONGUES CAN BE 21 INCHES (53 CM) LONG • THEY HAVE

7 COOL THINGS ABOUT AFRICA

1. The land occupied by China, Europe, and the United States could fit inside Africa—with room to spare!

2. The Great Pyramid of Khufu in Egypt was the world's tallest man-made structure for more than 4,400 years. It is still standing today.

3. The flag of Libya, an African country, is entirely green. It is the only national flag that is a solid color.

4. The Basenji, a dog from Africa, yodels instead of barking.

5. Most of the world's diamonds and gold come from mines in Africa.

6. The Goliath Frog, found in the rain forests of western Africa, can grow to be as big as some house cats!

7. Madagascar, Africa's largest island, is home to many unique animals such as lemurs, flying fox bats, and hissing cockroaches.

giraffe

VERY HIGH BLOOD PRESSURE TO PUMP BLOOD UP THEIR LONG NECKS

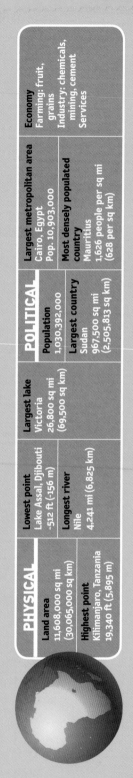

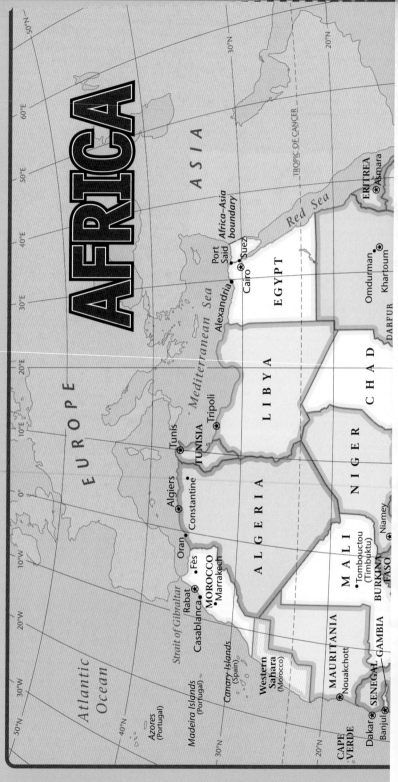

PHYSICAL

Land area
11,608,000 sq mi
(30,065,000 sq km)

Highest point
Kilimanjaro, Tanzania
19,340 ft (5,895 m)

Lowest point
Lake Assal, Djibouti
-512 ft (-156 m)

Longest river
Nile
4,241 mi (6,825 km)

Largest lake
Victoria
26,800 sq mi
(69,500 sq km)

POLITICAL

Population
1,030,392,000

Largest country
Sudan
967,500 sq mi
(2,505,813 sq km)

Largest metropolitan area
Cairo, Egypt
Pop. 10,903,000

Most densely populated country
Mauritius
1,626 people per sq mi
(628 per sq km)

Economy
Farming: fruit, grains
Industry: chemicals, mining, cement
Services

Gulf of Aden

SOMALIA

Mogadishu
(historic capital;
no central
government
since 1991)

Victoria

SEYCHELLES

DJIBOUTI
Djibouti

Addis
Ababa

ETHIOPIA

MAURITIUS
Port Louis
Réunion
(France)

Antananarivo

MADAGASCAR

COMOROS
Moroni

Mombasa

Dar es Salaam

KENYA
Nairobi

Indian
Ocean

SUDAN

SOUTHERN
SUDAN

UGANDA

Kampala

RWANDA
Kigali

BURUNDI
Bujumbura

Kisangani

Bangui

CENTRAL
AFRICAN REPUBLIC

DEMOCRATIC
REPUBLIC
OF THE CONGO

Kananga

Mbuji-Mayi

Dodoma

TANZANIA

MALAWI
Lilongwe

Mozambique Channel

MOZAMBIQUE

Lubumbashi

ZAMBIA
Lusaka

Kitwe

Kolwezi

Harare

ZIMBABWE

SWAZILAND
Mbabane
Lobamba

Maputo

Durban

LESOTHO
Maseru

SOUTH
AFRICA

Pretoria
(Tshwane)

Johannesburg

Gaborone

BOTSWANA

Bloemfontein

Port
Elizabeth

N'Djamena

CAMEROON
Yaoundé
Douala

CONGO

GABON
Libreville

Brazzaville

Kinshasa

Pointe-Noire

Cabinda
(Angola)

Luanda

ANGOLA

NAMIBIA

Windhoek

Cape Town

NIGERIA

Kano

Abuja

Ogbomosho
Lagos

BENIN
Porto-
Novo

TOGO
Lomé Cotonou

GHANA
Accra

Ouagadougou

Malabo

EQUATORIAL GUINEA

SAO TOME & PRINCIPE
São Tomé

Atlantic
Ocean

St. Helena
(U.K.)

Ascension
(U.K.)

EQUATOR

Bamako

GUINEA-
BISSAU
Bissau

GUINEA
Conakry

SIERRA
LEONE
Freetown

LIBERIA
Monrovia

CÔTE D'IVOIRE
(IVORY COAST)
Yamoussoukro
Abidjan

TROPIC OF CAPRICORN

Map Key
⊛ National capital
• Other city

800 Miles
800 Kilometers

Azimuthal Equal-Area Projection

ANTARC

T his frozen continent may be an interesting place to see, but unless you're a penguin, you probably wouldn't want to hang out in Antarctica for long. The fact that it's the coldest, windiest, and driest continent helps explain why humans never colonized this ice-covered land surrounding the South Pole.

No country actually owns Antarctica. Dozens of countries work together to study and care for its barren landscape. Antarctica is the only continent without a permanent population. Photographers and tourists visit. Scientists live there temporarily to study such things as weather, environment, and wildlife.

Visitors can observe several species of penguins that breed in Antarctica, including the emperor penguin. Antarctica's shores also serve as breeding grounds for six kinds of seals. And the surrounding waters provide food for whales.

People and animals share Antarctica. But there are still places on this vast, icy continent that have yet to be explored.

Weddell seal

2	NUMBER OF AUTOMATED TELLER MACHINES (ATMs) IN ANTARCTICA
3 MILES (4.8 KM)	DEPTH OF THICKEST ICE COVERING THE CONTINENT
MORE THAN 25,000	AVERAGE NUMBER OF TOURISTS WHO VISIT ANTARCTICA ANNUALLY

ADÉLIE PENGUINS LINE THEIR NESTS WITH SMALL ROCKS •

TICA

Adélie penguins

7 COOL THINGS ABOUT ANTARCTICA

1. During the warmer months, melting snow helps more than 3,000 species of algae bloom. This includes red algae, which makes the usually white snow look pink.

2. For nine months of the year, intense cold makes it too dangerous for planes to land on the continet.

3. All water at the South Pole is melted ice, some of the purest and coldest water on Earth.

4. The largest land animal in Antarctica is a wingless insect (penguins and seals are marine animals).

5. Mount Erebus is the southernmost volcano in the world.

6. Truly a frozen continent, Antarctica contains 90 percent of the world's ice.

7. Most of the world has signed the Antarctic Treaty, which says countries can only use the continent for peaceful reasons.

IN SPRING, FEMALE ADÉLIE PENGUINS LAY TWO EGGS AT A TIME

PHYSICAL

Land area
5,100,000 sq mi
(13,209,000 sq km)

Highest point
Vinson Massif
16,067 ft (4,897 m)

Lowest point
Bentley Subglacial
Trench
-8,383 ft (-2,555 m)

Coldest place
Plateau Station, annual
average temperature
−70°F (-56.7°C)

**Average precipitation
on the polar plateau**
Less than 2 in (5 cm)
per year

POLITICAL

Population
There are no indig-
enous inhabitants,
but there are both
permanent and
summer-only staffed
research stations.

**Number of
independent countries**
0

**Number of countries
claiming land**
7

**Number of countries
operating year-round
research stations**
19

**Number of year-round
research stations**
45

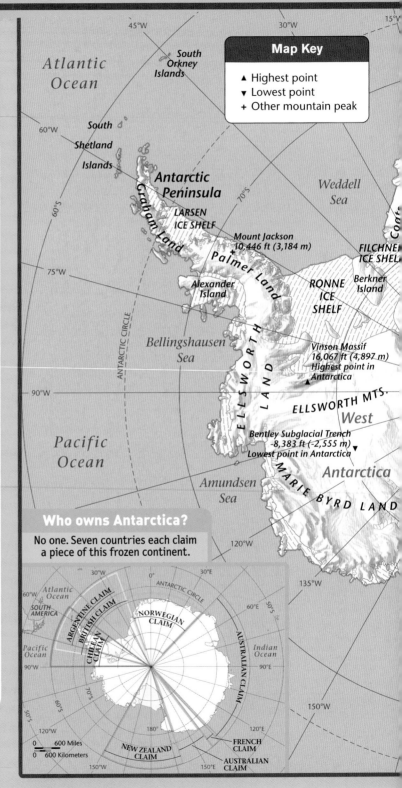

Map Key
▲ Highest point
▼ Lowest point
+ Other mountain peak

Atlantic
Ocean

South
Orkney
Islands

South
Shetland
Islands

Antarctic
Peninsula

Graham Land

LARSEN
ICE SHELF

Weddell
Sea

Mount Jackson
10,446 ft (3,184 m)
+

FILCHNER
ICE SHELF

Palmer Land

Coats

Alexander
Island

RONNE
ICE
SHELF

Berkner
Island

Bellingshausen
Sea

Vinson Massif
16,067 ft (4,897 m)
Highest point in
Antarctica
▲

ELLSWORTH LAND

ELLSWORTH MTS.

West

ANTARCTIC CIRCLE

Pacific
Ocean

Bentley Subglacial Trench
-8,383 ft (-2,555 m) ▼
Lowest point in Antarctica

Antarctica

Amundsen
Sea

MARIE BYRD LAND

Who owns Antarctica?

No one. Seven countries each claim
a piece of this frozen continent.

Atlantic
Ocean

ANTARCTIC CIRCLE

SOUTH
AMERICA

ARGENTINE CLAIM

BRITISH CLAIM

NORWEGIAN
CLAIM

Pacific
Ocean

CHILEAN
CLAIM

Indian
Ocean

AUSTRALIAN CLAIM

0   600 Miles
0   600 Kilometers

NEW ZEALAND
CLAIM

FRENCH
CLAIM

AUSTRALIAN
CLAIM

ANTARCTICA

FIMBUL
ICE SHELF

RIISER-LARSEN
ICE SHELF

Land

QUEEN MAUD LAND

ENDERBY
LAND

Indian
Ocean

0°

15°E

30°E

45°E

60°E

Valkyrie
Dome

MacKenzie Bay

75°E

Lambert
Glacier

AMERY ICE SHELF

AMERICAN

HIGHLAND

WEST
ICE SHELF

TRANSANTARCTIC MOUNTAINS

POLAR PLATEAU

South Pole

East

Antarctica

90°E

SHACKLETON
ICE SHELF

ROSS
ICE
SHELF

Roosevelt
Island

Taylor
Glacier

Ross Island

Mount Erebus
12,448 ft
(3,794 m)

Ross
Sea

VICTORIA LAND

Talos
Dome

80°S

70°S

WILKES LAND

105°E

120°E

60°S

165°W

180°

0   600 Miles

0   600 Kilometers

Azimuthal Equidistant Projection

150°E

135°E

*South
Magnetic
Pole (2012)

Indian
Ocean

7 COOL THINGS ABOUT ASIA

1. The Asian country of Brunei is home to the biggest inhabited palace on Earth, with 1,788 rooms.

2. All of today's pet hamsters can be traced to one hamster family that lived in Syria in 1930.

3. A 56-leaf clover was discovered in Japan.

4. The 10 tallest mountains in the world are all in Asia.

5. Nepal's flag is the only national flag in the world that is not rectangular in shape.

6. The Philippines—a group of more than 7,000 small islands in the Pacific Ocean—is home to a fig tree that grows fruit from its trunk instead of on its branches.

7. Dinosaur bones were mistaken for dragon bones when they were discovered in China more than 2,000 years ago.

WORLD'S TALLEST SKYSCRAPER!

Burj Khalifa skyscraper, Dubai, United Arab Emirates

ADULT JAPANESE MACAQUES ARE ABOUT 2 FEET (0.6 METERS) TALL

ASIA

From western Turkey to the eastern tip of Russia, Asia sprawls across nearly 180 degrees of longitude—almost half the globe! It boasts the highest (Mount Everest) and the lowest (the Dead Sea) places on Earth's surface.

Home to more than 40 countries, Asia is the world's largest continent, with more than four billion people. Three out of five people on the planet live here—that's more than live on all the other continents combined.

Asia is a land of contrasts. The continent's expansive rural areas are home to the most farmers in the world. Contemporary, commercial, and sacred cities also cover its vast lands. Asia boasts the most million-plus cities, including Tokyo, Japan; Riyadh, Saudi Arabia; Jakarta, Indonesia; and Beijing, China.

The world's first civilization arose in Sumer, in what is now Iraq. Rich cultures also emerged along rivers in present-day India and China, strongly influencing the world ever since. Asia is also home to a large number of religions, such as Islam, Buddhism, Hinduism, Judaism, and Christianity. Dozens of languages—from Arabic to Xiang—are spoken here.

The Asian economy is growing rapidly. Several Asian nations, such as China and South Korea, are near the top of the global marketplace.

Japanese macaques

Buddhist prayer flags in Tibet, China

60 — PERCENT OF THE WORLD'S POPULATION THAT LIVES IN ASIA

1,500 — NUMBER OF SPECIES OF PLANTS AND ANIMALS THAT LIVE IN LAKE BAIKAL IN RUSSIA

8.6 — PERCENT OF EARTH'S TOTAL SURFACE AREA THAT ASIA COVERS

JAPANESE MACAQUES LIVE FARTHER NORTH THAN ANY OTHER MONKEY

PHYSICAL

Land area
17,208,000 sq mi
(44,570,000 sq km)

Highest point
Mount Everest,
China-Nepal
29,035 ft (8,850 m)

Lowest point
Dead Sea, Israel-
Jordan
-1,385 ft (-422 m)

Longest river
Yangtze (Chang), China
3,964 mi (6,380 km)

**Largest lake entirely
in Asia**
Lake Baikal
12,200 sq mi
(31,500 sq km)

POLITICAL

Population
4,157,292,000

**Largest metropolitan
area**
Tokyo, Japan
Pop. 36,507,000

**Largest country
entirely in Asia**
China 3,705,405 sq mi
(9,596,960 sq km)

**Most densely
populated country**
Singapore
19,485 people
per sq mi
(7,526 per sq km)

Economy
Farming: rice, wheat
Industry: petroleum,
  electronics
Services

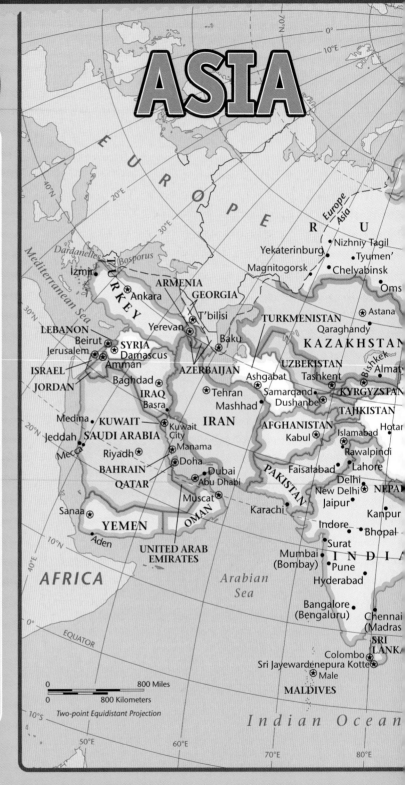

ASIA

EUROPE

Dardanelles
Bosporus
Mediterranean Sea
Izmir
TURKEY
Ankara
ARMENIA
GEORGIA
T'bilisi
Yerevan
Baku
TURKMENISTAN
Qaraghandy
KAZAKHSTAN
Yekaterinburg
Nizhniy Tagil
Tyumen'
Chelyabinsk
Magnitogorsk
Oms
Astana
LEBANON
Beirut
SYRIA
Damascus
Jerusalem
Amman
ISRAEL
JORDAN
Baghdad
IRAQ
Basra
AZERBAIJAN
UZBEKISTAN
Ashgabat
Tashkent
Bishkek
Almat
Tehran
Samarqand
Dushanbe
KYRGYZSTAN
Mashhad
TAJIKISTAN
Medina
KUWAIT
Kuwait
City
IRAN
AFGHANISTAN
Hotar
Jeddah
SAUDI ARABIA
Kabul
Islamabad
Mecca
Manama
Rawalpindi
Riyadh
Doha
Faisalabad
Lahore
BAHRAIN
Dubai
Delhi
QATAR
Abu Dhabi
New Delhi
NEPAL
PAKISTAN
Jaipur
Muscat
Karachi
Kanpur
Sanaa
OMAN
Indore
Bhopal
YEMEN
Surat
Aden
UNITED ARAB
EMIRATES
Mumbai
(Bombay)
Pune
INDIA
AFRICA
Arabian
Sea
Hyderabad
Bangalore
(Bengaluru)
Chennai
(Madras
EQUATOR
SRI
LANKA
Colombo
Sri Jayewardenepura Kotte
Male
MALDIVES
Two-point Equidistant Projection
Indian Ocean

0   800 Miles
0   800 Kilometers

★ North Pole

Arctic Ocean

Map Key

⊛ National capital
◎ Other capital
• Other city

Magadan

Sea of Okhotsk

R U S S I A

A commonly accepted division between Asia and Europe—marked here by a maroon, dashed line—is formed by the Ural Mountains, Ural River, Caspian Sea, Caucasus Mountains, and the Black Sea with its outlets, the Bosporus and Dardanelles.

ARCTIC CIRCLE

Tomsk
Novosibirsk
Lake Baikal
Irkutsk
Ulan Ude

Khabarovsk

Sapporo

Qiqihar
Harbin
Changchun
Fushun
Jilin
Vladivostok
Shenyang
NORTH KOREA
Sendai
JAPAN
Kyoto
Tokyo
Nagoya

Ulaanbaatar ⊛
M O N G O L I A
Anshan
P'yŏngyang ◎

Ürümqi
Beijing ⊛
Shijiazhuang
Dalian
Seoul ⊛
SOUTH KOREA
Osaka
Hiroshima
Fukuoka
Taiyuan
Zhengzhou
Qingdao

Lanzhou
Luoyang
Xuzhou
East China Sea
Nanjing
Xi'an
Shanghai

C H I N A
Chengdu
Nanchang

Kathmandu
BHUTAN
Lhasa
Thimphu ⊛
Chongqing
Guiyang
Changsha
Fuzhou
Taipei ◎
Taiwan
Kaohsiung

The People's Republic of China claims Taiwan as its 23rd province. Taiwan's government (Republic of China) maintains that there are two political entities.

BANGLADESH ⊛
Dhaka ⊛
Kunming
Nanning
Guangzhou
Shantou
Macau
Hong Kong

Kolkata (Calcutta)
Chittagong
MYANMAR (BURMA)
LAOS
Hanoi
Haiphong
South China Sea
Quezon City

Nay Pyi Taw
Vientiane
Da Nang
Manila ⊛
PHILIPPINES
Pacific Ocean

Yangon (Rangoon)
THAILAND
VIETNAM
Cagayan de Oro

Bangkok ⊛
CAMBODIA
Phnom Penh ⊛
Ho Chi Minh City (Saigon)

EQUATOR
Jayapura
Oceania Asia

Bandar Seri Begawan
Manado

Banda Aceh
BRUNEI
M A L A Y S I A
Medan
Kuala Lumpur
Balikpapan

SINGAPORE ⊛
I N D O N E S I A
Jambi
Palembang
Bandung
Semarang
Dili
TIMOR-LESTE (EAST TIMOR)
AUSTRALIA
Jakarta ⊛
Surabaya

TROPIC OF CANCER

AUSTRA
NEW ZEALAND, AND

This vast region includes Australia—the world's smallest and flattest continent—New Zealand, and a fleet of mostly tiny islands scattered across the Pacific Ocean. Apart from Australia, New Zealand, and Papua New Guinea, Oceania's other 11 independent countries cover about 25,000 square miles (65,000 sq km), an area only slightly larger than half of New Zealand's North Island. Twenty-one other island groups are dependencies of the United States, France, Australia, New Zealand, or the United Kingdom.

Australia has a strong indigenous population of Aborigines but is also heavily influenced by Anglo-Western culture. "Aussies," as Australians like to call themselves, nicknamed their continent the "land down under." That's because the entire continent lies south of, or "under," the Equator. Most Australians live in cities along the coast. But Australia also has huge cattle and sheep ranches. Many ranch children live far from school. They get their lessons by mail or over the Internet or radio. Their doctors even visit by airplane!

Maori man in traditional dress. Maoris are indigenous people of New Zealand.

Bora-Bora, French Polynesia

KANGAROOS DON'T HOP BACKWARD • A NEWBORN KANGAROO IS ABOUT AS

LIA,
OCEANIA,

7 COOL THINGS ABOUT
AUSTRALIA, NEW ZEALAND,
AND OCEANIA

a kangaroo and joey

1. Australia was once a British prison colony.

2. There is a hill in New Zealand named Taumatawhakatangihangakoauauota-mateapokaiwhenuakitanatahu.

3. Tonga, in the South Pacific, has some 170 islands, but only 36 are inhabited.

4. Australia's Great Barrier Reef, the largest coral reef structure on Earth, can be seen from space.

5. The middle of Australia, known as the Outback, is the driest part of the country and gets less than 10 inches (25 cm) of rain per year.

6. It's mandatory for everyone over 18 in Australia to vote. Those who don't are fined by the government.

7. Many Aussies refer to their country by the nickname "Oz."

1,200 MILES (1,930 KM)	DISTANCE BETWEEN AUSTRALIA AND NEW ZEALAND
516	NATIONAL PARKS IN AUSTRALIA
ABOUT 830	INDIGENOUS LANGUAGES SPOKEN IN PAPUA NEW GUINEA

LONG AS A PAPER CLIP ∗ KANGAROOS GATHER IN GROUPS CALLED MOBS

PHYSICAL

Land area
3,278,000 sq mi
(8,490,000 sq km)

Highest point
Mount Wilhelm,
Papua New Guinea
14,793 ft (4,509 m)

Lowest point
Lake Eyre, Australia
-52 ft (-16 m)

Longest river
Murray-Darling,
Australia 2,310 mi
(3,718 km)

Largest lake
Lake Eyre, Australia
3,430 sq mi
(8,884 sq km)

POLITICAL

Population
36,672,000

**Largest metropolitan
area**
Sydney, Australia
Pop. 4,395,000

Largest country
Australia
2,969,906 sq mi
(7,692,024 sq km)

**Most densely
populated country**
Nauru
1,313 people per sq mi
(507 per sq km)

Economy
Farming: livestock,
    wheat, fruit
Industry: mining,
    wool, oil
Services

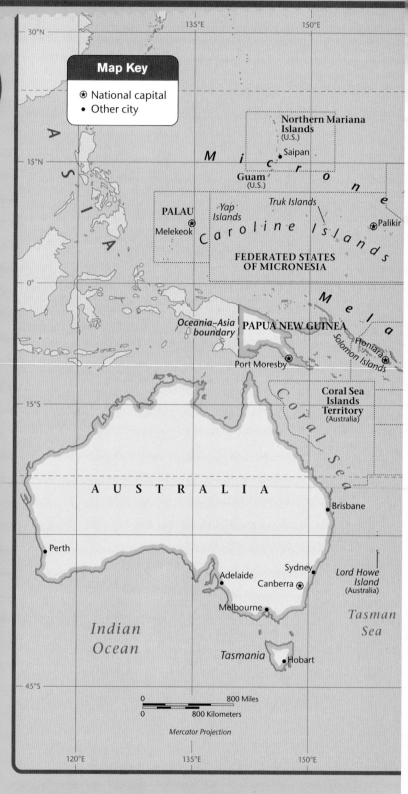

Map Key

⊗ National capital
• Other city

30°N
135°E
150°E

Northern Mariana
Islands
(U.S.)
• Saipan

15°N

M i c r o n e

Guam
(U.S.)

PALAU
Melekeok ⊗

·Yap
Islands

Truk Islands

Caroline Islands

⊗ Palikir

FEDERATED STATES
OF MICRONESIA

0°

M e l a

Oceania–Asia
boundary

PAPUA NEW GUINEA

Solomon Islands

Honiara ⊗

Port Moresby ⊗

15°S

Coral Sea
Islands
Territory
(Australia)

C o r a l   S e a

A U S T R A L I A

• Brisbane

• Perth

Adelaide
•

Sydney •
Canberra ⊗

Lord Howe
Island
(Australia)

Melbourne •

Tasman
Sea

Indian
Ocean

Tasmania

• Hobart

45°S

0   800 Miles
0   800 Kilometers

Mercator Projection

120°E
135°E
150°E

165°E 180° 165°W 150°W 135°W

North Pacific Ocean

Midway Is. (U.S.)

TROPIC OF CANCER

Monday | Sunday

Wake Island (U.S.)

Honolulu
Hawai'i • Hilo
(U.S.)

Johnston Atoll (U.S.)

15°N

Bikini Atoll

MARSHALL ISLANDS

Ralik Chain | Ratak Chain

⊛ Majuro

Kingman Reef (U.S.)

Palmyra Atoll (U.S.)

Line Islands

Howland Island (U.S.)

Baker Island (U.S.)

Kiritimati

EQUATOR 0°

Gilbert Islands

⊛ Tarawa

Jarvis I. (U.S.)

⊛ Yaren
NAURU

Phoenix Is.

KIRIBATI

SOLOMON ISLANDS

TUVALU
Funafuti ⊛

Tokelau (N.Z.)

Santa Cruz Islands

Wallis and Futuna Is. (France)

SAMOA
Apia ⊛

American Samoa (U.S.)
Pago Pago

Cook Islands (N.Z.)

Marquesas Islands

15°S

VANUATU

Port-Vila ⊛

⊛ Suva

TONGA

Niue (N.Z.)

Avarua •

Society Is.

Papeete •

French Polynesia (France)

Tuamotu Archipelago

FIJI ISLANDS

Nuku'alofa

Austral Is.

TROPIC OF CAPRICORN

• Nouméa

New Caledonia (France)

Norfolk Island (Australia)

South Pacific Ocean

Pitcairn Island (U.K.)

30°S

Kermadec Islands (N.Z.)

AUSTRALIA,
NEW ZEALAND, AND OCEANIA

Auckland •

NEW ZEALAND

⊛ Wellington

Christchurch •

Chatham Island (N.Z.)

45°S

Date Line

165°E 180° 165°W 150°W 135°W

EUROPE

A cluster of islands and peninsulas jutting west from Asia, Europe is bordered by the Atlantic and Arctic Oceans and more than a dozen seas. These bodies of water are linked to inland areas by canals and navigable rivers such as the Rhine and the Danube. The continent boasts a bounty of landscapes. Sweeping west from the Ural Mountains in Russia and Kazakhstan is the fertile Northern European Plain. Rugged uplands form part of Europe's western coast, while the Alps shield Mediterranean lands from frigid northern winds.

Europe is geographically small but is home to more than 700 million people in almost 50 countries, representing a mosaic of cultures, languages, and borders. Some of the most widely spoken languages in Europe include German, French, Italian, Spanish, Polish, Russian, and Dutch.

Here, first Greek and then Roman civilizations laid Europe's cultural foundation. Its colonial powers built vast empires, while its inventors and thinkers revolutionized world industry, economy, and politics. Today, the 27-member European Union seeks to unite the continent's diversity.

Saint Basil's Cathedral in Moscow, Russia

COOL CLICK

Go online to learn more about the countries of Europe.
travel.nationalgeographic.com/travel/continents/europe

reindeer herder from the indigenous Sami culture of northern Europe

REINDEER ARE FAST SWIMMERS • THEY CAN WALK 3,000 MILES (5,000 KM)

7 COOL THINGS ABOUT EUROPE

1. The minute hand of London's Big Ben clock travels about 118 miles (190 km) a year.

2. The first circus was held in Rome, Italy.

3. More chocolate is consumed in Switzerland than anywhere else in the world—12.4 pounds (5.6 kg) of chocolate per person every year.

4. The largest known ant supercolony stretches nearly 4,000 miles through Portugal, Spain, France, and Italy.

5. The word "purple" comes from a Greek word for a type of shellfish.

6. The first jet plane was flown in Germany.

7. About 85 percent of homes in Iceland are warmed using underground heat from geo-thermal hot springs.

Basilica of Santa Maria della Salute in Venice, Italy

143,200 SQUARE MILES (370,886 SQ KM)	AREA OF CASPIAN SEA, THE LARGEST LAKE ON EARTH
5,354 FEET (1,632 M)	DEPTH OF THE DEEPEST CAVE IN EUROPE, AUSTRIA'S LAMPRECHTSOFENVOGELSCHACHT
76 MILLION	NUMBER OF FOREIGN TOURISTS VISITING FRANCE EACH YEAR

A YEAR • REPORTS OF "FLYING REINDEER" DATE TO A.D. 1052

PHYSICAL

Land area
3,841,000 sq mi
(9,947,000 sq km)

Highest point
El'brus, Russia
18,510 ft (5,642 m)

Lowest point
Caspian Sea
-92 ft (-28 m)

Longest river
Volga, Russia
2,290 mi
(3,685 km)

**Largest lake
entirely in Europe**
Ladoga, Russia
6,835 sq mi
(17,703 sq km)

POLITICAL

Population
738,579,000

**Largest metropolitan
area**
Moscow, Russia
Pop. 10,523,000

**Largest country
entirely in Europe**
Ukraine
233,090 sq mi
(603,700 sq km)

**Most densely
populated country**
Monaco
48,231 people per sq mi
(18,622 per sq km)

Economy
Farming: vegetables,
fruit, grains
Industry: chemicals,
machinery
Services

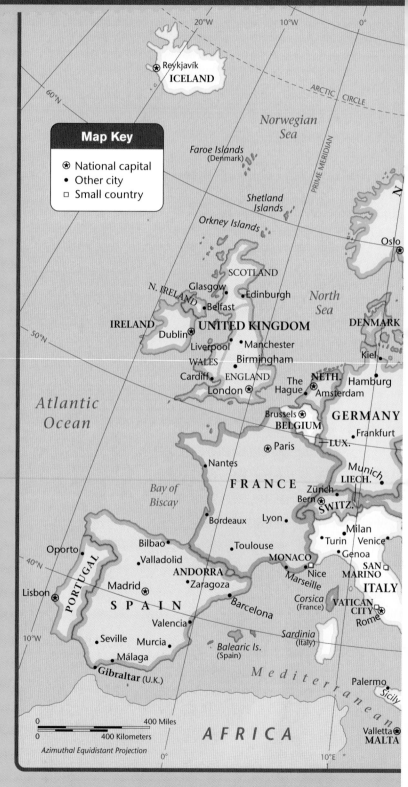

Map Key

⊛ National capital
• Other city
□ Small country

Reykjavík
ICELAND

ARCTIC CIRCLE

Norwegian
Sea

Faroe Islands
(Denmark)

PRIME MERIDIAN

N.

Shetland
Islands

Oslo

Orkney Islands

SCOTLAND

North
Sea

Glasgow •Edinburgh

N. IRELAND
Belfast

DENMARK

IRELAND
Dublin ⊛ UNITED KINGDOM

Kiel.

Liverpool •Manchester
WALES Birmingham

Hamburg

NETH.

Cardiff• ENGLAND

The
Hague•

Amsterdam

London ⊛

Atlantic
Ocean

Brussels ⊛ GERMANY
BELGIUM

⊛ Paris

•Frankfurt
LUX.

•Nantes

Munich

FRANCE

LIECH.

Zürich

Bay of
Biscay

Bern •

SWITZ.

•Bordeaux

Lyon•

Oporto

•Milan
•Turin Venice

Bilbao•

•Toulouse

•Genoa
MONACO

ANDORRA

•Valladolid

•Zaragoza

Nice

SAN
MARINO

Marseille

Lisbon•

Madrid ⊛

Barcelona

ITALY

PORTUGAL

SPAIN

Corsica
(France)

VATICAN
CITY
Rome

Valencia•

•Seville Murcia•

Sardinia
(Italy)

Balearic Is.
(Spain)

•Málaga

Gibraltar (U.K.)

Palermo

M e d i t e r r a n e a n

Sicily

Valletta ⊛

0   400 Miles

MALTA

0   400 Kilometers

AFRICA

Azimuthal Equidistant Projection

EUROPE

A commonly accepted division
between Asia and Europe—
marked here by a maroon,
dashed line—is formed by the
Ural Mountains, Ural River, Caspian
Sea, Caucasus Mountains, and
the Black Sea with its outlets, the
Bosporus and Dardanelles.

NORTH AMERICA

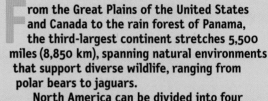

Canada lynx

From the Great Plains of the United States and Canada to the rain forest of Panama, the third-largest continent stretches 5,500 miles (8,850 km), spanning natural environments that support diverse wildlife, ranging from polar bears to jaguars.

North America can be divided into four large regions: the Great Plains, the mountainous West, the Canadian Shield of the Northeast, and the eastern region.

Before Columbus even "discovered" the New World, it was a land of abundance for its inhabitants. Cooler, less seasonal, and more thickly forested than today, it contained a wide variety of species. Living off the land, Native Americans spread across these varied landscapes. Although some native groups remain, the majority of North Americans today are descendants of immigrants.

North America is home to many large industrialized cities, including two of the largest metropolitan areas in the world: Mexico City, Mexico, and New York City, New York, U.S.A.

While abundant resources and fast-changing technologies have brought prosperity to Canada and the United States, other North American countries wrestle with the most basic needs. Promise and problems abound across this contrasting realm of 23 countries and more than 530 million people.

COOL CLICK

Learn more about North America online.
travel.nationalgeographic
.com/travel/continents/
north-america/

1,300 — AVERAGE NUMBER OF TORNADOES THAT OCCUR IN THE UNITED STATES EACH YEAR

9 MILLION — APPROXIMATE NUMBER OF CANADIANS WHO SPEAK FRENCH

2 INCHES (5 CM) — SIZE OF CUBA'S BEE HUMMINGBIRD, THE SMALLEST BIRD IN THE WORLD

THE TUFTS ON A LYNX'S EARS HELP IT HEAR MORE CLEARLY

7 COOL THINGS ABOUT NORTH AMERICA

1. More dinosaurs have been found in North America than anywhere else.

2. A 95-mile (153 km) -long underground river flows beneath Yucatán, Mexico.

3. A Canadian company bottles water that comes from 15,000-year-old icebergs.

4. The brightest light on a hotel is in Las Vegas, Nevada, and can be seen from airplanes 250 miles away.

5. About 35 species of sharks live off the coast of Cuba.

6. Cheetah ancestors roamed North America about four million years ago

7. An Aztec emperor in what is now Mexico introduced hot chocolate to Europeans.

Day of the Dead skeleton figurine from Mexico

NEW YORKER

Empire State Building (center), New York City, New York, U.S.A.

A LYNX'S LARGE, WIDE PAWS WORK LIKE SNOWSHOES

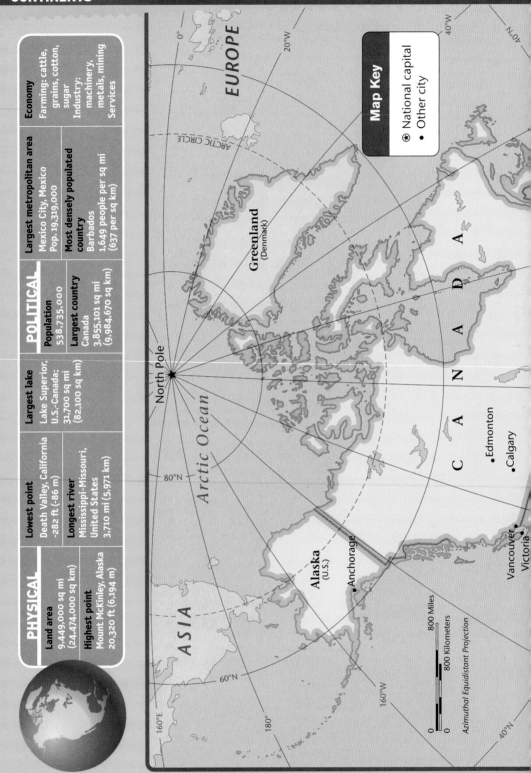

PHYSICAL

Lowest point
Death Valley, California
-282 ft (-86 m)

Highest point
Mount McKinley, Alaska
20,320 ft (6,194 m)

Longest river
Mississippi-Missouri,
United States
3,710 mi (5,971 km)

Largest lake
Lake Superior,
U.S.–Canada;
31,700 sq mi
(82,100 sq km)

POLITICAL

Population
538,735,000

Largest country
Canada
3,855,101 sq mi
(9,984,670 sq km)

Largest metropolitan area
Mexico City, Mexico
Pop. 19,319,000

**Most densely populated
country**
Barbados
1,649 people per sq mi
(637 per sq km)

Economy
Farming: cattle,
grains, cotton,
sugar
Industry:
machinery,
metals, mining
Services

Land area
9,449,000 sq mi
(24,474,000 sq km)

Map Key

⊛ National capital
• Other city

EUROPE

Greenland
(Denmark)

ARCTIC CIRCLE

North Pole

Arctic Ocean

80°N

ASIA

60°N

160°E

180°

160°W

C A N A D A

•Edmonton
•Calgary

Alaska
(U.S.)

•Anchorage

Vancouver•
Victoria•

800 Miles

800 Kilometers

Azimuthal Equidistant Projection

0°
20°W
40°W
40°N
20°E
40°N

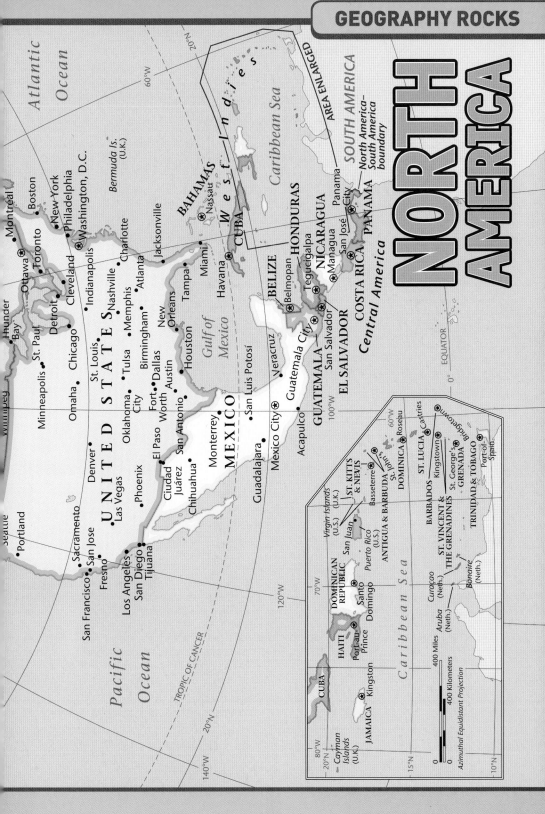

NORTH AMERICA

Atlantic Ocean

60°W

20°W

Bermuda Is. (U.K.)

Montréal
Ottawa
Toronto
Boston
New York
Philadelphia
Washington, D.C.
Detroit
Cleveland
Indianapolis
Charlotte
Jacksonville

Thunder Bay
Winnipeg
Minneapolis
St. Paul
Chicago
Omaha
St. Louis
Nashville
Memphis
Atlanta
Tampa
Miami

UNITED STATES

Denver
Las Vegas
Oklahoma City
Tulsa
Dallas
Fort Worth
Birmingham
New Orleans
Houston
Austin
San Antonio

Sacramento
San Jose
Fresno
San Francisco
Los Angeles
San Diego
Tijuana
Phoenix
El Paso
Ciudad Juárez
Chihuahua

Seattle
Portland

Pacific Ocean

120°W
140°W
20°N

TROPIC OF CANCER

Monterrey
MEXICO
Guadalajara
Mexico City
San Luis Potosí
Acapulco
Veracruz

Gulf of Mexico

100°W

BAHAMAS
Nassau
CUBA
Havana

West Indies

Caribbean Sea

BELIZE
Belmopan
GUATEMALA
Guatemala City
San Salvador
EL SALVADOR
HONDURAS
Tegucigalpa
NICARAGUA
Managua
San José
COSTA RICA
PANAMA
Panama City

Central America

AREA ENLARGED

SOUTH AMERICA
North America–South America boundary

EQUATOR
0°

289

SOUTH AMERICA

12,500 FEET (3,810 M) ABOVE SEA LEVEL	ELEVATION OF LAKE TITICACA, THE HIGHEST NAVIGABLE LAKE IN THE WORLD
2 MILLION SQUARE MILES (5.2 MILLION SQ KM)	SIZE OF THE AMAZON RAIN FOREST
7 MILLION	NUMBER OF LLAMAS AND ALPACAS IN SOUTH AMERICA

blue poison dart frog

POISON DART FROGS RAISED IN CAPTIVITY NEVER DEVELOP VENOM

The 12 countries of South America stretch from the warm waters of the Caribbean to the frigid ocean around Antarctica. The mighty Amazon carries more water than the world's next ten biggest rivers combined, draining a third of the continent. Its basin contains the planet's largest rain forest. The Andes tower along the continent's western edge from Colombia to southern Chile.

The gold-seeking Spaniards conquered the Amerindians when they arrived in the Andes in 1532. Along with the Portuguese, they ruled most of the continent for almost 300 years. The conquest of South America by Europeans took a heavy toll on its indigenous peoples.

Centuries of ethnic blending have woven Amerindian, European, African, and Asian heritage into South America's rich cultural fabric. Today's mix of colonial and indigenous languages demonstrates this unique blend.

Despite its relatively small population and wealth of natural resources, South America today is burdened by economic, social, and environmental problems. But with the majestic Andean mountain chain, the mighty Amazon River, and the most extensive rain forest on Earth, South America has nearly unlimited potential.

Peruvian girl in festival costume

Christ the Redeemer statue, Rio de Janeiro, Brazil

7 COOL THINGS ABOUT SOUTH AMERICA

1. One-quarter of all butterfly species on Earth live in South American rain forests.

2. Marine iguanas are found only in Ecuador's Galápagos Islands.

3. Guarani is the name of a people native to Paraguay, the country's basic unit of money, and one if its two official languages.

4. Rainbow-colored grasshoppers live in the rain forests of Peru.

5. The Amazon River is as long as the distance between New York City and Rome.

6. The guinea pig was first domesticated in South America.

7. Cape Horn, the southernmost tip of South America, is only 600 miles (965 km) away from Antarctica.

THEIR BRILLIANT COLORS WARN PREDATORS TO KEEP AWAY

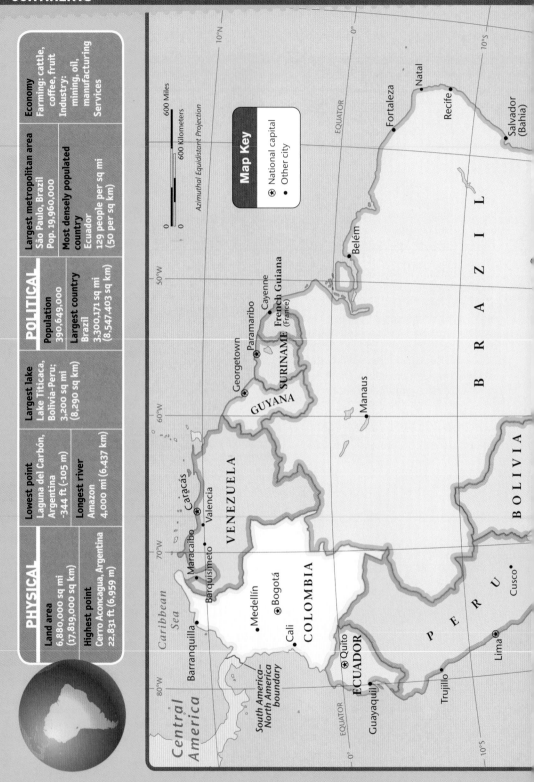

PHYSICAL

Land area
6,880,000 sq mi
(17,819,000 sq km)

Highest point
Cerro Aconcagua, Argentina
22,831 ft (6,959 m)

Lowest point
Laguna del Carbón, Argentina
-344 ft (-105 m)

Longest river
Amazon
4,000 mi (6,437 km)

Largest lake
Lake Titicaca, Bolivia-Peru;
3,200 sq mi
(8,290 sq km)

POLITICAL

Population
390,649,000

Largest country
Brazil
3,300,171 sq mi
(8,547,403 sq km)

Largest metropolitan area
São Paulo, Brazil
Pop. 19,960,000

Most densely populated country
Ecuador
129 people per sq mi
(50 per sq km)

Economy

Farming: cattle, coffee, fruit
Industry: mining, oil, manufacturing
Services

Map Key
⊛ National capital
• Other city

Azimuthal Equidistant Projection

600 Miles
600 Kilometers

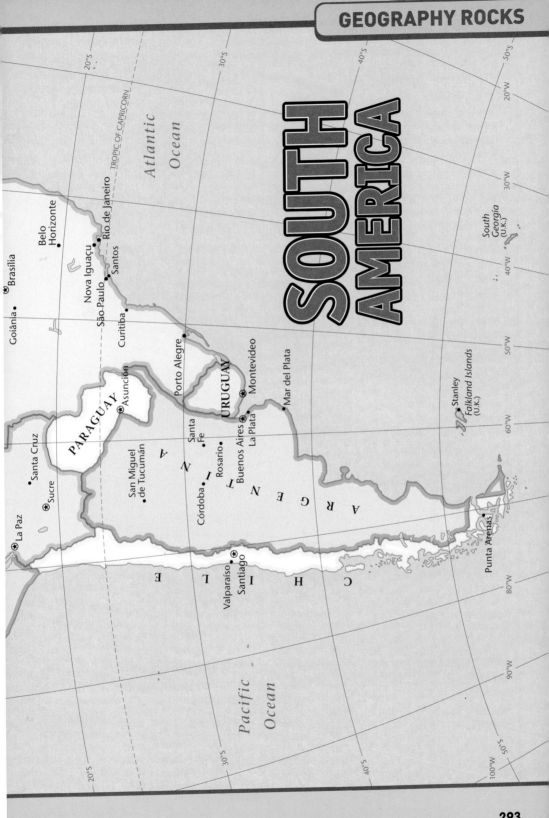

SOUTH AMERICA

Atlantic Ocean

Pacific Ocean

TROPIC OF CAPRICORN

Brazil cities: Brasília, Goiânia, Belo Horizonte, Rio de Janeiro, Nova Iguaçu, São Paulo, Santos, Curitiba, Porto Alegre

PARAGUAY — Asunción

URUGUAY — Montevideo

ARGENTINA — San Miguel de Tucumán, Córdoba, Santa Fe, Rosario, Buenos Aires, La Plata, Mar del Plata

CHILE — Valparaíso, Santiago, Punta Arenas

La Paz, Sucre, Santa Cruz

Falkland Islands (U.K.) — Stanley

South Georgia (U.K.)

20°S · 30°S · 40°S · 50°S

20°W · 30°W · 40°W · 50°W · 60°W · 80°W · 90°W · 100°W

COUNTRIES OF THE WORLD

The following pages present a general overview of all 194 independent countries recognized by the National Geographic Society, including the newest nation, Kosovo, which gained independence in 2008.

Flags of each independent country symbolize diverse cultures and histories. The statistical data provide highlights of geography and demography. They are a brief overview of each country. They present general characteristics and are not intended to be comprehensive. For example, not every language spoken in a specific country can be listed. Thus, languages shown are the most representative of that area. This is also true of the religions mentioned.

A country is defined as a political body with its own independent government, geographical space, and, in most cases, laws, military, and taxes.

Disputed areas such as Northern Cyprus and Taiwan, and dependencies of independent nations, such as Bermuda and Puerto Rico, are not included in this listing.

Note the color key at the bottom of the pages and the locator map below, which assign a color to each country based on the continent on which it is located. All information is based on 2009 to 2010 data—the most recent information available at press time.

Color Key by Continent

Afghanistan

Area: 251,773 sq mi (652,090 sq km)
Population: 29,121,000
Capital: Kabul, pop. 3,573,000
Currency: afghani
Religions: Sunni Muslim, Shiite Muslim
Languages: Afghan Persian (Dari), Pashto, Turkic languages (primarily Uzbek and Turkmen), Baluchi, 30 minor languages (including Pashai)

Albania

Area: 11,100 sq mi (28,748 sq km)
Population: 3,213,000
Capital: Tirana, pop. 433,000
Currency: lek
Religions: Muslim, Albanian Orthodox, Roman Catholic
Languages: Albanian, Greek, Vlach, Romani, Slavic dialects

Algeria

Area: 919,595 sq mi (2,381,741 sq km)
Population: 36,004,000
Capital: Algiers, pop. 2,740,000
Currency: Algerian dinar
Religion: Sunni Muslim
Languages: Arabic, French, Berber dialects

Andorra

Area: 181 sq mi (469 sq km)
Population: 84,000
Capital: Andorra la Vella, pop. 25,000
Currency: euro
Religion: Roman Catholic
Languages: Catalan, French, Castilian, Portuguese

Angola

Area: 481,354 sq mi (1,246,700 sq km)
Population: 18,993,000
Capital: Luanda, pop. 4,511,000
Currency: kwanza
Religions: indigenous beliefs, Roman Catholic, Protestant
Languages: Portuguese, Bantu, and other African languages

Antigua and Barbuda

Area: 171 sq mi (442 sq km)
Population: 91,000
Capital: St. John's, pop. 27,000
Currency: East Caribbean dollar
Religions: Anglican, Seventh-day Adventist, Pentecostal, Moravian, Roman Catholic, Methodist, Baptist, Church of God, other Christian
Languages: English, local dialects

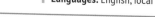

Argentina

Area: 1,073,518 sq mi
(2,780,400 sq km)
Population: 40,519,000
Capital: Buenos Aires,
pop. 12,988,000
Currency: Argentine peso
Religion: Roman Catholic
Languages: Spanish, English, Italian, German, French

Armenia

Area: 11,484 sq mi
(29,743 sq km)
Population: 3,110,000
Capital: Yerevan, pop. 1,110,000
Currency: dram
Religions: Armenian Apostolic, other Christian
Language: Armenian

Australia

Area: 2,969,906 sq mi
(7,692,024 sq km)
Population: 22,411,000
Capital: Canberra, pop. 384,000
Currency: Australian dollar
Religions: Roman Catholic, Anglican
Language: English

Austria

Area: 32,378 sq mi (83,858 sq km)
Population: 8,385,000
Capital: Vienna, pop. 1,693,000
Currency: euro
Religions: Roman Catholic, Protestant, Muslim
Language: German

Azerbaijan

Area: 33,436 sq mi
(86,600 sq km)
Population: 9,048,000
Capital: Baku, pop. 1,950,000
Currency: Azerbaijani manat
Religion: Muslim
Language: Azerbaijani (Azeri)

Bahamas

Area: 5,382 sq mi (13,939 sq km)
Population: 342,000
Capital: Nassau, pop. 248,000
Currency: Bahamian dollar
Religions: Baptist, Anglican, Roman Catholic,
Pentecostal, Church of God
Languages: English, Creole

Bahrain

Area: 277 sq mi (717 sq km)
Population: 1,254,000
Capital: Manama, pop. 163,000
Currency: Bahraini dinar
Religions: Shiite Muslim, Sunni Muslim, Christian
Languages: Arabic, English, Farsi, Urdu

Bangladesh

Area: 56,977 sq mi (147,570 sq km)
Population: 164,425,000
Capital: Dhaka, pop. 14,251,000
Currency: taka
Religions: Muslim, Hindu
Languages: Bangla (Bengali), English

Barbados

Area: 166 sq mi (430 sq km)
Population: 274,000
Capital: Bridgetown, pop. 112,000
Currency: Barbadian dollar
Religions: Anglican, Pentecostal, Methodist, other
Protestant, Roman Catholic
Language: English

Belarus

Area: 80,153 sq mi
(207,595 sq km)
Population: 9,470,000
Capital: Minsk, pop. 1,837,000
Currency: Belarusian ruble
Religions: Eastern Orthodox, other (includes Roman
Catholic, Protestant, Jewish, Muslim)
Languages: Belarusian, Russian

Belgium

Area: 11,787 sq mi (30,528 sq km)
Population: 10,811,000
Capital: Brussels, pop. 1,892,000
Currency: euro
Religions: Roman Catholic, other (includes Protestant)
Languages: Dutch, French

Bosnia and Herzegovina

Area: 19,741 sq mi (51,129 sq km)
Population: 3,843,000
Capital: Sarajevo, pop. 392,000
Currency: konvertibilna marka (convertible mark)
Religions: Muslim, Orthodox, Roman Catholic
Languages: Bosnian, Croatian, Serbian

Belize

Area: 8,867 sq mi (22,965 sq km)
Population: 345,000
Capital: Belmopan, pop. 20,000
Currency: Belizean dollar
Religions: Roman Catholic, Protestant (includes Pentecostal, Seventh-day Adventist, Mennonite, Methodist)
Languages: Spanish, Creole, Mayan dialects, English, Garifuna (Carib), German

Botswana

Area: 224,607 sq mi (581,730 sq km)
Population: 1,826,000
Capital: Gaborone, pop. 196,000
Currency: pula
Religions: Christian, Badimo
Languages: Setswana, Kalanga

Benin

Area: 43,484 sq mi (112,622 sq km)
Population: 9,801,000
Capitals: Porto-Novo, pop. 276,000; Cotonou, pop. 815,000
Currency: Communauté Financière Africaine franc
Religions: Christian, Muslim, Vodoun
Languages: French, Fon, Yoruba, tribal languages

Brazil

Area: 3,300,171 sq mi (8,547,403 sq km)
Population: 193,253,000
Capital: Brasília, pop. 3,789,000
Currency: real
Religions: Roman Catholic, Protestant
Language: Portuguese

Bhutan

Area: 17,954 sq mi (46,500 sq km)
Population: 695,000
Capital: Thimphu, pop. 89,000
Currencies: ngultrum; Indian rupee
Religions: Lamaistic Buddhist, Indian- and Nepalese-influenced Hindu
Languages: Dzongkha, Tibetan dialects, Nepalese dialects

Brunei

Area: 2,226 sq mi (5,765 sq km)
Population: 379,000
Capital: Bandar Seri Begawan, pop. 22,000
Currency: Bruneian dollar
Religions: Muslim, Buddhist, Christian, other (includes indigenous beliefs)
Languages: Malay, English, Chinese

Bolivia

Area: 424,164 sq mi (1,098,581 sq km)
Population: 10,426,000
Capitals: La Paz, pop. 1,642,000; Sucre, pop. 281,000
Currency: boliviano
Religions: Roman Catholic, Protestant (includes Evangelical Methodist)
Languages: Spanish, Quechua, Aymara

Bulgaria

Area: 42,855 sq mi (110,994 sq km)
Population: 7,542,000
Capital: Sofia, pop. 1,192,000
Currency: lev
Religions: Bulgarian Orthodox, Muslim
Languages: Bulgarian, Turkish, Roma

 COLOR KEY ● Africa ● Australia, New Zealand, and Oceania

Burkina Faso

Area: 105,869 sq mi (274,200 sq km)
Population: 16,242,000
Capital: Ouagadougou, pop. 1,777,000
Currency: Communauté Financière Africaine franc
Religions: Muslim, indigenous beliefs, Christian
Languages: French, native African languages

Burundi

Area: 10,747 sq mi (27,834 sq km)
Population: 8,519,000
Capital: Bujumbura, pop. 455,000
Currency: Burundi franc
Religions: Roman Catholic, indigenous beliefs, Muslim, Protestant
Languages: Kirundi, French, Swahili

Cambodia

Area: 69,898 sq mi (181,035 sq km)
Population: 15,053,000
Capital: Phnom Penh, pop. 1,519,000
Currency: riel
Religion: Theravada Buddhist
Language: Khmer

Cameroon

Area: 183,569 sq mi (475,442 sq km)
Population: 19,958,000
Capital: Yaoundé, pop. 1,739,000
Currency: Communauté Financière Africaine franc
Religions: indigenous beliefs, Christian, Muslim
Languages: 24 major African language groups, English, French

Canada

Area: 3,855,101 sq mi (9,984,670 sq km)
Population: 34,146,000
Capital: Ottawa, pop. 1,170,000
Currency: Canadian dollar
Religions: Roman Catholic, Protestant (includes United Church, Anglican), other Christian
Languages: English, French

Cape Verde

Area: 1,558 sq mi (4,036 sq km)
Population: 518,000
Capital: Praia, pop. 125,000
Currency: Cape Verdean escudo
Religions: Roman Catholic (infused with indigenous beliefs), Protestant (mostly Church of the Nazarene)
Languages: Portuguese, Crioulo

MOST POPULOUS COUNTRIES
(mid-2010 data)

1.	China	1,338,114,000
2.	India	1,188,831,000
3.	United States	309,636,000
4.	Indonesia	235,496,000
5.	Brazil	193,253,000
6.	Pakistan	184,753,000
7.	Bangladesh	164,425,000
8.	Nigeria	158,259,000

LEAST POPULOUS COUNTRIES
(mid-2010 data)

1.	Vatican City	798
2.	Tuvalu	10,000
3.	Nauru	11,000
4.	Palau	21,000
5.	San Marino	32,000
6.	Liechtenstein	36,000
7.	Monaco	36,000
8.	St. Kitts and Nevis	53,000

● Asia ● Europe ● North America ● South America

Central African Republic

Area: 240,535 sq mi (622,984 sq km)
Population: 4,845,000
Capital: Bangui, pop. 702,000
Currency: Communauté Financière Africaine franc
Religions: indigenous beliefs, Protestant, Roman Catholic, Muslim
Languages: French, Sangho, tribal languages

Chad

Area: 495,755 sq mi (1,284,000 sq km)
Population: 11,506,000
Capital: N'Djamena, pop. 808,000
Currency: Communauté Financière Africaine franc
Religions: Muslim, Catholic, Protestant, animist
Languages: French, Arabic, Sara, more than 120 languages and dialects

Chile

Area: 291,930 sq mi (756,096 sq km)
Population: 17,094,000
Capital: Santiago, pop. 5,883,000
Currency: Chilean peso
Religions: Roman Catholic, Evangelical
Language: Spanish

China

Area: 3,705,405 sq mi (9,596,960 sq km)
Population: 1,338,114,000
Capital: Beijing, pop. 12,214,000
Currency: renminbi (yuan)
Religions: Taoist, Buddhist, Christian
Languages: Standard Chinese or Mandarin, Yue, Wu, Minbei, Minnan, Xiang, Gan, Hakka dialects

Colombia

Area: 440,831 sq mi (1,141,748 sq km)
Population: 45,508,000
Capital: Bogotá, pop. 8,262,000
Currency: Colombian peso
Religion: Roman Catholic
Language: Spanish

Comoros

Area: 719 sq mi (1,862 sq km)
Population: 691,000
Capital: Moroni, pop. 49,000
Currency: Comoran franc
Religion: Sunni Muslim
Languages: Arabic, French, Shikomoro

Congo

Area: 132,047 sq mi (342,000 sq km)
Population: 3,938,000
Capital: Brazzaville, pop. 1,292,000
Currency: Communauté Financière Africaine franc
Religions: Christian, animist
Languages: French, Lingala, Monokutuba, local languages

Costa Rica

Area: 19,730 sq mi (51,100 sq km)
Population: 4,578,000
Capital: San José, pop. 1,416,000
Currency: Costa Rican colón
Religions: Roman Catholic, Evangelical
Languages: Spanish, English

5 cool things about **COSTA RICA**

1. It takes less than one hour to fly from one coast of Costa Rica to the other.

2. Costa Rica means "Rich Coast" in Spanish.

3. Costa Ricans refer to themselves as "Ticos" (males) or "Ticas" (females).

4. Arenal volcano in northwestern Costa Rica is one of the world's most active volcanoes.

5. Costa Rica is the only country in the Western Hemisphere without an army.

COLOR KEY ● Africa ● Australia, New Zealand, and Oceania

Côte d'Ivoire (Ivory Coast)

Area: 124,503 sq mi
(322,462 sq km)
Population: 22,000,000
Capitals: Abidjan, pop. 4,009,000;
Yamoussoukro, pop. 808,000
Currency: Communauté Financière Africaine franc
Religions: Muslim, indigenous beliefs, Christian
Languages: French, Dioula, other native dialects

Croatia

Area: 21,831 sq mi
(56,542 sq km)
Population: 4,424,000
Capital: Zagreb, pop. 685,000
Currency: kuna
Religions: Roman Catholic, Orthodox
Language: Croatian

Cuba

Area: 42,803 sq mi
(110,860 sq km)
Population: 11,246,000
Capital: Havana, pop. 2,140,000
Currency: Cuban peso
Religions: Roman Catholic, Protestant, Jehovah's
Witnesses, Jewish, Santería
Language: Spanish

Cyprus

Area: 3,572 sq mi (9,251 sq km)
Population: 1,096,000
Capital: Nicosia, pop. 240,000
Currencies: euro; new Turkish
lira in Northern Cyprus
Religions: Greek Orthodox, Muslim, Maronite,
Armenian Apostolic
Languages: Greek, Turkish, English

Czech Republic (Czechia)

Area: 30,450 sq mi (78,866 sq km)
Population: 10,527,000
Capital: Prague, pop. 1,162,000
Currency: koruny
Religion: Roman Catholic
Language: Czech

Democratic Republic of the Congo

Area: 905,365 sq mi
(2,344,885 sq km)
Population: 67,827,000
Capital: Kinshasa, pop. 8,401,000
Currency: Congolese franc
Religions: Roman Catholic, Protestant, Kimbanguist,
Muslim, syncretic sects, indigenous beliefs
Languages: French, Lingala, Kingwana, Kikongo, Tshiluba

Denmark

Area: 16,640 sq mi (43,098 sq km)
Population: 5,546,000
Capital: Copenhagen, pop. 1,174,000
Currency: Danish krone
Religions: Evangelical Lutheran, other Protestant,
Roman Catholic
Languages: Danish, Faroese, Greenlandic, German,
English as second language

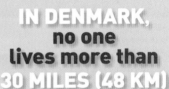

**IN DENMARK,
no one
lives more than
30 MILES (48 KM)
from THE SEA.**

Djibouti

Area: 8,958 sq mi
(23,200 sq km)
Population: 879,000
Capital: Djibouti, pop. 567,000
Currency: Djiboutian franc
Religions: Muslim, Christian
Languages: French, Arabic, Somali, Afar

Dominica

Area: 290 sq mi (751 sq km)
Population: 72,000
Capital: Roseau, pop. 14,000
Currency: East Caribbean
dollar
Religions: Roman Catholic, Seventh-day Adventist,
Pentecostal, Baptist, Methodist, other Christian
Languages: English, French patois

Dominican Republic

Area: 18,704 sq mi
(48,442 sq km)
Population: 9,884,000
Capital: Santo Domingo,
pop. 2,138,000
Currency: Dominican peso
Religion: Roman Catholic
Language: Spanish

Ecuador

Area: 109,483 sq mi
(283,560 sq km)
Population: 14,205,000
Capital: Quito, pop. 1,801,000
Currency: U.S. dollar
Religion: Roman Catholic
Languages: Spanish, Quechua, other
Amerindian languages

Egypt

Area: 386,874 sq mi
(1,002,000 sq km)
Population: 80,384,000
Capital: Cairo, pop. 10,903,000
Currency: Egyptian pound
Religions: Muslim (mostly Sunni), Coptic Christian
Languages: Arabic, English, French

El Salvador

Area: 8,124 sq mi (21,041 sq km)
Population: 6,194,000
Capital: San Salvador,
pop. 1,534,000
Currency: U.S. dollar
Religions: Roman Catholic, Protestant
Languages: Spanish, Nahua

Equatorial Guinea

Area: 10,831 sq mi (28,051 sq km)
Population: 693,000
Capital: Malabo, pop. 128,000
Currency: Communauté
Financière Africaine franc
Religions: Christian (predominantly Roman Catholic),
pagan practices
Languages: Spanish, French, Fang, Bubi

Eritrea

Area: 46,774 sq mi (121,144 sq km)
Population: 5,224,000
Capital: Asmara, pop. 649,000
Currency: nakfa
Religions: Muslim, Coptic Christian, Roman Catholic,
Protestant
Languages: Afar, Arabic, Tigre, Kunama, Tigrinya, other
Cushitic languages

Estonia

Area: 17,462 sq mi (45,227 sq km)
Population: 1,340,000
Capital: Tallinn, pop. 399,000
Currency: euro
Religions: Evangelical Lutheran, Orthodox
Languages: Estonian, Russian

Ethiopia

Area: 437,600 sq mi
(1,133,380 sq km)
Population: 84,976,000
Capital: Addis Ababa,
pop. 2,863,000
Currency: birr
Religions: Christian, Muslim, traditional
Languages: Amharic, Oromigna, Tigrinya, Guaragigna

Fiji Islands

Area: 7,095 sq mi (18,376 sq km)
Population: 850,000
Capital: Suva, pop. 174,000
Currency: Fijian dollar
Religions: Christian (Methodist, Roman Catholic,
Assembly of God), Hindu (Sanatan), Muslim (Sunni)
Languages: English, Fijian, Hindustani

Finland

Area: 130,558 sq mi
(338,145 sq km)
Population: 5,364,000
Capital: Helsinki, pop. 1,107,000
Currency: euro
Religion: Lutheran Church of Finland
Languages: Finnish, Swedish

France

Area: 210,026 sq mi (543,965 sq km)
Population: 62,956,000
Capital: Paris, pop. 10,410,000
Currency: euro
Religions: Roman Catholic, Muslim
Language: French

Gabon

Area: 103,347 sq mi (267,667 sq km)
Population: 1,501,000
Capital: Libreville, pop. 619,000
Currency: Communauté Financière Africaine franc
Religions: Christian, animist
Languages: French, Fang, Myene, Nzebi, Bapounou/Eschira, Bandjabi

Gambia

Area: 4,361 sq mi (11,295 sq km)
Population: 1,751,000
Capital: Banjul, pop. 436,000
Currency: dalasi
Religions: Muslim, Christian
Languages: English, Mandinka, Wolof, Fula, other indigenous vernaculars

Georgia

Area: 26,911 sq mi (69,700 sq km)
Population: 4,638,000
Capital: T'bilisi, pop. 1,115,000
Currency: lari
Religions: Orthodox Christian, Muslim, Armenian-Gregorian
Languages: Georgian, Russian, Armenian, Azeri, Abkhaz

Germany

Area: 137,847 sq mi (357,022 sq km)
Population: 81,624,000
Capital: Berlin, pop. 3,438,000
Currency: euro
Religions: Protestant, Roman Catholic, Muslim
Language: German

Ghana

Area: 92,100 sq mi (238,537 sq km)
Population: 23,992,000
Capital: Accra, pop. 2,269,000
Currency: Ghana cedi
Religions: Christian (Pentecostal/Charismatic, Protestant, Roman Catholic, other), Muslim, traditional beliefs
Languages: Asante, Ewe, Fante, Boron (Brong), Dagomba, Dangme, Dagarte (Dagaba), Akyem, Ga, English

Greece

Area: 50,949 sq mi (131,957 sq km)
Population: 11,331,000
Capital: Athens, pop. 3,252,000
Currency: euro
Religion: Greek Orthodox
Languages: Greek, English, French

Grenada

Area: 133 sq mi (344 sq km)
Population: 110,000
Capital: St. George's, pop. 40,000
Currency: East Caribbean dollar
Religions: Roman Catholic, Anglican, other Protestant
Languages: English, French patois

Guatemala

Area: 42,042 sq mi (108,889 sq km)
Population: 14,362,000
Capital: Guatemala City, pop. 1,075,000
Currency: quetzal
Religions: Roman Catholic, Protestant, indigenous Maya beliefs
Languages: Spanish, 23 official Amerindian languages

Guinea

Area: 94,926 sq mi (245,857 sq km)
Population: 10,817,000
Capital: Conakry, pop. 1,597,000
Currency: Guinean franc
Religions: Muslim, Christian, indigenous beliefs
Languages: French, ethnic languages

COOL CLICK

Want to see interactive maps and videos of the countries? Go online to National Geographic. travel.nationalgeographic.com/ travel/countries/

Hungary

Area: 35,919 sq mi (93,030 sq km)
Population: 10,004,000
Capital: Budapest, pop. 1,705,000
Currency: forint
Religions: Roman Catholic, Calvinist, Lutheran
Language: Hungarian

Guinea-Bissau

Area: 13,948 sq mi (36,125 sq km)
Population: 1,647,000
Capital: Bissau, pop. 302,000
Currency: Communauté Financière Africaine franc
Religions: indigenous beliefs, Muslim, Christian
Languages: Portuguese, Crioulo, African languages

Iceland

Area: 39,769 sq mi (103,000 sq km)
Population: 317,000
Capital: Reykjavík, pop. 198,000
Currency: Icelandic krona
Religion: Lutheran Church of Iceland
Languages: Icelandic, English, Nordic languages, German

Guyana

Area: 83,000 sq mi (214,969 sq km)
Population: 772,000
Capital: Georgetown, pop. 132,000
Currency: Guyanese dollar
Religions: Christian, Hindu, Muslim
Languages: English, Amerindian dialects, Creole, Hindustani, Urdu

India

Area: 1,269,221 sq mi (3,287,270 sq km)
Population: 1,188,831,000
Capital: New Delhi, pop. 21,720,000 (part of Delhi metropolitan area)
Currency: Indian rupee
Religions: Hindu, Muslim
Languages: Hindi, 21 other official languages, Hindustani (popular Hindi/Urdu variant in the north)

Haiti

Area: 10,714 sq mi (27,750 sq km)
Population: 9,785,000
Capital: Port-au-Prince, pop. 2,643,000
Currency: gourde
Religions: Roman Catholic, Protestant (Baptist, Pentecostal, other)
Languages: French, Creole

Indonesia

Area: 742,308 sq mi (1,922,570 sq km)
Population: 235,496,000
Capital: Jakarta, pop. 9,121,000
Currency: Indonesian rupiah
Religions: Muslim, Protestant, Roman Catholic
Languages: Bahasa Indonesia (modified form of Malay), English, Dutch, Javanese, local dialects

Honduras

Area: 43,433 sq mi (112,492 sq km)
Population: 7,616,000
Capital: Tegucigalpa, pop. 1,000,000
Currency: lempira
Religions: Roman Catholic, Protestant
Languages: Spanish, Amerindian dialects

Iran

Area: 636,296 sq mi (1,648,000 sq km)
Population: 75,078,000
Capital: Tehran, pop. 7,190,000
Currency: Iranian rial
Religions: Shiite Muslim, Sunni Muslim
Languages: Persian, Turkic, Kurdish, Luri, Baluchi, Arabic

COLOR KEY ● Africa ● Australia, New Zealand, and Oceania

Iraq

Area: 168,754 sq mi
(437,072 sq km)
Population: 31,467,000
Capital: Baghdad, pop. 5,751,000
Currency: Iraqi dinar
Religions: Shiite Muslim, Sunni Muslim
Languages: Arabic, Kurdish, Assyrian, Armenian

Ireland

Area: 27,133 sq mi
(70,273 sq km)
Population: 4,505,000
Capital: Dublin, pop. 1,084,000
Currency: euro
Religions: Roman Catholic, Church of Ireland
Languages: Irish (Gaelic), English

5 cool things about IRELAND

1. The shamrock (a three-leaf clover) is the national plant of Ireland.

2. Ireland's nickname is the Emerald Isle because of its green landscape.

3. Muckanaghederdaughaulia is a place-name in Ireland.

4. Thousands of people kiss Ireland's famous Blarney Stone every year. It's said to bring the gift of eloquence.

5. Some of Ireland's major cities were originally Viking settlements.

Israel

Area: 8,550 sq mi (22,145 sq km)
Population: 7,634,000
Capital: Jerusalem, pop. 768,000
Currency: new Israeli sheqel
Religions: Jewish, Muslim
Languages: Hebrew, Arabic, English

Italy

Area: 116,345 sq mi
(301,333 sq km)
Population: 60,506,000
Capital: Rome, pop. 3,357,000
Currency: euro
Religions: Roman Catholic, Protestant, Jewish, Muslim
Languages: Italian, German, French, Slovene

Jamaica

Area: 4,244 sq mi
(10,991 sq km)
Population: 2,708,000
Capital: Kingston, pop. 580,000
Currency: Jamaican dollar
Religions: Protestant (Church of God, Seventh-day Adventist, Pentecostal, Baptist, Anglican, other)
Languages: English, English patois

Japan

Area: 145,902 sq mi (377,887 sq km)
Population: 127,370,000
Capital: Tokyo, pop. 36,507,000
Currency: yen
Religions: Shinto, Buddhist
Language: Japanese

Jordan

Area: 34,495 sq mi
(89,342 sq km)
Population: 6,496,000
Capital: Amman, pop. 1,088,000
Currency: Jordanian dinar
Religions: Sunni Muslim, Christian
Languages: Arabic, English

Kazakhstan

Area: 1,049,155 sq mi
(2,717,300 sq km)
Population: 16,315,000
Capital: Astana, pop. 650,000
Currency: tenge
Religions: Muslim, Russian Orthodox
Languages: Kazakh (Qazaq), Russian

Kenya

Area: 224,081 sq mi (580,367 sq km)
Population: 40,047,000
Capital: Nairobi, pop. 3,375,000
Currency: Kenyan shilling
Religions: Protestant, Roman Catholic, Muslim, indigenous beliefs
Languages: English, Kiswahili, many indigenous languages

Kosovo

Area: 4,203 sq mi (10,887 sq km)
Population: 2,252,000
Capital: Prishtina, pop. 600,000
Currency: euro
Religions: Muslim, Serbian Orthodox, Roman Catholic
Languages: Albanian, Serbian, Bosnian, Turkish, Roma

Kiribati

Area: 313 sq mi (811 sq km)
Population: 101,000
Capital: Tarawa, pop. 43,000
Currency: Australian dollar
Religions: Roman Catholic, Protestant (Congregational)
Languages: I-Kiribati, English

Kuwait

Area: 6,880 sq mi (17,818 sq km)
Population: 3,117,000
Capital: Kuwait City, pop. 2,230,000
Currency: Kuwaiti dinar
Religions: Sunni Muslim, Shiite Muslim
Languages: Arabic, English

You Are There!

Masai Mara National Reserve
Kenya, Africa

Just about a four-hour drive from the Kenyan capital of Nairobi, this vast stretch of savanna might as well be a world away from the hustle-and-bustle of city life. A safari through the 600 square miles (1,554 sq km) of grasslands gives you the opportunity to see some of Earth's most elusive creatures. Look closely and you may see leopards or even the endangered black rhino. And over there by the acacia tree? It's a pride of lions lazing around in the sun. Here, hippos bathe alongside Nile crocodiles in the Mara River, while African elephants cool off by its banks.

Near the Reserve, the people of the Maasai live in huts roofed with grass. Known for their elegant beads and colorful dress, the Maasai are considered semi-nomadic, often traveling with their herds as the cattle seek out fresh grass to graze—a journey much like that of the many wild animals that live on their land!

COLOR KEY ● Africa ● Australia, New Zealand, and Oceania

Kyrgyzstan

Area: 77,182 sq mi
(199,900 sq km)
Population: 5,339,000
Capital: Bishkek, pop. 854,000
Currency: som
Religions: Muslim, Russian Orthodox
Languages: Kyrgyz, Uzbek, Russian

Laos

Area: 91,429 sq mi
(236,800 sq km)
Population: 6,436,000
Capital: Vientiane, pop. 799,000
Currency: kip
Religions: Buddhist, animist
Languages: Lao, French, English, various ethnic languages

Latvia

Area: 24,938 sq mi
(64,589 sq km)
Population: 2,242,000
Capital: Riga, pop. 711,000
Currency: Latvian lat
Religions: Lutheran, Roman Catholic, Russian Orthodox
Languages: Latvian, Russian, Lithuanian

Lebanon

Area: 4,036 sq mi (10,452 sq km)
Population: 4,255,000
Capital: Beirut, pop. 1,909,000
Currency: Lebanese pound
Religions: Muslim, Christian
Languages: Arabic, French, English, Armenian

Lesotho

Area: 11,720 sq mi (30,355 sq km)
Population: 1,920,000
Capital: Maseru, pop. 220,000
Currencies: loti; South African rand
Religions: Christian, indigenous beliefs
Languages: Sesotho, English, Zulu, Xhosa

Liberia

Area: 43,000 sq mi
(111,370 sq km)
Population: 4,102,000
Capital: Monrovia,
pop. 882,000
Currency: Liberian dollar
Religions: Christian, indigenous beliefs, Muslim
Languages: English, some 20 ethnic languages

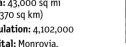

Libya

Area: 679,362 sq mi
(1,759,540 sq km)
Population: 6,546,000
Capital: Tripoli, pop. 1,095,000
Currency: Libyan dinar
Religion: Sunni Muslim
Languages: Arabic, Italian, English

Liechtenstein

Area: 62 sq mi (160 sq km)
Population: 36,000
Capital: Vaduz, pop. 5,000
Currency: Swiss franc
Religions: Roman Catholic, Protestant
Languages: German, Alemannic dialect

Lithuania

Area: 25,212 sq mi
(65,300 sq km)
Population: 3,317,000
Capital: Vilnius, pop. 546,000
Currency: litas
Religions: Roman Catholic, Russian Orthodox
Languages: Lithuanian, Russian, Polish

Luxembourg

Area: 998 sq mi (2,586 sq km)
Population: 508,000
Capital: Luxembourg, pop. 90,000
Currency: euro
Religions: Roman Catholic, Protestant, Jewish, Muslim
Languages: Luxembourgish, German, French

Macedonia

Area: 9,928 sq mi
(25,713 sq km)
Population: 2,054,000
Capital: Skopje, pop. 480,000
Currency: Macedonian denar
Religions: Macedonian Orthodox, Muslim
Languages: Macedonian, Albanian, Turkish

Malaysia

Area: 127,355 sq mi (329,847 sq km)
Population: 28,858,000
Capital: Kuala Lumpur,
pop. 1,494,000
Currency: ringgit
Religions: Muslim, Buddhist, Christian, Hindu
Languages: Bahasa Malaysia, English, Chinese, Tamil,
Telugu, Malayalam, Panjabi, Thai, indigenous languages

Madagascar

Area: 226,658 sq mi
(587,041 sq km)
Population: 20,146,000
Capital: Antananarivo,
pop. 1,816,000
Currency: Madagascar ariary
Religions: indigenous beliefs, Christian, Muslim
Languages: English, French, Malagasy

Maldives

Area: 115 sq mi (298 sq km)
Population: 319,000
Capital: Male, pop. 120,000
Currency: rufiyaa
Religion: Sunni Muslim
Languages: Maldivian Dhivehi, English

5 cool things about MADAGASCAR

1. Madagascar's 50 lemur species make up nearly half of the island's mammals.

2. A lizard in Madagascar has a third eye on top of its head.

3. Researchers in Madagascar recently discovered a fossil of a beach-ball-size amphibian, believed to be the largest frog to ever have lived.

4. Madagascar is home to nearly half of the world's known chameleon species.

5. Madagascar was a colony of France from 1896 to 1960.

Mali

Area: 478,841 sq mi (1,240,192 sq km)
Population: 15,185,000
Capital: Bamako, pop. 1,628,000
Currency: Communauté Financière Africaine franc
Religions: Muslim, indigenous beliefs
Languages: Bambara, French, numerous African languages

Malta

Area: 122 sq mi (316 sq km)
Population: 419,000
Capital: Valletta, pop. 199,000
Currency: euro
Religion: Roman Catholic
Languages: Maltese, English

Malawi

Area: 45,747 sq mi
(118,484 sq km)
Population: 15,448,000
Capital: Lilongwe, pop. 821,000
Currency: Malawian kwacha
Religions: Christian, Muslim
Languages: Chichewa, Chinyanja, Chiyao, Chitumbuka

Marshall Islands

Area: 70 sq mi (181 sq km)
Population: 54,000
Capital: Majuro, pop. 30,000
Currency: U.S. dollar
Religions: Protestant, Assembly of God, Roman Catholic
Language: Marshallese

COLOR KEY ● Africa ● Australia, New Zealand, and Oceania

Mauritania

Area: 397,955 sq mi
(1,030,700 sq km)
Population: 3,366,000
Capital: Nouakchott, pop. 709,000
Currency: ouguiya
Religion: Muslim
Languages: Arabic, Pulaar, Soninke, French, Hassaniya, Wolof

Mauritius

Area: 788 sq mi (2,040 sq km)
Population: 1,281,000
Capital: Port Louis, pop. 149,000
Currency: Mauritian rupee
Religions: Hindu, Roman Catholic, Muslim, other Christian
Languages: Creole, Bhojpuri, French

Monaco

Area: 0.8 sq mi (2.0 sq km)
Population: 36,000
Capital: Monaco, pop. 33,000
Currency: euro
Religion: Roman Catholic
Languages: French, English, Italian, Monegasque

The **AVERAGE PERSON** can **WALK** across the country of **MONACO** in less than an **HOUR.**

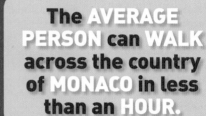

Mexico

Area: 758,449 sq mi
(1,964,375 sq km)
Population: 110,645,000
Capital: Mexico City, pop. 19,319,000
Currency: Mexican peso
Religions: Roman Catholic, Protestant
Languages: Spanish, Mayan, Nahuatl, other indigenous

Mongolia

Area: 603,909 sq mi
(1,564,116 sq km)
Population: 2,764,000
Capital: Ulaanbaatar, pop. 949,000
Currency: togrog/tugrik
Religions: Buddhist Lamaist, Shamanist, Christian
Languages: Khalkha Mongol, Turkic, Russian

Micronesia

Area: 271 sq mi (702 sq km)
Population: 111,000
Capital: Palikir, pop. 7,000
Currency: U.S. dollar
Religions: Roman Catholic, Protestant
Languages: English, Trukese, Pohnpeian, Yapese, other indigenous languages

Montenegro

Area: 5,415 sq mi
(14,026 sq km)
Population: 632,000
Capital: Podgorica, pop. 144,000
Currency: euro
Religions: Orthodox, Muslim, Roman Catholic
Languages: Serbian (Ijekavian dialect), Bosnian, Albanian, Croatian

Moldova

Area: 13,050 sq mi
(33,800 sq km)
Population: 4,117,000
Capital: Chisinau, pop. 650,000
Currency: Moldovan leu
Religion: Eastern Orthodox
Languages: Moldovan, Russian, Gagauz

Morocco

Area: 274,461 sq mi
(710,850 sq km)
Population: 31,851,000
Capital: Rabat, pop. 1,770,000
Currency: Moroccan dirham
Religion: Muslim
Languages: Arabic, Berber dialects, French

Mozambique

Area: 308,642 sq mi
(799,380 sq km)
Population: 23,406,000
Capital: Maputo, pop. 1,589,000
Currency: metical
Religions: Roman Catholic, Muslim, Zionist Christian
Languages: Emakhuwa, Xichangana, Portuguese,
Elomwe, Cisena, Echuwabo, other local languages

Namibia

Area: 318,261 sq mi
(824,292 sq km)
Population: 2,212,000
Capital: Windhoek, pop. 342,000
Currencies: Namibian dollar;
South African rand
Religions: Lutheran, other Christian, indigenous beliefs
Languages: Afrikaans, German, English

Myanmar (Burma)

Area: 261,218 sq mi
(676,552 sq km)
Population: 53,414,000
Capitals: Nay Pyi Taw, pop.
992,000; Yangon (Rangoon), pop. 4,088,000
Currency: kyat
Religions: Buddhist, Christian, Muslim
Languages: Burmese, minority ethnic languages

Nauru

Area: 8 sq mi (21 sq km)
Population: 11,000
Capital: Yaren, pop. 10,000
Currency: Australian dollar
Religions: Protestant, Roman Catholic
Languages: Nauruan, English

You Are There!

Mount Everest South Base Camp

NEPAL

It's near freezing and dipping here at Mount Everest South Base Camp in Nepal, a destination visited by thousands of people each year. At an elevation of 18,000 feet (5,486 m), the base camp is higher than the highest peaks in Europe. But for some of the climbers, it's only the starting point! Just getting to Base Camp is an epic adventure in itself. While some people choose to take a helicopter, others opt to take several-day tours guided by Sherpas—natives of Nepal and expert climbers—all the way up to Base Camp (and back).

Because it's so physically tough to tackle Everest, only about 150 people make it to the top each year. That's why it's important to spend a few days at Base Camp gearing up for the trip. Here you begin to adjust to the thin air that only gets thinner as you make your way to the tippy-top of Everest, looming 29,035 feet (8,850 m) above sea level.

COLOR KEY ● Africa ● Australia, New Zealand, and Oceania

Nepal

Area: 56,827 sq mi
(147,181 sq km)
Population: 28,044,000
Capital: Kathmandu, pop. 990,000
Currency: Nepalese rupee
Religions: Hindu, Buddhist, Muslim, Kirant
Languages: Nepali, Maithali, Bhojpuri, Tharu, Tamang,
Newar, Magar

Netherlands

Area: 16,034 sq mi
(41,528 sq km)
Population: 16,618,000
Capital: Amsterdam, pop. 1,044,000
Currency: euro
Religions: Roman Catholic, Dutch Reformed,
Calvinist, Muslim
Languages: Dutch, Frisian

New Zealand

Area: 104,454 sq mi
(270,534 sq km)
Population: 4,375,000
Capital: Wellington, pop. 391,000
Currency: New Zealand dollar
Religions: Anglican, Roman Catholic, Presbyterian,
other Christian
Languages: English, Maori

Nicaragua

Area: 50,193 sq mi
(130,000 sq km)
Population: 5,996,000
Capital: Managua, pop. 934,000
Currency: gold cordoba
Religions: Roman Catholic, Evangelical
Language: Spanish

Niger

Area: 489,191 sq mi (1,267,000 sq km)
Population: 15,861,000
Capital: Niamey, pop. 1,004,000
Currency: Communauté
Financière Africaine franc
Religions: Muslim, other (includes indigenous
beliefs and Christian)
Languages: French, Hausa, Djerma

Nigeria

Area: 356,669 sq mi
(923,768 sq km)
Population: 158,259,000
Capital: Abuja, pop. 1,857,000
Currency: naira
Religions: Muslim, Christian, indigenous beliefs
Languages: English, Hausa, Yoruba, Igbo (Ibo), Fulani

North Korea

Area: 46,540 sq mi
(120,538 sq km)
Population: 21,757,000
Capital: Pyongyang,
pop. 2,828,000
Currency: North Korean won
Religions: Buddhist, Confucianist, some Christian
and syncretic Chondogyo
Language: Korean

Norway

Area: 125,004 sq mi
(323,758 sq km)
Population: 4,888,000
Capital: Oslo, pop. 875,000
Currency: Norwegian krone
Religion: Church of Norway (Lutheran)
Languages: Bokmal Norwegian, Nynorsk
Norwegian, Sami

Oman

Area: 119,500 sq mi
(309,500 sq km)
Population: 3,132,000
Capital: Muscat, pop. 634,000
Currency: Omani rial
Religions: Ibadhi Muslim, Sunni Muslim,
Shiite Muslim, Hindu
Languages: Arabic, English, Baluchi, Urdu, Indian dialects

Pakistan

Area: 307,374 sq mi
(796,095 sq km)
Population: 184,753,000
Capital: Islamabad, pop. 832,000
Currency: Pakistani rupee
Religions: Sunni Muslim, Shiite Muslim
Languages: Punjabi, Sindhi, Siraiki, Pashto, Urdu,
Baluchi, Hindko, English

Palau

Area: 189 sq mi (489 sq km)
Population: 21,000
Capital: Melekeok, 1,000
Currency: U.S. dollar
Religions: Roman Catholic, Protestant, Modekngei, Seventh-day Adventist
Languages: Palauan, Filipino, English, Chinese

Panama

Area: 29,157 sq mi (75,517 sq km)
Population: 3,509,000
Capital: Panama City, pop. 1,346,000
Currencies: balboa; U.S. dollar
Religions: Roman Catholic, Protestant
Languages: Spanish, English

Papua New Guinea

Area: 178,703 sq mi (462,840 sq km)
Population: 6,765,000
Capital: Port Moresby, pop. 314,000
Currency: kina
Religions: indigenous beliefs, Roman Catholic, Lutheran, other Protestant
Languages: Melanesian Pidgin, 820 indigenous languages

Paraguay

Area: 157,048 sq mi (406,752 sq km)
Population: 6,451,000
Capital: Asunción, pop. 1,977,000
Currency: guarani
Religions: Roman Catholic, Protestant
Languages: Spanish, Guarani

Peru

Area: 496,224 sq mi (1,285,216 sq km)
Population: 29,461,000
Capital: Lima, pop. 8,769,000
Currency: nuevo sol
Religion: Roman Catholic
Languages: Spanish, Quechua, Aymara, minor Amazonian languages

Philippines

Area: 115,831 sq mi (300,000 sq km)
Population: 94,013,000
Capital: Manila, pop. 11,449,000
Currency: Philippine peso
Religions: Roman Catholic, Muslim, other Christian
Languages: Filipino (based on Tagalog), English

Poland

Area: 120,728 sq mi (312,685 sq km)
Population: 38,186,000
Capital: Warsaw, pop. 1,710,000
Currency: zloty
Religion: Roman Catholic
Language: Polish

Portugal

Area: 35,655 sq mi (92,345 sq km)
Population: 10,655,000
Capital: Lisbon, pop. 2,808,000
Currency: euro
Religion: Roman Catholic
Languages: Portuguese, Mirandese

Qatar

Area: 4,448 sq mi (11,521 sq km)
Population: 1,674,000
Capital: Doha, pop. 427,000
Currency: Qatari rial
Religions: Muslim, Christian
Languages: Arabic; English commonly a second language

Romania

Area: 92,043 sq mi (238,391 sq km)
Population: 21,454,000
Capital: Bucharest, pop. 1,933,000
Currency: new leu
Religions: Eastern Orthodox, Protestant, Roman Catholic
Languages: Romanian, Hungarian

COLOR KEY   ● Africa   ● Australia, New Zealand, and Oceania

Russia

Area: 6,592,850 sq mi
(17,075,400 sq km)
Population: 141,920,000
Capital: Moscow, pop. 10,523,000
Currency: ruble
Religions: Russian Orthodox, Muslim
Languages: Russian, many minority languages
Note: Russia is in both Europe and Asia, but its capital is in Europe, so it is classified here as a European country.

RUSSIA has COASTS on THREE OCEANS— THE ATLANTIC, PACIFIC, AND ARCTIC.

Rwanda

Area: 10,169 sq mi
(26,338 sq km)
Population: 10,413,000
Capital: Kigali, pop. 909,000
Currency: Rwandan franc
Religions: Roman Catholic, Protestant, Adventist, Muslim
Languages: Kinyarwanda, French, English, Kiswahili

San Marino

Area: 24 sq mi (61 sq km)
Population: 32,000
Capital: San Marino, pop. 4,000
Currency: euro
Religion: Roman Catholic
Language: Italian

Samoa

Area: 1,093 sq mi (2,831 sq km)
Population: 192,000
Capital: Apia, pop. 36,000
Currency: tala
Religions: Congregationalist, Roman Catholic, Methodist, Church of Jesus Christ of Latter-day Saints, Assembly of God, Seventh-day Adventist
Languages: Samoan (Polynesian), English

Sao Tome and Principe

Area: 386 sq mi (1,001 sq km)
Population: 164,000
Capital: São Tomé, pop. 60,000
Currency: dobra
Religions: Roman Catholic, Evangelical
Language: Portuguese

MEET THE NAT GEO EXPLORER

SPENCER WELLS

A leading population geneticist and director of the Genographic Project (genographic.nationalgeographic.com), Wells is studying humankind's family tree.

What was your closest call in the field?

I've had a few, but the most physically difficult experience was when I lived with Chukchi reindeer herders in Russia's Far East, inside the Arctic Circle. The temperatures fell as low as -94°F (-70°C), which freezes unprotected skin and can kill you in minutes.

How would you suggest kids follow in your footsteps?

Find something in school you are passionate about, focus on it, and study hard. Don't let people tell you that it's not a practical subject to study—if you are excited enough about it, you will find a way to do it for a living. Take risks. Challenging yourself will give you confidence, and you'll learn something that may be useful in your future work.

● Asia ● Europe ● North America ● South America

Saudi Arabia

Area: 756,985 sq mi (1,960,582 sq km)
Population: 29,207,000
Capital: Riyadh, pop. 4,725,000
Currency: Saudi riyal
Religion: Muslim
Language: Arabic

Senegal

Area: 75,955 sq mi (196,722 sq km)
Population: 12,509,000
Capital: Dakar, pop. 2,777,000
Currency: Communauté Financière Africaine franc
Religions: Muslim, Christian (mostly Roman Catholic)
Languages: French, Wolof, Pulaar, Jola, Mandinka

Serbia

Area: 29,913 sq mi (77,474 sq km)
Population: 7,288,000
Capital: Belgrade, pop. 1,115,000
Currency: Serbian dinar
Religions: Serbian Orthodox, Roman Catholic, Muslim
Languages: Serbian, Hungarian

Seychelles

Area: 176 sq mi (455 sq km)
Population: 88,000
Capital: Victoria, pop. 26,000
Currency: Seychelles rupee
Religions: Roman Catholic, Anglican, other Christian
Languages: Creole, English

Sierra Leone

Area: 27,699 sq mi (71,740 sq km)
Population: 5,836,000
Capital: Freetown, pop. 875,000
Currency: leone
Religions: Muslim, indigenous beliefs, Christian
Languages: English, Mende, Temne, Krio

Singapore

Area: 255 sq mi (660 sq km)
Population: 5,140,000
Capital: Singapore, pop. 4,737,000
Currency: Singapore dollar
Religions: Buddhist, Muslim, Taoist, Roman Catholic, Hindu, other Christian
Languages: Mandarin, English, Malay, Hokkien, Cantonese, Teochew, Tamil

Slovakia

Area: 18,932 sq mi (49,035 sq km)
Population: 5,429,000
Capital: Bratislava, pop. 428,000
Currency: euro
Religions: Roman Catholic, Protestant, Greek Catholic
Languages: Slovak, Hungarian

Slovenia

Area: 7,827 sq mi (20,273 sq km)
Population: 2,054,000
Capital: Ljubljana, pop. 260,000
Currency: euro
Religion: Roman Catholic, Muslim, Orthodox
Languages: Slovene, Croatian, Serbian

Solomon Islands

Area: 10,954 sq mi (28,370 sq km)
Population: 546,000
Capital: Honiara, pop. 72,000
Currency: Solomon Islands dollar
Religions: Church of Melanesia, Roman Catholic, South Seas Evangelical, other Christian
Languages: Melanesian pidgin, 120 indigenous languages

Somalia

Area: 246,201 sq mi (637,657 sq km)
Population: 9,359,000
Capital: Mogadishu, pop. 1,353,000
Currency: Somali shilling
Religion: Sunni Muslim
Languages: Somali, Arabic, Italian, English

COLOR KEY   ● Africa ● Australia, New Zealand, and Oceania

South Africa

Area: 470,693 sq mi (1,219,090 sq km)
Population: 49,851,000
Capitals: Pretoria (Tshwane), pop. 1,404,000; Bloemfontein, pop. 436,000; Cape Town, pop. 3,353,000
Currency: rand
Religions: Zion Christian, Pentecostal, Catholic, Methodist, Dutch Reformed, Anglican, other Christian
Languages: IsiZulu, IsiXhosa, Afrikaans, Sepedi, English

South Korea

Area: 38,321 sq mi (99,250 sq km)
Population: 48,875,000
Capital: Seoul, pop. 9,778,000
Currency: South Korean won
Religions: Christian, Buddhist
Languages: Korean, English

JEJU ISLAND in South Korea is FAMOUS for its WOMEN DIVERS, called HAENYOS.

Spain

Area: 195,363 sq mi (505,988 sq km)
Population: 47,055,000
Capital: Madrid, pop. 5,762,000
Currency: euro
Religion: Roman Catholic
Languages: Castilian Spanish, Catalan, Galician, Basque

Sri Lanka

Area: 25,299 sq mi (65,525 sq km)
Population: 20,686,000
Capital: Colombo, pop. 681,000
Currency: Sri Lankan rupee
Religions: Buddhist, Muslim, Hindu, Christian
Languages: Sinhala, Tamil

St. Kitts and Nevis

Area: 104 sq mi (269 sq km)
Population: 53,000
Capital: Basseterre, pop. 13,000
Currency: East Caribbean dollar
Religions: Anglican, other Protestant, Roman Catholic
Language: English

St. Lucia

Area: 238 sq mi (616 sq km)
Population: 176,000
Capital: Castries, pop. 15,000
Currency: East Caribbean dollar
Religions: Roman Catholic, Seventh-day Adventist, Pentecostal
Languages: English, French patois

St. Vincent and the Grenadines

Area: 150 sq mi (389 sq km)
Population: 107,000
Capital: Kingstown, pop. 28,000
Currency: East Caribbean dollar
Religions: Anglican, Methodist, Roman Catholic
Languages: English, French patois

Sudan

Area: 967,500 sq mi (2,505,813 sq km)
Population: 43,192,000
Capital: Khartoum, pop. 5,021,000
Currency: Sudanese pound
Religions: Sunni Muslim, indigenous beliefs, Christian
Languages: Arabic, Nubian, Ta Bedawie, many diverse dialects of Nilotic, Nilo-Hamitic, Sudanic languages

Suriname

Area: 63,037 sq mi (163,265 sq km)
Population: 524,000
Capital: Paramaribo, pop. 259,000
Currency: Suriname dollar
Religions: Hindu, Protestant (predominantly Moravian), Roman Catholic, Muslim, indigenous beliefs
Languages: Dutch, English, Sranang Tongo, Hindustani, Javanese

Swaziland

Area: 6,704 sq mi (17,363 sq km)
Population: 1,202,000
Capitals: Mbabane, pop. 74,000;
Lobamba, pop. 4,557
Currency: lilangeni
Religions: Zionist, Roman Catholic, Muslim
Languages: English, siSwati

Sweden

Area: 173,732 sq mi (449,964 sq km)
Population: 9,382,000
Capital: Stockholm, pop. 1,279,000
Currency: Swedish krona
Religion: Lutheran
Languages: Swedish, Sami, Finnish

Switzerland

Area: 15,940 sq mi
(41,284 sq km)
Population: 7,824,000
Capital: Bern, pop. 346,000
Currency: Swiss franc
Religions: Roman Catholic, Protestant, Muslim
Languages: German, French, Italian, Romansh

Syria

Area: 71,498 sq mi (185,180 sq km)
Population: 22,505,000
Capital: Damascus, pop. 2,527,000
Currency: Syrian pound
Religions: Sunni, other Muslim (includes Alawite,
Druze), Christian
Languages: Arabic, Kurdish, Armenian, Aramaic,
Circassian

Tajikistan

Area: 55,251 sq mi
(143,100 sq km)
Population: 7,617,000
Capital: Dushanbe, pop. 704,000
Currency: somoni
Religions: Sunni Muslim, Shiite Muslim
Languages: Tajik, Russian

Tanzania

Area: 364,900 sq mi (945,087 sq km)
Population: 45,040,000
Capitals: Dar es Salaam,
pop. 2,930,000; Dodoma, pop. 200,000
Currency: Tanzanian shilling
Religions: Muslim, indigenous beliefs, Christian
Languages: Kiswahili, Kiunguja, English, Arabic, local
languages

Thailand

Area: 198,115 sq mi
(513,115 sq km)
Population: 68,139,000
Capital: Bangkok, pop. 6,902,000
Currency: baht
Religions: Buddhist, Muslim
Languages: Thai, English, ethnic dialects

Timor-Leste (East Timor)

Area: 5,640 sq mi
(14,609 sq km)
Population: 1,150,000
Capital: Díli, pop. 166,000
Currency: U.S. dollar
Religion: Roman Catholic
Languages: Tetum, Portuguese, Indonesian, English,
indigenous languages

Togo

Area: 21,925 sq mi (56,785 sq km)
Population: 6,780,000
Capital: Lomé, pop. 1,593,000
Currency: Communauté
Financière Africaine franc
Religions: indigenous beliefs, Christian, Muslim
Languages: French, Ewe, Mina, Kabye, Dagomba

Tonga

Area: 289 sq mi (748 sq km)
Population: 104,000
Capital: Nuku'alofa,
pop. 24,000
Currency: pa'anga
Religion: Christian
Languages: Tongan, English

COLOR KEY ● Africa ● Australia, New Zealand, and Oceania

Trinidad and Tobago

Area: 1,980 sq mi (5,128 sq km)
Population: 1,319,000
Capital: Port of Spain, pop. 57,000
Currency: Trinidad and Tobago dollar
Religions: Roman Catholic, Hindu, Anglican, Baptist
Languages: English, Caribbean Hindustani, French, Spanish, Chinese

Tunisia

Area: 63,170 sq mi (163,610 sq km)
Population: 10,541,000
Capital: Tunis, pop. 759,000
Currency: Tunisian dinar
Religion: Muslim
Languages: Arabic, French

Turkey

Area: 300,948 sq mi (779,452 sq km)
Population: 73,621,000
Capital: Ankara, pop. 3,846,000
Currency: new Turkish lira
Religion: Muslim (mostly Sunni)
Languages: Turkish, Kurdish, Dimli (Zaza), Azeri, Kabardian, Gagauz

Turkmenistan

Area: 188,456 sq mi (488,100 sq km)
Population: 5,177,000
Capital: Ashgabat, pop. 637,000
Currency: Turkmen manat
Religions: Muslim, Eastern Orthodox
Languages: Turkmen, Russian, Uzbek

Tuvalu

Area: 10 sq mi (26 sq km)
Population: 10,000
Capital: Funafuti, pop. 5,000
Currencies: Australian dollar; Tuvaluan dollar
Religion: Church of Tuvalu (Congregationalist)
Languages: Tuvaluan, English, Samoan, Kiribati

Uganda

Area: 93,104 sq mi (241,139 sq km)
Population: 33,796,000
Capital: Kampala, pop. 1,535,000
Currency: Ugandan shilling
Religions: Protestant, Roman Catholic, Muslim
Languages: English, Ganda, other local languages, Kiswahili, Arabic

Ukraine

Area: 233,090 sq mi (603,700 sq km)
Population: 45,864,000
Capital: Kyiv (Kiev), pop. 2,779,000
Currency: hryvnia
Religions: Ukrainian Orthodox, Orthodox, Ukrainian Greek Catholic
Languages: Ukrainian, Russian

United Arab Emirates

Area: 30,000 sq mi (77,700 sq km)
Population: 5,386,000
Capital: Abu Dhabi, pop. 666,000
Currency: Emirati dirham
Religion: Muslim
Languages: Arabic, Persian, English, Hindi, Urdu

United Kingdom

Area: 93,788 sq mi (242,910 sq km)
Population: 62,207,000
Capital: London, pop. 8,615,000
Currency: British pound
Religions: Anglican, Roman Catholic, Presbyterian, Methodist
Languages: English, Welsh, Scottish form of Gaelic

United States

Area: 3,794,083 sq mi (9,826,630 sq km)
Population: 309,636,000
Capital: Washington, D.C., pop. 601,723
Currency: U.S. dollar
Religions: Protestant, Roman Catholic
Languages: English, Spanish

Uruguay

Area: 68,037 sq mi
(176,215 sq km)
Population: 3,357,000
Capital: Montevideo, pop. 1,633,000
Currency: Uruguayan peso
Religion: Roman Catholic
Language: Spanish

Uzbekistan

Area: 172,742 sq mi
(447,400 sq km)
Population: 28,120,000
Capital: Tashkent,
pop. 2,201,000
Currency: Uzbekistani sum
Religions: Muslim (mostly Sunni), Eastern Orthodox
Languages: Uzbek, Russian, Tajik

Vanuatu

Area: 4,707 sq mi (12,190 sq km)
Population: 245,000
Capital: Port Vila, pop. 44,000
Currency: vatu
Religions: Presbyterian, Anglican, Roman Catholic, other Christian, indigenous beliefs
Languages: more than 100 local languages, pidgin (known as Bislama or Bichelama)

Vatican City

Area: 0.2 sq mi (0.4 sq km)
Population: 798
Capital: Vatican City, pop. 798
Currency: euro
Religion: Roman Catholic
Languages: Italian, Latin, French

Venezuela

Area: 352,144 sq mi
(912,050 sq km)
Population: 28,834,000
Capital: Caracas, pop. 3,051,000
Currency: bolivar
Religion: Roman Catholic
Languages: Spanish, numerous indigenous dialects

Vietnam

Area: 127,844 sq mi
(331,114 sq km)
Population: 88,851,000
Capital: Hanoi, pop. 2,668,000
Currency: dong
Religions: Buddhist, Roman Catholic
Languages: Vietnamese, English, French, Chinese, Khmer

Yemen

Area: 207,286 sq mi
(536,869 sq km)
Population: 23,584,000
Capital: Sanaa, pop. 2,229,000
Currency: Yemeni rial
Religions: Muslim, including Shaf'i (Sunni) and Zaydi (Shiite)
Language: Arabic

Zambia

Area: 290,586 sq mi
(752,614 sq km)
Population: 13,279,000
Capital: Lusaka, pop. 1,413,000
Currency: Zambian kwacha
Religions: Christian, Muslim, Hindu
Languages: English, Bemba, Kaonda, Lozi, Lunda, Luvale, Nyanja, Tonga, about 70 other indigenous languages

Zimbabwe

Area: 150,872 sq mi
(390,757 sq km)
Population: 12,644,000
Capital: Harare, pop. 1,606,000
Currency: Zimbabwean dollar
Religions: Syncretic (part Christian, part indigenous beliefs), Christian, indigenous beliefs
Languages: English, Shona, Sindebele, tribal dialects

COOL CLICK

Want to see National Geographic photographs from around the world? Go online.
travel.nationalgeographic.com/travel/travel-photos

COLOR KEY ● Africa ● Australia, New Zealand, and Oceania

Bet you didn't know

8 ways
people try to get
good luck
around the globe

1
CARRYING
bat bones
IN YOUR POCKET
in **Greece**

2
HOLDING
leopard teeth
in **Liberia**

3
touching
A CHIMNEY SWEEP'S BRUSH
in **Germany**

4
EATING lasagna
on New Year's Day
in **Sicily, Italy**

5
RECEIVING
the gift of a
WHITE EGG
in **England**

6
watching a ladybug
fly into your bedroom
in **Italy**

7
riding a camel
in **Turkey**

8
breaking GLASS
in **Bulgaria**

● Asia ● Europe ● North America ● South America

317

THE POLITICAL UNITED STATES

9:00AM PACIFIC TIME

Cape Flattery

10:00AM
MOUNTAIN TIME

Seattle
Olympia ● Tacoma
WASHINGTON ● Spokane
Yakima
Portland ●
Salem ⊛
Eugene ●
OREGON
Medford ●
● Klamath Falls
Eureka ●
Redding ●

Lewiston ●
I D A H O
● Boise
Idaho
Falls
Pocatello ●

Great Falls ●
Butte ● ● Helena
M O N T A N A
R O C K Y
Billings ●
● Cody
Yellowstone L.
W Y O M I N G
Casper ●

Minot ●
Grand Forks ●
N O R T H D A K O T A
⊛ Bismarck Fargo
Aberdeen ●
S O U T H D A K O T A
● Pierre
Rapid
City ● Sioux Fall

Sacramento ●
San ● Oakland
Francisco ● San Jose
Salinas ●
Fresno ●
Bakersfield ●
Point
Conception
Los Angeles ●
Long Beach ● ● Riverside
San Diego ●

Reno ●
● Carson City
Lake Tahoe
N E V A D A
Great
Salt
Lake
Ogden ●
⊛ Salt Lake
City
● Provo
U T A H
Grand
Junction ●
Lake
Powell
St. George ●
Las
Vegas ●
Lake
Mead
D e s e r t
Grand Canyon
Flagstaff ●
A R I Z O N A
Phoenix ⊛● Mesa
Yuma ●
Tucson ●

G r e a t B a s i n
M o j a v e

Cheyenne ●
Laramie ●
⋈ Fort Collins
Denver ● Boulder
⊛
C O L O R A D O
Colorado Springs ●
● Pueblo

N E B R A S K A
Grand
Island ● Linco
Platte
S. Platte

K A N S A S
Dodge City ●
Arkansas Wichi

Santa Fe ● ⋈
● Albuquerque
N E W M E X I C O
Las Cruces ●
El Paso ●

O K L A H
Amarillo ● Oklahom
Lawton ● City
Wichita Falls ●
Lubbock ● Red
Roswell ● Dalla
Midland ● Abilene Fort Worth ●
Odessa ●
Waco ●
T E X A S

7:00AM
HAWAI'I-
ALEUTIAN
TIME

North Slope
Brooks Range
Alaska Range
● Juneau
● Anchorage
ALASKA
Alaska Peninsula
0   400 miles
0   400 kilometers
ALEUTIAN ISLANDS

8:00AM
ALASKA TIME

Kaua'i
Ni'ihau O'ahu
● Honolulu Moloka'i
Lana'i Maui
HAWAI'I Kaho'olawe ● Hilo ● Hawai'i
0   150 mi
0   150 km

7:00AM
HAWAI'I-
ALEUTIAN
TIME

San ⊛
Antonio Austi
●
Corp
Chris
Laredo ●
Brownsvi

Like a giant quilt, the United States is made up of 50 states. Each is unique, but together they make a national fabric held together by a constitution and a federal government. State boundaries, outlined in dotted lines on the map, set apart internal political units within the country. The national capital—Washington, D.C.—is marked by a star in a double circle. The capital of each state is marked by a star in a single circle.

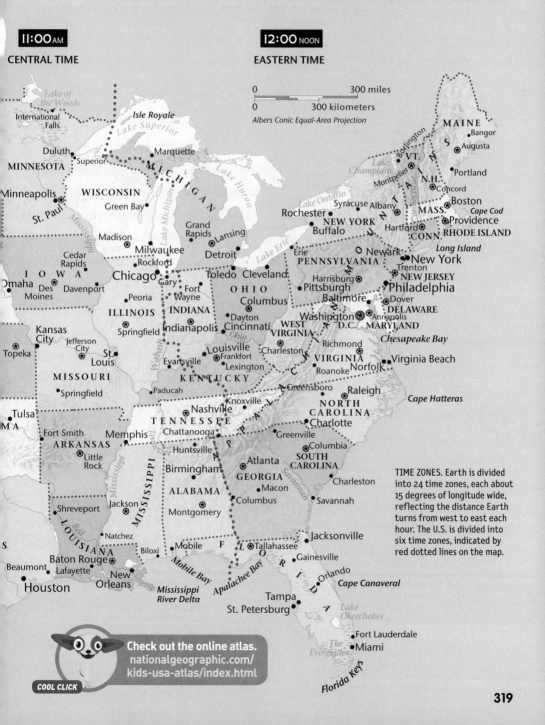

11:00 AM
CENTRAL TIME

12:00 NOON
EASTERN TIME

0   300 miles
0   300 kilometers
Albers Conic Equal-Area Projection

TIME ZONES. Earth is divided into 24 time zones, each about 15 degrees of longitude wide, reflecting the distance Earth turns from west to east each hour. The U.S. is divided into six time zones, indicated by red dotted lines on the map.

Check out the online atlas.
nationalgeographic.com/
kids-usa-atlas/index.html

COOL CLICK

319

THE PHYSICAL UNITED STATES

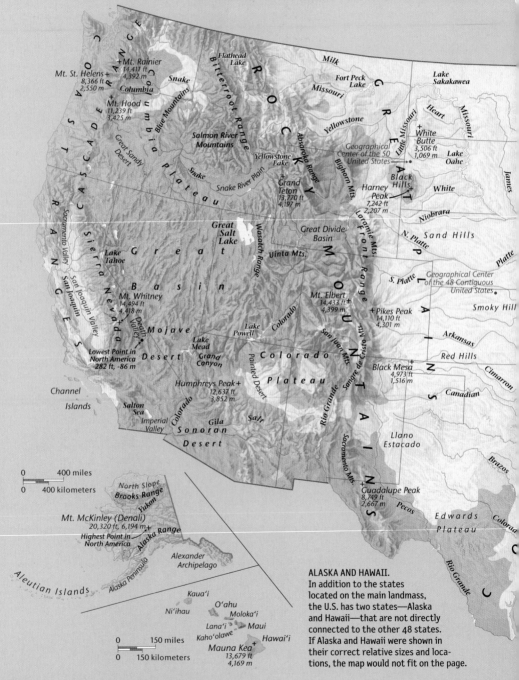

Mt. Rainier
14,411 ft
4,392 m

Mt. St. Helens +
8,366 ft
2,550 m

Columbia

Snake

Flathead
Lake

Milk

Fort Peck
Lake

Lake
Sakakawea

Mt. Hood
11,239 ft
3,425 m

Blue Mountains

Bitterroot Range

Salmon River
Mountains

Missouri

Yellowstone

Little Missouri

Heart

Missouri

Great Sandy
Desert

Snake

Snake River Plain

Yellowstone
Lake

Absaroka Range

Geographical
Center of the 50
United States

White
Butte
3,506 ft
1,069 m

Lake
Oahe

Grand
Teton
13,770 ft
4,197 m

Bighorn Mts.

Harney
Peak
7,242 ft
2,207 m

Black
Hills

White

James

Great
Salt
Lake

Wasatch Range

Uinta Mts.

Great Divide
Basin

Niobrara

N. Platte

Sand Hills

Platte

Lake
Tahoe

G r e a t

Mt. Whitney
14,494 ft
4,418 m

B a s i n

Mt. Elbert
14,433 ft
4,399 m

Laramie Mts.

Front Range

S. Platte

Geographical Center
of the 48 Contiguous
United States

Smoky Hill

Pikes Peak
14,110 ft
4,301 m

Sacramento Valley

San Joaquin Valley

Sierra Nevada

Death
Valley

Mojave

Lake
Powell

Colorado

San Juan Mts.

Arkansas

Red Hills

Lowest Point in
North America
-282 ft, -86 m

Desert

Lake
Mead

Grand
Canyon

Painted Desert

C o l o r a d o

P l a t e a u

Sangre de Cristo Mts.

Black Mesa
4,973 ft
1,516 m

Canadian

Cimarron

Channel

Islands

Salton
Sea

Imperial
Valley

Humphreys Peak +
12,637 ft
3,852 m

Colorado

Gila

S o n o r a n

Salt

Rio Grande

Llano
Estacado

Brazos

Desert

Sacramento Mts.

Guadalupe Peak
8,749 ft
2,667 m

Pecos

Edwards

Plateau

Colorado

0   400 miles

0   400 kilometers

North Slope

Brooks Range

Yukon

Mt. McKinley (Denali)
20,320 ft, 6,194 m

Highest Point in
North America

Alaska Range

Alexander
Archipelago

Aleutian Islands

Alaska Peninsula

Rio Grande

Kaua'i

Ni'ihau

O'ahu

Moloka'i

Lana'i

Kaho'olawe

Maui

Hawai'i

0   150 miles

0   150 kilometers

Mauna Kea
13,679 ft
4,169 m

ALASKA AND HAWAII.
In addition to the states
located on the main landmass,
the U.S. has two states—Alaska
and Hawaii—that are not directly
connected to the other 48 states.
If Alaska and Hawaii were shown in
their correct relative sizes and locations, the map would not fit on the page.

Stretching from the Atlantic Ocean in the east to the Pacific Ocean in the west, the United States is the third-largest country (by area) in the world. Its physical diversity ranges from mountains to fertile plains and dry deserts. Shading on the map indicates changes in elevation, while colors show different vegetation patterns.

0   400 miles

0   400 kilometers

Albers Conic Equal-Area Projection

NATURAL VEGETATION

- NEEDLELEAF FOREST
- BROADLEAF FOREST
- MIXED FOREST
- GRASSLAND
- TROPICAL VEGETATION
- DESERT
- TUNDRA

To see more great maps, go online. maps.national geographic.com/maps

COOL CLICK

THE STATES

From sea to shining sea, the United States of America is a nation of diversity. In the more than 235 years since its creation, the nation has grown to become home to a wide range of peoples, industries, and cultures. The following pages present a general overview of all 50 states in the U.S.

The country is generally divided into five large regions: the Northeast, the Southeast, the Midwest, the Southwest, and the West. Though loosely defined, these zones tend to share important similarities, including climate, history, and geography. The color key below provides a guide to which states are in each region.

Flags of each state and highlights of demography and industry are also included. These details offer a brief overview of each state.

In addition, each state's official flower and bird are indentified.

*Note: U.S. population figures do not reflect the 2010 census.

Color Key by Region

Arizona

Area: 113,998 sq mi (295,256 sq km)
Population: 6,392,017
Capital: Phoenix, pop. 1,593,659
Largest city: Phoenix, pop. 1,593,659
Industry: Real estate, manufactured goods, retail, state and local government, transportation and public utilities, wholesale trade, health services, tourism
State flower/bird: Saguaro/cactus wren

Arkansas

Area: 53,179 sq mi (137,732 sq km)
Population: 2,915,918
Capital: Little Rock, pop. 191,933
Largest city: Little Rock, pop. 191,933
Industry: Services, food processing, paper products, transportation, metal products, machinery, electronics
State flower/bird: Apple blossom/mockingbird

California

Area: 163,696 sq mi (423,972 sq km)
Population: 37,253,956
Capital: Sacramento, pop. 466,676
Largest city: Los Angeles, pop. 3,831,868
Industry: Electronic components and equipment, computers and computer software, tourism, food processing, entertainment, clothing
State flower/bird: Golden poppy/California quail

Alabama

Area: 52,419 sq mi (135,765 sq km)
Population: 4,779,736
Capital: Montgomery, pop. 202,124
Largest city: Birmingham, pop. 230,131
Industry: Retail and wholesale trade, services, government, finance, insurance, real estate, transportation, construction, communication
State flower/bird: Camellia/northern flicker

Alaska

Area: 663,267 sq mi (1,717,862 sq km)
Population: 710,231
Capital: Juneau, pop. 30,796
Largest city: Anchorage, pop. 286,174
Industry: Petroleum products, government, services, trade
State flower/bird: Forget-me-not/willow ptarmigan

5 cool things about ALASKA

1. The 22 smallest U.S. states could all fit inside Alaska.

2. Alaska was purchased from Russia for about two cents an acre.

3. There are 100-foot-tall sand dunes in Alaska.

4. A 13-year-old kid designed Alaska's flag.

5. Katmai National Park and Preserve in King Salmon, Alaska, is home to more than 2,000 brown bears.

COLOR KEY ● Northeast ● Southeast

Colorado

Area: 104,094 sq mi (269,602 sq km)
Population: 5,029,196
Capital: Denver, pop. 610,345
Largest city: Denver, pop. 610,345
Industry: Real estate, government, durable goods, communications, health and other services, nondurable goods, transportation
State flower/bird: Columbine/lark bunting

Connecticut

Area: 5,543 sq mi (14,357 sq km)
Population: 3,574,097
Capital: Hartford, pop. 124,060
Largest city: Bridgeport, pop. 137,298
Industry: Transportation equipment, metal products, machinery, electrical equipment, printing and publishing, scientific instruments, insurance
State flower/bird: Mountain laurel/robin

Delaware

Area: 2,489 sq mi (6,447 sq km)
Population: 897,934
Capital: Dover, pop. 36,560
Largest city: Wilmington, pop. 73,069
Industry: Food processing, chemicals, rubber and plastic products, scientific instruments, printing and publishing, financial services
State flower/bird: Peach blossom/blue hen chicken

Florida

Area: 65,755 sq mi (170,304 sq km)
Population: 18,801,310
Capital: Tallahassee, pop. 172,574
Largest city: Jacksonville, pop. 813,518
Industry: Tourism, health services, business services, communications, banking, electronic equipment, insurance
State flower/bird: Orange blossom/mockingbird

Georgia

Area: 59,425 sq mi (153,910 sq km)
Population: 9,687,653
Capital: Atlanta, pop. 540,922
Largest city: Atlanta, pop. 540,922
Industry: Textiles and clothing, transportation equipment, food processing, paper products, chemicals, electrical equipment, tourism
State flower/bird: Cherokee rose/brown thrasher

Hawaii

Area: 10,931 sq mi (28,311 sq km)
Population: 1,360,301
Capital: Honolulu, pop. 374,658
Largest city: Honolulu, pop. 374,658
Industry: Tourism, trade, finance, food processing, petroleum refining, stone, clay, glass products
State flower/bird: Hibiscus/Hawaiian goose (nene)

Idaho

Area: 83,570 sq mi (216,447 sq km)
Population: 1,567,582
Capital: Boise, pop. 205,707
Largest city: Boise, pop. 205,707
Industry: Electronics and computer equipment, tourism, food processing, forest products, mining
State flower/bird: Syringa (Lewis's mock orange)/ mountain bluebird

Illinois

Area: 57,914 sq mi (149,998 sq km)
Population: 12,830,632
Capital: Springfield, pop. 118,033
Largest city: Chicago, pop. 2,851,268
Industry: Industrial machinery, electronic equipment, food processing, chemicals, metals, printing and publishing, rubber and plastics, motor vehicles
State flower/bird: Violet/cardinal

Indiana

Area: 36,418 sq mi (94,322 sq km)
Population: 6,483,802
Capital: Indianapolis, pop. 807,584
Largest city: Indianapolis, pop. 807,584
Industry: Transportation equipment, steel, pharmaceutical and chemical products, machinery, petroleum, coal
State flower/bird: Peony/cardinal

There is a TOWN called POPCORN, INDIANA.

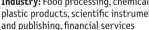

COOL CLICK

Check out great state facts online.
state.me.us
This is for Maine. For each state insert the two-letter state abbreviation (see p. 329) where "me" is now.

Maine

Area: 35,385 sq mi (91,646 sq km)
Population: 1,328,361
Capital: Augusta, pop. 18,444
Largest city: Portland, pop. 63,008
Industry: Health services, tourism, forest products, leather products, electrical equipment, food processing
State flower/bird: White pine cone and tassel/chickadee

Iowa

Area: 56,272 sq mi (145,743 sq km)
Population: 3,046,355
Capital: Des Moines, pop. 200,538
Largest city: Des Moines, pop. 200,538
Industry: Real estate, health services, industrial machinery, food processing, construction
State flower/bird: Wild rose/American goldfinch

Maryland

Area: 12,407 sq mi (32,133 sq km)
Population: 5,773,552
Capital: Annapolis, pop. 36,879
Largest city: Baltimore, pop. 637,418
Industry: Real estate, federal government, health services, business services, engineering services
State flower/bird: Black-eyed Susan/northern (Baltimore) oriole

Kansas

Area: 82,277 sq mi (213,097 sq km)
Population: 2,853,118
Capital: Topeka, pop. 124,331
Largest city: Wichita, pop. 372,186
Industry: Aircraft manufacturing, transportation equipment, construction, food processing, printing and publishing, health care
State flower/bird: Sunflower/western meadowlark

Massachusetts

Area: 10,555 sq mi (27,336 sq km)
Population: 6,547,629
Capital: Boston, pop. 645,169
Largest city: Boston, pop. 645,169
Industry: Electrical equipment, machinery, metal products, scientific instruments, printing and publishing, tourism
State flower/bird: Mayflower/chickadee

Kentucky

Area: 40,409 sq mi (104,659 sq km)
Population: 4,339,367
Capital: Frankfort, pop. 27,382
Largest city: Louisville, pop. 566,503
Industry: Manufacturing, services, government, finance, insurance, real estate, retail trade, transportation, wholesale trade, construction, mining
State flower/bird: Goldenrod/cardinal

The BOSTON CREAM PIE is the state dessert of Massachusetts.

Louisiana

Area: 51,840 sq mi (134,265 sq km)
Population: 4,533,372
Capital: Baton Rouge, pop. 225,388
Largest city: New Orleans, pop. 354,850
Industry: Chemicals, petroleum products, food processing, health services, tourism, oil and natural gas extraction, paper products
State flower/bird: Magnolia/brown pelican

Michigan

Area: 96,716 sq mi (250,495 sq km)
Population: 9,883,640
Capital: Lansing, pop. 113,802
Largest city: Detroit, pop. 910,921
Industry: Motor vehicles and parts, machinery, metal products, office furniture, tourism, chemicals
State flower/bird: Apple blossom/robin

COLOR KEY ● Northeast ● Southeast

Minnesota

Area: 86,939 sq mi (225,172 sq km)
Population: 5,303,925
Capital: St. Paul, pop. 281,253
Largest city: Minneapolis, pop. 385,378
Industry: Real estate, banking and insurance, industrial machinery, printing and publishing, food processing, scientific equipment
State flower/bird: Showy lady's slipper/common loon

Mississippi

Area: 48,430 sq mi (125,434 sq km)
Population: 2,967,297
Capital: Jackson, pop. 175,021
Largest city: Jackson, pop. 175,021
Industry: Petroleum products, health services, electronic equipment, transportation, banking, forest products, communications
State flower/bird: Magnolia/mockingbird

Missouri

Area: 69,704 sq mi (180,534 sq km)
Population: 5,988,927
Capital: Jefferson City, pop. 41,297
Largest city: Kansas City, pop. 482,299
Industry: Transportation equipment, food processing, chemicals, electrical equipment, metal products
State flower/bird: Hawthorn/eastern bluebird

Montana

Area: 147,042 sq mi (380,840 sq km)
Population: 989,415
Capital: Helena, pop. 29,939
Largest city: Billings, pop. 105,845
Industry: Forest products, food processing, mining, construction, tourism
State flower/bird: Bitterroot/western meadowlark

Nebraska

Area: 77,354 sq mi (200,346 sq km)
Population: 1,826,341
Capital: Lincoln, pop. 254,001
Largest city: Omaha, pop. 454,731
Industry: Food processing, machinery, electrical equipment, printing and publishing
State flower/bird: Goldenrod/western meadowlark

Nevada

Area: 110,561 sq mi (286,352 sq km)
Population: 2,700,551
Capital: Carson City, pop. 55,176
Largest city: Las Vegas, pop. 567,641
Industry: Tourism and gaming, mining, printing and publishing, food processing, electrical equipment
State flower/bird: Sagebrush/mountain bluebird

New Hampshire

Area: 9,350 sq mi (24,216 sq km)
Population: 1,316,470
Capital: Concord, pop. 42,546
Largest city: Manchester, pop. 109,279
Industry: Machinery, electronics, metal products
State flower/bird: Purple lilac/purple finch

New Jersey

Area: 8,721 sq mi (22,588 sq km)
Population: 8,791,894
Capital: Trenton, pop. 83,242
Largest city: Newark, pop. 278,154
Industry: Machinery, electronics, metal products, chemicals
State flower/bird: Violet/American goldfinch

New Mexico

Area: 121,590 sq mi (314,917 sq km)
Population: 2,059,179
Capital: Santa Fe, pop. 73,979
Largest city: Albuquerque, pop. 529,219
Industry: Electronic equipment, state and local government, real estate, business services, federal government, oil and gas extraction, health services
State flower/bird: Yucca/roadrunner

New York

Area: 54,556 sq mi (141,300 sq km)
Population: 19,378,102
Capital: Albany, pop. 93,836
Largest city: New York City, pop. 8,391,881
Industry: Printing and publishing, machinery, computer products, finance, tourism
State flower/bird: Rose/eastern bluebird

North Carolina

Area: 53,819 sq mi (139,390 sq km)
Population: 9,535,483
Capital: Raleigh, pop. 405,612
Largest city: Charlotte, pop. 704,422
Industry: Real estate, health services, chemicals, tobacco products, finance, textiles
State flower/bird: Flowering dogwood/cardinal

North Dakota

Area: 70,700 sq mi (183,113 sq km)
Population: 672,591
Capital: Bismarck, pop. 61,217
Largest city: Fargo, pop. 95,556
Industry: Services, government, finance, construction, transportation, oil and gas
State flower/bird: Wild prairie rose/western meadowlark

Ohio

Area: 44,825 sq mi (116,097 sq km)
Population: 11,536,504
Capital: Columbus, pop. 769,332
Largest city: Columbus, pop. 769,332
Industry: Transportation equipment, metal products, machinery, food processing, electrical equipment
State flower/bird: Scarlet carnation/cardinal

Oklahoma

Area: 69,898 sq mi (181,036 sq km)
Population: 3,751,351
Capital: Oklahoma City, pop. 560,333
Largest city: Oklahoma City, pop. 560,333
Industry: Manufacturing, services, government, finance, insurance, real estate
State flower/bird: Mistletoe/scissor-tailed flycatcher

Oregon

Area: 98,381 sq mi (254,806 sq km)
Population: 3,831,074
Capital: Salem, pop. 155,469
Largest city: Portland, pop. 566,143
Industry: Real estate, retail and wholesale trade, electronic equipment, health services, construction, forest products, business services
State flower/bird: Oregon grape/western meadowlark

Pennsylvania

Area: 46,055 sq mi (119,283 sq km)
Population: 12,702,379
Capital: Harrisburg, pop. 47,418
Largest city: Philadelphia, pop. 1,547,297
Industry: Machinery, printing and publishing, forest products, metal products
State flower/bird: Mountain laurel/ruffed grouse

The SLINKY is Pennsylvania's OFFICIAL STATE TOY.

Rhode Island

Area: 1,545 sq mi (4,002 sq km)
Population: 1,052,567
Capital: Providence, pop. 171,909
Largest city: Providence, pop. 171,909
Industry: Health services, business services, silver and jewelry products, metal products
State flower/bird: Violet/Rhode Island red

South Carolina

Area: 32,020 sq mi (82,932 sq km)
Population: 4,625,364
Capital: Columbia, pop. 129,333
Largest city: Columbia, pop. 129,333
Industry: Service industries, tourism, chemicals, textiles, machinery, forest products
State flower/bird: Yellow jessamine/Carolina wren

South Dakota

Area: 77,117 sq mi (199,732 sq km)
Population: 814,180
Capital: Pierre, pop. 14,072
Largest city: Sioux Falls, pop. 158,008
Industry: Finance, services, manufacturing, government, retail trade, transportation and utilities, wholesale trade, construction, mining
State flower/bird: Pasqueflower/ring-necked pheasant

COLOR KEY   Northeast   Southeast

Tennessee

Area: 42,143 sq mi (109,151 sq km)
Population: 6,346,105
Capital: Nashville, pop. 605,473
Largest city: Memphis, pop. 676,640
Industry: Service industries, chemicals, transportation equipment, processed foods, machinery
State flower/bird: Iris/mockingbird

Texas

Area: 268,581 sq mi (695,624 sq km)
Population: 25,145,561
Capital: Austin, pop. 786,386
Largest city: Houston, pop. 2,257,926
Industry: Chemicals, machinery, electronics and computers, food products, petroleum and natural gas, transportation equipment
State flower/bird: Bluebonnet/mockingbird

Utah

Area: 84,899 sq mi (219,888 sq km)
Population: 2,763,885
Capital: Salt Lake City, pop. 183,102
Largest city: Salt Lake City, pop. 183,102
Industry: Government, manufacturing, real estate, construction, health services, business services, banking
State flower/bird: Sego lily/California gull

Vermont

Area: 9,614 sq mi (24,901 sq km)
Population: 625,741
Capital: Montpelier, pop. 7,705
Largest city: Burlington, pop. 38,647
Industry: Health services, tourism, finance, real estate, computer components, electrical parts, printing and publishing, machine tools
State flower/bird: Red clover/hermit thrush

Virginia

Area: 42,774 sq mi (110,785 sq km)
Population: 8,001,024
Capital: Richmond, pop. 204,451
Largest city: Virginia Beach, pop. 433,575
Industry: Food processing, communication and electronic equipment, transportation equipment, printing, shipbuilding, textiles
State flower/bird: Flowering dogwood/cardinal

Washington

Area: 71,300 sq mi (184,666 sq km)
Population: 6,724,540
Capital: Olympia, pop. 46,100
Largest city: Seattle, pop. 616,627
Industry: Aerospace, tourism, food processing, forest products, paper products, industrial machinery, printing and publishing, metals, computer software
State flower/bird: Coast rhododendron/Amer. goldfinch

West Virginia

Area: 24,230 sq mi (62,755 sq km)
Population: 1,852,994
Capital: Charleston, pop. 50,268
Largest city: Charleston, pop. 50,268
Industry: Tourism, coal mining, chemicals, metal manufacturing, forest products, stone, clay, oil, glass products
State flower/bird: Rhododendron/cardinal

Wisconsin

Area: 65,498 sq mi (169,639 sq km)
Population: 5,686,986
Capital: Madison, pop. 235,419
Largest city: Milwaukee, pop. 605,013
Industry: Industrial machinery, paper products, food processing, metal products, electronic equipment, transportation
State flower/bird: Wood violet/robin

WISCONSIN is HOME to a MUSEUM all about mustard.

Wyoming

Area: 97,814 sq mi (253,337 sq km)
Population: 563,626
Capital: Cheyenne, pop. 57,478
Largest city: Cheyenne, pop. 57,478
Industry: Oil and natural gas, mining, generation of electricity, chemicals, tourism
State flower/bird: Indian paintbrush/western meadowlark

 Midwest 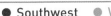 Southwest West

THE TERRITORIES

The United States has 14 territories—political divisions that are not states. Three of these are in the Caribbean Sea, and the other eleven are in the Pacific Ocean.

St. John, U.S. Virgin Islands

U.S. CARIBBEAN TERRITORIES

Puerto Rico

Area: 3,508 sq mi (9,086 sq km)
Population: 3,725,789
Capital: San Juan (proper), pop. 420,326
Languages: Spanish, English

U.S. Virgin Islands

Area: 149 sq mi (386 sq km)
Population: 110,000
Capital: Charlotte Amalie, pop. 54,000
Languages: English, Spanish or Spanish Creole, French or French Creole

U.S. PACIFIC TERRITORIES

American Samoa

Area: 77 sq mi (199 sq km)
Population: 68,000
Capital: Pago Pago, pop. 60,000
Language: Samoan

Guam

Area: 217 sq mi (561 sq km)
Population: 189,000
Capital: Hagåtña (Agana), pop. 153,000
Languages: English, Chamorro, Philippine languages

Northern Mariana Islands

Area: 184 sq mi (477 sq km)
Population: 88,000
Capital: Saipan, pop. 79,000
Languages: Philippine languages, Chinese, Chamorro, English

Other U.S. Territories

Baker Island, Howland Island, Jarvis Island, Johnston Atoll, Kingman Reef, Midway Islands, Palmyra Atoll, Wake Island, Navassa Island (in the Caribbean)

THE NATION'S CAPITAL

District of Columbia

Area: 68 sq mi (177 sq km)
Population: 601,723

Abraham Lincoln, who was President during the Civil War and a strong opponent of slavery, is remembered in the Lincoln Memorial, located at the opposite end of the National Mall from the U.S. Capitol Building.

The Smithsonian Institution, the world's largest museum, is actually made up of 19 museums. Established in 1846, the Smithsonian is sometimes referred to as the nation's attic because of its large collections.

COLOR KEY ● Territories ● Northeast

MR. POTATO HEAD ran for MAYOR of BOISE, IDAHO, in 1985.

TEXAS is the only state to allow residents to VOTE FROM SPACE.

4,000-YEAR-OLD POPCORN was found in a cave in NEW MEXICO.

Oregon's **D RIVER** is only 120 feet long—SHORTER than an **Olympic-size** SWIMMING POOL.

Green Bay, Wisconsin, is unofficially **KNOWN** as the "TOILET PAPER CAPITAL OF THE WORLD."

VERMONT's name comes from TWO FRENCH WORDS meaning "GREEN MOUNTAIN."

The world's first UNDERWATER HOTEL is in KEY LARGO, FLORIDA.

Two-Letter Postal Abbreviations

AK	Alaska
AL	Alabama
AR	Arkansas
AS	American Samoa
AZ	Arizona
CA	California
CO	Colorado
CT	Connecticut
DC	District of Columbia
DE	Delaware
FL	Florida
GA	Georgia
GU	Guam
HI	Hawaii
IA	Iowa
ID	Idaho
IL	Illinois
IN	Indiana
KS	Kansas
KY	Kentucky
LA	Louisiana
MA	Massachusetts
MD	Maryland
ME	Maine
MI	Michigan
MN	Minnesota
MO	Missouri
MP	Northern Mariana Islands
MS	Mississippi
MT	Montana
NC	North Carolina
ND	North Dakota
NE	Nebraska
NH	New Hampshire
NJ	New Jersey
NM	New Mexico
NV	Nevada
NY	New York
OH	Ohio
OK	Oklahoma
OR	Oregon
PA	Pennsylvania
PR	Puerto Rico
RI	Rhode Island
SC	South Carolina
SD	South Dakota
TN	Tennessee
TX	Texas
UT	Utah
VA	Virginia
VI	U.S. Virgin Islands
VT	Vermont
WA	Washington
WI	Wisconsin
WV	West Virginia
WY	Wyoming

URBAN GIANT

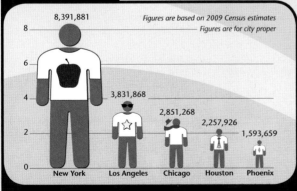

Figures are based on 2009 Census estimates
Figures are for city proper

8,391,881 — New York
3,831,868 — Los Angeles
2,851,268 — Chicago
2,257,926 — Houston
1,593,659 — Phoenix

With more than twice the population of the next-largest city, New York—known as the Big Apple—is the country's largest city.

Wacky
Road Trip

Check out these **5** strange-but-true roadside attractions.

You're riding in the car listening to your favorite tune and daydreaming about the next cool stop on this family vacation. Suddenly your dad slows down. Peering into an alley, you see an entire wall covered in gum! Huh? Actually, this sticky attraction is just one of many wacky art displays scattered across the country. So buckle your seat belt and get ready for a wild ride.

Bubblegum Alley
SAN LUIS OBISPO, CALIFORNIA, U.S.A.

Some call it art; others call it just plain gross. Bubblegum Alley is covered from top to bottom with wads of chewed gum, a tradition that was started mysteriously by locals in the 1950s. Some artists even created images of funny faces and the American flag. Unamused community members had the "masterpiece" removed—twice! But the cleanup didn't stick, and soon more gum appeared. Now the alley has more than two million pieces of gum on it.

Giant Trumpet
SCHLADMING, AUSTRIA

This trumpet can't play music, but it sure does get a lot of attention. Located in a mining town, the 49-foot (15-m) -long instrument is the largest trumpet in the world.

Mac the Moose

3

MOOSE JAW, SASKATCHEWAN, CANADA

You probably wouldn't be that surprised to see a moose in Canada, but what if it were 32 feet (10 m) tall? Well, that's what you'll find when you head to the Moose Jaw, Saskatchewan, information center. Built in 1984 to help welcome visitors to this tourist town, Mac weighs in at a hearty 10 tons (9,072 t).

4

Giant Penguin

CUT BANK, MONTANA, U.S.A.

Bundle up when you visit this statue, because temperatures here can get as low as -47°F (-44°C). As a nod to the frosty conditions, a local businessman built the 27-foot (8-m) -tall penguin out of 10,000 pounds (4,536 kg) of concrete. The creator left for warmer weather, but the statue—seven times taller than a real emperor penguin—still stands, welcoming visitors to its chilly home.

Paul Bunyan

5

AKELEY, MINNESOTA, U.S.A.

You can't miss this giant statue of Paul Bunyan, the mythological, larger-than-life lumberjack. One of the biggest Bunyan landmarks in the United States, the fiberglass statue measures 25 feet (7.6 m)—that's taller than a two-story building! Need another reason to visit this landmark? It's right across the street from Paul's Purple Cow ice-cream parlor. Yum!

Great Barrier Reef
VACATION
and more!

Imagine being whisked away on a dream vacation to Australia's Great Barrier Reef. A world of wonder awaits you—both on land and underwater.

First, take a fast ride over the reef in a low-flying helicopter, getting a unique aerial view of the biggest living structure on Earth. Then throw on some snorkel gear and jump in the water to be welcomed by the awesome sight of the colorful coral reef. You look at—but don't touch—the frilly, knobby, odd-shaped corals. Watch as the fish flutter and dart away from you as you spot a striped zebra shark. Don't worry—it's not an aggressive fish that could harm you, unlike the lionfish, with its venomous spines to warn you away.

Next, you're off to explore the rain forest, where you take a dip in a creek and climb a tower into the canopy. On your visit to a wildlife park, you're allowed to hand-feed kangaroos and wallabies. You top off your visit by cuddling a koala at a nature park.

A trip to Australia is an adventure of a lifetime!

VACATION Hot Spots

CHECK OUT SOME OF THE MOST POPULAR ATTRACTIONS IN THE WORLD.

Times Square
New York City, NY
36 million visitors a year

National Mall & Memorial Parks
Washington, DC
24 million

Golden Gate National Recreation Area
San Francisco, CA
17 million

Walt Disney World Magic Kingdom
Lake Buena Vista, FL
17 million

Trafalgar Square
London, England
15 million

Notre Dame de Paris
Paris, France
13 million

Niagara Falls
New York State and Ontario, Canada
12 million

For more on these and other exciting destinations, go online.
traveler.nationalgeographic.com

Q Where do **crayons** go on **vacation?**

A To a wax museum.

Skip the BUBBLE GUM in Singapore— buying it is ILLEGAL.

The ORIGINAL 7 WONDERS of the WORLD

More than 2,000 years ago, many travelers wrote about sights they had seen on their journeys. Over time, seven of those places made history as the "wonders of the ancient world." There are seven because the Greeks, who made the list, believed the number seven to be magical.

THE PYRAMIDS OF GIZA, EGYPT
BUILT: ABOUT 2600 B.C.
MASSIVE TOMBS OF EGYPTIAN PHARAOHS, THE PYRAMIDS ARE THE ONLY ANCIENT WONDERS STILL STANDING TODAY.

HANGING GARDENS OF BABYLON, IRAQ
BUILT: DATE UNKNOWN
LEGEND HAS IT THAT THIS GARDEN PARADISE WAS PLANTED ON AN ARTIFICIAL MOUNTAIN, BUT MANY EXPERTS SAY IT NEVER REALLY EXISTED.

TEMPLE OF ARTEMIS AT EPHESUS, TURKEY
BUILT: SIXTH CENTURY B.C.
THIS TOWERING TEMPLE WAS BUILT TO HONOR ARTEMIS, THE GREEK GODDESS OF THE HUNT.

STATUE OF ZEUS, GREECE
BUILT: FIFTH CENTURY B.C.
THIS 40-FOOT (12-M) STATUE DEPICTED THE KING OF THE GREEK GODS.

MAUSOLEUM AT HALICARNASSUS, TURKEY
BUILT: FOURTH CENTURY B.C.
THIS ELABORATE TOMB WAS BUILT FOR KING MAUSOLUS.

COLOSSUS OF RHODES, RHODES (AN ISLAND IN THE AEGEAN SEA)
BUILT: FOURTH CENTURY B.C.
A 110-FOOT (34-M) STATUE HONORED THE GREEK SUN GOD HELIOS.

LIGHTHOUSE OF ALEXANDRIA, EGYPT
BUILT: THIRD CENTURY B.C.
THE WORLD'S FIRST LIGHTHOUSE, IT USED MIRRORS TO REFLECT SUNLIGHT FOR MILES OUT TO SEA.

The NEW 7 WONDERS of the WORLD

Why name new wonders of the world? Most of the original ancient wonders no longer exist. To be eligible for the new list, the wonders had to be man-made before the year 2000 and in preservation. They were selected in 2007 through a poll of more than 100 million voters!

TAJ MAHAL, INDIA
COMPLETED: 1648
THIS LAVISH TOMB WAS BUILT AS A FINAL RESTING PLACE FOR THE BELOVED WIFE OF EMPEROR SHAH JAHAN.

PETRA, SOUTHWEST JORDAN
COMPLETED: ABOUT 200 B.C.
SOME 30,000 PEOPLE ONCE LIVED IN THIS ROCK CITY CARVED INTO CLIFF WALLS.

MACHU PICCHU, PERU
COMPLETED: ABOUT 1450
OFTEN CALLED THE "LOST CITY IN THE CLOUDS," MACHU PICCHU IS PERCHED 7,972 FEET (2,430 M) HIGH IN THE ANDES.

THE COLOSSEUM, ITALY
COMPLETED: A.D. 80
WILD ANIMALS—AND HUMANS— FOUGHT EACH OTHER TO THE DEATH BEFORE 50,000 SPECTATORS IN THIS ARENA.

CHRIST THE REDEEMER STATUE, BRAZIL
COMPLETED: 1931
TOWERING ATOP CORCOVADO MOUNTAIN, THIS STATUE IS TALLER THAN A 12-STORY BUILDING AND WEIGHS ABOUT 2.5 MILLION POUNDS (1.1 MILLION KG).

CHICHÉN ITZÁ, MEXICO
COMPLETED: TENTH CENTURY
ONCE THE CAPITAL CITY OF THE ANCIENT MAYA EMPIRE, CHICHÉN ITZÁ IS HOME TO THE FAMOUS PYRAMID OF KUKULCÁN.

GREAT WALL OF CHINA, CHINA
COMPLETED: 1644
THE LONGEST MAN-MADE STRUCTURE EVER BUILT, IT WINDS OVER AN ESTIMATED 4,500 MILES (7,000 KM).

WORLD'S COOLEST

CHECK OUT THIS AMAZING ROTATING BUILDING

Humans have built incredible structures, including the Great Wall of China and the pyramids of Egypt. But there's one thing that even the world's most amazing structures can't do: alter their shapes. Well, that could change.

Someday, you could live in a shape-shifting skyscraper that never stays still. The first of these buildings, which are called Dynamic Towers, will be built in Dubai, a city in the United Arab Emirates in the Middle East. It will be about two and a half times taller than the Washington Monument. Each floor will be in constant motion, rotating independently and at different speeds—like an 80-story Rubik's Cube forever being twisted by invisible hands. "These buildings will never look the same," according to David Fisher, the architect behind the idea.

EVER-CHANGING

This may sound like fantasy, but in a few years the Dynamic Tower is expected to become a reality. The first 35 floors will consist of offices and a luxury hotel. Floors 36 through 70 will house numerous apartments, but each of the top ten floors in the 80-story tower will be a single apartment. While the architect will control the movement of most of the floors, anyone who owns one of the top ten apartments will be able to move them however he or she likes.

Each luxury apartment, expected to cost about $36 million, will cover an expansive 10,700 square feet (1,000 sq m).

IT ROTATES!

SKYSCRAPERS

GREENEST SKYSCRAPER

Wind will power the tower's motion, making it the first self-powered skyscraper in history. To generate electricity, the Dubai skyscraper will place windmill blades horizontally between each floor of the building (below). There will be 79 wind turbines. In addition, the roofs will have solar panels to capture the sun's energy. Combined, this will make enough electricity to power the entire tower—and several nearby as well.

SKYSCRAPER FACTORIES

Skyscrapers are usually built one floor at a time—but not the Dynamic Tower: It will be the world's first skyscraper to be built in a factory. Only the enormous concrete core cylinder will be built on-site, while each floor will be made at a factory. They will be shipped to the construction site ready to go: Even the furniture will be inside. All of this will make construction safer, faster, and less expensive.

SUPERSTRUCTURES

Take a look at these remarkable facts about six of the world's skyscrapers.

TAIPEI 101 IN TAIWAN, CHINA: IT'S BUILT TO WITHSTAND 130-MILE-AN-HOUR (209 KPH) WINDS.

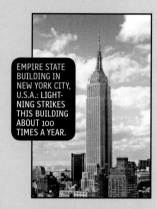

EMPIRE STATE BUILDING IN NEW YORK CITY, U.S.A.: LIGHTNING STRIKES THIS BUILDING ABOUT 100 TIMES A YEAR.

WILLIS (FORMERLY SEARS) TOWER IN CHICAGO, ILLINOIS, U.S.A.: AT 1,450 FEET (442 M), IT IS THE TALLEST BUILDING IN NORTH AMERICA.

PETRONAS TOWERS IN KUALA LUMPUR, MALAYSIA: THE TOWERS HAVE 32,000 WINDOWS. IT TAKES WINDOW WASHERS A MONTH TO CLEAN EACH TOWER.

TWO INTERNATIONAL FINANCE CENTRE IN HONG KONG, CHINA: THERE ARE 62 ELEVATORS IN THE 1,362-FOOT (415-M)-TALL BUILDING.

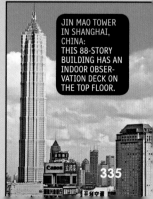

JIN MAO TOWER IN SHANGHAI, CHINA: THIS 88-STORY BUILDING HAS AN INDOOR OBSERVATION DECK ON THE TOP FLOOR.

Finding Your Way Around

Every map has a story to tell, but first you have to know how to read one. Maps represent information by using a language of symbols. Knowing how to read these symbols provides access to a wide range of information. Look at the scale and compass rose or arrow to understand distance and direction (see box below).

To find out what each symbol on a map means, you must use the key. It's your secret decoder—identifying information by each symbol on the map.

Latitude

Longitude

90°N (North Pole)
75°N
60°N
45°N
30°N
15°N
0° (Equator)
15°S
30°S
45°S

LATITUDE AND LONGITUDE

Latitude and Longitude lines (above) help us determine locations on Earth. Every place on Earth has a special address called absolute location. Imaginary lines called lines of latitude run west to east, parallel to the Equator. These lines measure distance in degrees north or south from the Equator (0° latitude) to the North Pole (90°N) or to the South Pole (90°S). One degree of latitude is approximately 70 miles (113 km).

Lines of longitude run north to south, meeting at the poles. These lines measure distance in degrees east or west from 0° longitude (prime meridian) to 180° longitude. The prime meridian runs through Greenwich, England.

SCALE & DIRECTION

The scale on a map is shown as a fraction, as words, or as a line or bar. It relates distance on the map to distance in the real world. Sometimes the scale identifies the type of map projection. Maps may include an arrow or compass rose to indicate north on the map.

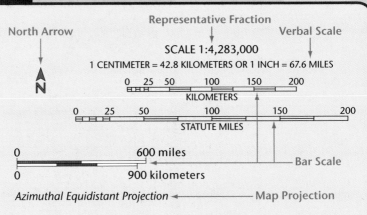

North Arrow

N

Representative Fraction

SCALE 1:4,283,000

1 CENTIMETER = 42.8 KILOMETERS OR 1 INCH = 67.6 MILES

Verbal Scale

0 25 50 100 150 200
KILOMETERS

0 25 50 100 150 200
STATUTE MILES

0 600 miles
0 900 kilometers

Bar Scale

Azimuthal Equidistant Projection ← Map Projection

SYMBOLS

There are three main types of map symbols: points, lines, and areas. Points, which can be either dots or small icons, represent locations of things, such as schools, cities, or landmarks. Lines are used to show boundaries, roads, or rivers and can vary in color or thickness. Area symbols use patterns or color to show regions, such as a sandy area or a neighborhood.

POINT
A point symbol, a black dot, indicates a city, such as Omdurman.

LINE
Sudan's country boundary appears as a line symbol: a dotted line with a colored edge.

AREA
Sandy places, such as parts of the Sahara Desert, are shown by a tan, speckled area.

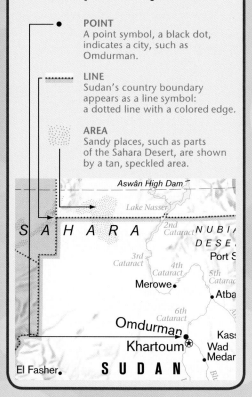

What's an ATLAS?

An atlas, or collection of maps, is usually chock-full of information, charts, and illustrations. You can look up specific places or just browse. For example, the *National Geographic World Atlas for Young Explorers* is full of photographs, statistics, quick facts, and—most of all—lots of detailed maps and charts.

MAKING A PROJECTION. Globes present a model of Earth as it is—a sphere—but they are bulky and can be difficult to use and store. Flat maps are much more convenient but certain problems can result from transferring Earth's curved surface to a flat piece of paper, a process called projection. Imagine a globe that has been cut in half like this one has. If a light is shined into it, the lines of latitude and longitude and the shapes of the continent will cast shadows that can be "projected" onto a piece of paper, as shown here. Depending on how the paper is positioned, the shadows will be distorted in different ways.

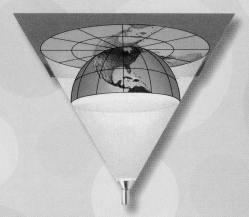

ABSOLUTE LOCATION. The imaginary grid composed of lines of latitude and longitude helps us locate places on a map. Suppose you are playing a game of global scavenger hunt. The clue says the prize is hidden at absolute location 30°S, 60°W. You know that the first number is south of the Equator, and the second is west of the prime meridian. On the map at left, find the line of latitude labeled 30°S. Now find the line of longitude labeled 60°W. Trace these lines with your fingers until they meet. Identify this spot. The prize must be located in central Argentina (see arrow, right).

GAME ANSWERS

Galaxy Quest, pages 164–165

Lost and Found, page 166

Signs of the Times, page 168
Signs #2 and #6 are fake.

Mousetrap, page 169

What in the World? Seeing Spots! page 170
Top row: twister, feather, gecko.
Middle row: ladybug, Dalmatian, domino.
Bottom row: fish, candy buttons,
                    mushroom.

Stump Your Parents, page 171
1. B; 2. D; 3. F; 4. D (The show has never
revealed which state the Simpsons live in.);
5. B; 6. A; 7. A.

A Piece of Cake, page 172
From left to right, top to bottom: boy, birthday
cake, bulldog, bicycle, bubbles, bread, barrel,
ball, broom, beret, book, bear, belt, buns,
ballerina, balloons, box, bow tie, bones,
basket, buttons, bagels, baker, bowl, butter.

We Gave It a Swirl, page 174

1. clown fish, 2. cheetah, 3. duckling,
4. polar bear, 5. caterpillar.

A Wintry Mix-Up, page 175

Animal Jam, pages 176–177

Having a Blast!, page 178

Double Take, page 180

Pet Project, page 181

SS; 114 (LO), Photosani/SS; 115 (LE), Corey Ford/ Dreamstime.com; 115 (RT), IS; 116, Bob Thomas/ Popperfoto/GI; 117 (UP), Annie Griffiths; 117 (LO), Graham Smith/ArtMasters; 119 (UP), Mary Terriberry/SS; 119 (LO), Andrew Howe/IS; 120 (A), Jan Hopgood/SS; 120 (B), Taylor S. Kennedy/ NGS; 120 (C), SS; 120 (D), Peterphoto/IS; 120 (E), CB; 120 (F), SS; 120 (G), De Visu/SS; 120 (H), SS; 121 (I), Gregor Schuster/CB; 121 (J), Ríoghán/SS; 121 (K), Josh Westrich/CB; 121 (L), Angarato/SS; 121 (UP RT), AP Images/Foto AP/Museo Brit·nico, PA; 122, David Ryan/Lonely Planet Images; 123 (UP), JTB Photo/PL; 123 (CTR), AP Photo/Charles City Press/Mark Wicks; 123 (LO LE), AP Photo/ The Alpena News/Amy Lisenbe; 123 (LO RT), AP Photo/Al Grillo; 124 (ALL), Harrod Blank; 124–125 (LO), Hunter Mann/Harrod Blank; 126 (UP LE, UP RT), Tom Nick Cococtos; 126 (LO), Ron Nickel/Design Pic/CB; 127 (UP),Tom Nick Cococtos; 127 (CTR), Comet Photography Inc.; 127 (RT CTR), Rebecca Hale/NGS Staff; 127 (LO), Comet Photography Inc.; 128, Brand X/SUS; 129 (UP), Adrian Weinbrecht/GI; 129 (LO), Donald Erickson/IS; 130 (UP), Route 66/SS; 130 (CTR), Joel Blit/SS; 130 (LO), Joanne van Hoof/SS

Super Science (132–161)
132–133, Nick Kaloterakis; 134, DA; 135 (A), Sebastian Kaulitzki/SS; 135 (B), Steve Gschmeissner/PR; 135 (C), Volker Steger/Christian Bardele/PR; 135 (D), Fedor A. Sidorov/SS; 135 (E), Marie C. Fields/SS; 135 (F), sgame/SS; 135 (G), Benjamin Jessop/IS; 136–137 (Background), Take 27 Ltd/PR; 137 (ALL), DA; 138 (UP), Michael Taylor/SS; 138 (CTR), NASA; 138 (LO), NASA; 139–141 (ALL) DA; 142 (A), Giovanni Benintende/SS; 142 (B), Tony & Daphne Hallas/PR; 142 (C), peresanz/ SS; 142 (Background), Gabe Palmer/CB; 143 (ALL), DA; 144 (Background), AlaskaStock/CB; 146 (UP), NASA; 146 (LO), NASA; 147, courtesy of Lockheed Martin; 147 (RT), Johnee Bee; 148 (UP), Sebastian Kaulitzki/SS; 148 (LO), Westend61/ SUS; 149, Mondolithic Studios; 150 (UP), Dennis Cooper/IS; 150 (LO), Linda Nye; 152, Robert J. Demarest; 153, Blake Thornton; 154, Jani Bryson/IS; 155 (A), Lisa F. Young/SS; 155 (B), Mark Thiessen/NGS Staff; 155 (C), Elena Elisseeva/SS; 155 (D), Erik Lam/SS; 155 (E), 06photo/SS; 155 (F), Marc Dietrich/SS; 155 (G), Roxana Bashyrova/SS; 155 (H), Rebecca Hale/NGS Staff; 155 (I), FoodCollection/SUS; 155 (Background), Jean Michel Labat/Ardea; 156–157, Mondolithic Studios; 158–159 (UP), Mondolithic Studios; 158 (LO), Mondolithic Studios; 158–159 (Background), Don Farrall/GI; 159 (LO LE), NASA; 159 (LO RT), Pat Rawlings; 160 (LO), Chris Gorgio/IS; 160 (UP), Rob Marmion/ SS; 160 (LO), Chris Gorgio/IS; 161,pixhook/IS

Little Big Book of Fun (162–181)
162 (A), Pat Moriarty; 162 (B), Dan Sipple; 162 (C), SeaWorld Orlando; 162 (D), Smart Bomb Interactive; 162 (E), Clayton Hanmer; 162 (F), Howard Davies/CB; 162 (G), Ron Kimball Studios; 162 (H), Pat Moriarty; 163 (A), Pat Moriarty; 163 (B), Clayton Hanmer; 163 (C), Dan Sipple; 163 (D), Clayton Hanmer; 163 (E), Smart Bomb Interactive; 163 (F), Julie Habel/CB; 163 (G), Marty Baumann; 163 (H), Aaron Reiner; 163 (I), Nagy Melinda/ SS; 163 (J), Aaron Reiner; 164–165, Clayton Hanmer; 166, Pat Moriarty; 167, Marty Baumann; 168 (UP LE), Julie Habel/CB; 168 (UP CTR), Stockbyte/PictureQuest; 168 (UP RT), Pat O'Hara/CB; 168 (LE CTR), Howard Davies/CB; 168 (RT CTR), Joseph Sohm/PictureQuest; 168 (LO LE), Dale O'Dell/Alamy; 168 (LO RT), David Keaton/CB; 169, James Yamasaki; 170 (UP LE), Rebecca Hale/NGS Staff; 170 (UP RT), Art Wolfe/GI; 170 (UP RT), Derek P Redfearn/GI;

170 (LE CTR), Photri/Ann & Rob Simpson; 170 (CTR), Ron Kimball Studios; 170 (RT CTR), Image Source/PictureQuest; 170 (LO LE), Linda Dunk/ Taxi/GI; 170 (LO CTR), Steven Mark Needham/ FoodPix; 170 (LO RT), Rosemary Calvert/GI; 171 (UP LE), Bettmann/CB; 171 (LE CTR), David Davis Photo Productions/Alamy; 171 (LO LE), NASA; 171 (UP RT), Barry King/Wire Image/GI; 171 (RT CTR), SeaWorld Orlando; 171 (LO RT), Thomas Mangelsen/MP; 172, Aaron Reiner; 173 (UP LE), Alec Longstreth; 173 (UP RT), Karen Sneider; 173 (LO LE), Clayton Hanmer; 173 (RT CTR), Karen Sneider; 173 (LO RT), Karen Sneider; 174 (UP LE), cbpix/SS; 174 (UP RT), Christian Musat/SS; 174 (RT CTR), FloridaStock/SS; 174 (LO LE), Nagy Melinda/SS; 174 (CTR), Christian Musat/SS; 175, James Yamasaki; 176–177, Smart Bomb Interactive; 178, James Yamasaki; 179, Dan Sipple; 180, S. Remain/Matton Images; 181, Pat Moriarty

Wonders of Nature (182–209)
182–183, Michael Melford/NGS; 184, Jarvis Gray/ SS; 185, Stuart Armstrong; 186–187, Jason Edwards/NGS; 188 (UP), Image 100/SUS; 188 (LO), Brandon Cole/Workbook Stock/Jupiter Images; 188–189 (Background), John A. Anderson/ IS; 189 (UP), Paul Souders/CB; 189 (LO), Zafer Kizilkaya; 191 (A), Shusei Nagaoka/NGS; 191 (B), Susan Sanford/NGS; 191 (C), Susan Sanford/NGS; 191 (D), Susan Sanford/NGS; 191 (E), Susan Sanford/NGS; 193, JewelryStock/Alamy; 193 (LO RT), Knaupe/IS; 194 (UP), AVTG/IS; 194 (LO), Brad Wynnyk/SS; 195 (A), Rich Carey/SS; 195 (B), Richard Walters/IS; 195 (C), Karen Graham/IS; 195 (D), Michio Hoshino/MP/NGS; 196, PR; 197 (UP), David Tipling/NPL/MP; 197 (A), Donald L Fackler Jr./Alamy; 197 (B), Nigel Cattlin/Alamy; 197 (C), Imagebroker/Alamy; 197 (D), John Glover/ Alamy; 198, Klimapark; 199 (LE), Artem Efimov/SS; 199 (CTR), Weiss and Overpeck, The University of Arizona; 199 (RT), Weiss and Overpeck, The University of Arizona; 200 (UP), Arctic-Images/ CB; 200 (CTR), Jim Reed/PR, Inc; 200 (LO), Spectrumphotofile.com/Photographers Direct; 201 (UP), U.S. Navy photo; 201 (CTR), PhotoTake Inc./Alamy; 201 (LO LE), Spectrumphotofile. com/Photographers Direct; 201 (LO RT), Cathy & Gordon ILLG/ Adventure Photography; 202, Thomas Allen/GI; 203, NOAA; 204 (UP), AP Images/ Kyodo; 204 (LO), Richard Olsenius/NGS; 205 (UP), sdecoret/SS; 205 (Background), Orvar Atli Thorgeirsson/Nordicphotos/CB; 206, Galen Rowell/ CB; 207, Eric Dietrich/MP; 209, AVAVA/SS

Awesome Adventure (210–229)
210–211, Michael Melford/NGS Staff; 212 (UP LE), Mark Thiessen/NGS Staff; 212 (UP RT), Mark Thiessen/NGS Staff; 212–213 (CTR), Aladin Abdel Naby/Reuters; 213 (UP LE), Mark Thiessen/NGS; 213 (UP RT), Beverly Joubert/NGS; 214 (LE), www. macfreefilms.com; 214 (RT), Stephen L. Alvarez; 215 (UP), George Steinmetz/SS; 215 (LO), photo courtesy of Luke Dollar; 216 (UP), Yoshino Tomi Photo Studio/PL; 216 (LO LE), JTB Photo/PL; 216 (Background), Robert Clark; 217 (UP), Skyscan/CB; 217 (A), CB; 217 (B), Bettmann/CB; 217 (C), Bettmann/CB; 218–219, Peter Carsten/ Speleo Research & Films/NGS; 220–221 (ALL), TR; 220–221 (globes), Martin Walz; 222, Mark Downey/Lucid Images; 222 (A), Neil L. Rettig/ NGS; 222 (B), Mattias Klum/NGS; 222 (C), David A. Northcott/CB; 222 (D), Michael Dick/ Animals Animals; 223 (LE), Ian Austin/Aurora Photos; 223 (RT), Annie Griffiths; 224 (A), Amy Toensing/NGS Staff; 224 (B), Amy Toensing/ NGS Staff; 224 (C), Lijah Hanley; 224 (D), Fabio Liverani/NPL; 225 (UP), Renee Lynn/GI; 225 (LO), Barbara Kinney; 226, Martin Harvey/www.wildimagesonline.co.za; 227

(UP), Nicole Duplaix/NGS; 227 (CTR), Stephen Frink/CB; 227 (LO), Jason Edwards/NGS; 228, Killroy Productions/SS

History Happens (230–257)
230–231, Kenneth Garrett; 232, Wang da Gang; 233 (UP LE), OLM/NGS; 233 (UP RT), OLM/NGS; 233 (LO LE), Wang da Gang; 233 (RT CTR), OLM; 233 (LO RT), OLM/NGS; 234 (UP), ADLWS; 234 (LO LE), ADLWS; 234 (LO CTR LE), ADLWS; 234 (LO CTR RT), ADLWS; 234 (LO RT), ADLWS; 235 (UP LE), ADLWS; 235 (UP CTR), ADLWS; 235 (UP RT), Elisabetta Ferrero/White Star; 235 (LO), Art by Elisabeth Daynés; 236, Matthias Breiter/MP/ NGS; 238–239 (UP), Mondolithic Studios; 239 (UP RT), Seamas Culligan/Zuma/CB; 239 (LO), Roger Ressmeyer/CB; 240, Clayton Hanmer; 242, AP Images/Adam Butler; 244 (UP), Scott Rothstein/SS; 244 (LO), Courtesy of Declaration of Independence Road Inc.; 245 (UP), Cristina Ciochina/SS; 245 (LO), Stephen Coburn/SS; 246 (LE), Gary Blakely/SS; 246 (RT), S. Borisov/ SS; 247 (LE), Cory Thoman/SS; 247 (RT), Cory Thoman/SS; 248–251 (ALL), WHHA; 252 (A-E), WHHA; 252 (F), AP Photo/Pablo Martinez Monsivais; 252 (G, H), The White House; 253, Aga/SS; 254 (UP), Bettmann/CB; 254 (LO), Bettmann/CB; 255 (UP), AP Photo/Gene Herrick; 255 (LE CTR), Central Press/GI; 255 (RT CTR), Topham/The Image Works; 255 (LO), Central Press/GI; 256, AP Photo/Ben Curtis; 257, bluehill/SS

Geography Rocks (258–337)
258–259, C & M Denis-Huot/Peter Arnold Images/ PL; 265 (A), Maria Stenzel/NGS; 265 (B), Bill Hatcher/NGS; 265 (C), Carsten Peter/SS; 265 (D), Carsten Peter/SS; 265 (E), Gordon Wiltsie/ NGS; 265 (F), James P. Blair/NGS; 265 (G), Thomas J. Abercrombie/NGS; 265 (H), Bill Curtsinger/SS; 266, George F. Mobley/NGS; 267, Jeff Vanuga/NPL; 270 (UP), Joel Simon/ Digital Vision/GI; 271–270, Daniel Cox/Oxford Scientific/PL; 274, Gavin Hellier/Robert Harding World Imagery/CB; 275 (UP), Stephen Belcher/ Foto Natura/MP; 275 (LO), rest/IS; 278 (UP), Frans Lanting; 279 (LO), Jim Zuckerman/CB; 279, Kitch Bain/SS; 282 (UP), Pozstos Janos/IS; 282 (LO), Jorma Jaemsen/zefa/CB; 283, Index Stock/SS; 286, DLILLC/CB; 287 (Inset), ML Harris/Iconica/GI; 287 (Background), Alan Schein Photography/CB; 290, ZSSD/MP/NGS; 291 (UP), John & Lisa Merrill/DanitaDelimont.com; 291 (LO), Glowimages/GI; 304, R. Martens/IS; 308, Robert Preston/Alamy; 311, David Evans; 323, Steve Cukrov/SS; 328 (UP), Panoramic Images/GI; 328 (LO LE), PhotoDisc; 328 (LO RT), PhotoDisc; 330–331 (UP RT), Matt Boulton; 330 (LO), Zoltan Szabo; 330 (CTR), Paul Harris/GI; 331 (LE), RoadsideAmerica.com; 331 (RT), RoadsideAmerica.com; 332 (UP), Trevor Smithers ARPS/Alamy; 332 (LO LE), Image Source/GI; 333 (A), David Sutherland/GI; 333 (B), Ferdinand Knab/ GI; 333 (C), Ferdinand Knab/GI; 333 (D), Ferdinand Knab/GI; 333 (E), Wilhelm van Ehrenberg/GI; 333 (F), Ferdinand Knab/GI; 333 (G), DEA Picture Library/GI; 333 (H), Holger Mette/SS; 333 (I), Holger Mette/SS; 333 (J), Jarno Gonzalez Zarraonandia/SS; 333 (K), David Iliff/SS; 333 (L), Ostill/SS; 333 (M), Hannamariah/SS; 333 (N), Jarno Gonzalez Zarraonandia/SS; 334–335, Dynamic Architecture TM/David Fisher Architect/ All Rights Reserved 2008 © International Patent Pending; 335 (A), Digital Vision/Alamy; 335 (B), Sandra Baker/Alamy; 335 (C), Jon Arnold/ Alamy; 335 (D), International Photobank/Alamy; 335 (E), Daniel Hewlett/Alamy; 335 (F), Digital Vision/Alamy; 335 (G-H), Dynamic Architecture TM/David Fisher Architect/All Rights Reserved 2008 © International Patent Pending

346

Published by the
National Geographic Society

John M. Fahey, Jr.
Chairman of the Board and Chief Executive Officer

Timothy T. Kelly
President

Declan Moore
Executive Vice President; President, Publishing

Melina Gerosa Bellows
Chief Creative Officer, Kids and Family, Global Media

Prepared by the Book Division

Nancy Laties Feresten, *Senior Vice President,*
Editor in Chief, Children's Books
Jonathan Halling, *Design Director,*
Children's Publishing
Jennifer Emmett, *Editorial Director,*
Children's Books
Carl Mehler, *Director of Maps*
R. Gary Colbert, *Production Director*
Jennifer A. Thornton, *Managing Editor*

Staff for This Book

Robin Terry, *Project Manager*
Mary Varilla Jones, *Project Editor*
James Hiscott, Jr., *Art Director*
Ruthie Thompson, *Designer*
Lori Epstein, *Senior Illustrations Editor*
Kris Hanneman, *Illustrations Editor*
Sarah Wassner Flynn, *Contributing Writer*
Michelle Harris, *Researcher*
Kate Olesin, *Editorial Assistant*
Hillary Moloney, *Illustrations Assistant*
Kathryn Robbins, *Design Production Assistant*
Michael McNey and David B. Miller,
Map Research and Production
Stuart Armstrong, *Graphics Illustrator*
Grace Hill, *Associate Managing Editor*
Lewis R. Bassford, *Production Manager*
Susan Borke, *Legal and Business Affairs*

Manufacturing and Quality Management

Christopher A. Liedel, *Chief Financial Officer*
Phillip L. Schlosser, *Senior Vice President*
Chris Brown, *Technical Director*
Nicole Elliott, *Manager*
Rachel Faulise, *Manager*
Robert L. Barr, *Manager*

In Partnership with
NATIONAL GEOGRAPHIC KIDS Magazine

Julie Vosburgh Agnone, *Vice President*
Rachel Buchholz, *Executive Editor*
Catherine D. Hughes, *Science Editor*
Robin Terry, *Senior Editor*
Photo: Jay Sumner, *Photo Director,*
Children's Publishing; Karine Aigner, *Senior Editor*;
Kelley Miller, *Editor*

Art: Eva Absher, *Associate Design Director*;
Nicole M. Lazarus, *Associate Art Director*;
Julide Obuz Dengel, *Designer*;
Stewart Bean, *Art Production Assistant*
Sharon Thompson, *Copy Editor*
Margaret J. Krauss, *Assistant Editor*
Administration: Tammi Colleary, *Business Specialist*
Production: David V. Showers, *Director*

The National Geographic Society is one of the world's
largest nonprofit scientific and educational organizations.
Founded in 1888 to "increase and diffuse geographic
knowledge," the Society works to inspire people to care
about the planet. National Geographic reflects the world
through its magazines, television programs, films, music
and radio, books, DVDs, maps, exhibitions, live events,
school publishing programs, interactive media and
merchandise. *National Geographic* magazine, the Society's
official journal, published in English and 33 local-language
editions, is read by more than 38 million people each
month. The National Geographic Channel reaches 320
million households in 34 languages in 166 countries.
National Geographic Digital Media receives more than 15
million visitors a month. National Geographic has funded
more than 9,400 scientific research, conservation and
exploration projects and supports an education program
promoting geography literacy. For more information,
visit nationalgeographic.com.

For more information, please call
1-800-NGS LINE (647-5463)
or write to the following address:
NATIONAL GEOGRAPHIC SOCIETY
1145 17th Street NW
Washington, D.C. 20036-4688 U.S.A.

Visit us online at nationalgeographic.com/books
For librarians and teachers: ngchildrensbooks.org

More for kids from National Geographic:
kids.nationalgeographic.com

For information about special discounts for bulk
purchases, please contact National Geographic Books
Special Sales: ngspecsales@ngs.org

For rights or permissions inquiries, please contact
National Geographic Books Subsidiary Rights:
ngbookrights@ngs.org

Paperback ISBN: 978-1-4263-0783-6
Hardcover ISBN: 978-1-4263-0784-3
ISSN: 2153-7364

Printed in the United States of America
11/QGT-CML/1